Fading into the
limelight

FADING *into* *the* LIMELIGHT

FADING *into* *the* LIMELIGHT

PETER SALLIS

in collaboration with John Miller

First published in Great Britain in 2006
by Orion Books
an imprint of the Orion Publishing Group Ltd
Orion House
5 Upper Saint Martin's Lane
London, WC2H 9EA

3 5 7 9 10 8 6 4 2

ISBN-13 978 0 75287 596 5
ISBN-10 0 75287 596 5

Typeset by Input Data Services Ltd, Frome

Printed in Great Britain by Clays Ltd, St Ives plc

The Orion Publishing Group's policy is to use papers that
are natural, renewable and recyclable products and made
from wood grown in sustainable forests. The logging and
manufacturing processes are expected to conform to the
environmental regulations of the country of origin.

Contents

Acknowledgements   vii

Foreword by Roy Clarke   ix

Preface   1

ONE   Acting in the RAF   4

TWO   Cranwell to RADA   28

THREE   Fortnightly Rep   48

FOUR   'He Might be Green'   60

FIVE   Moby Dick Rehearsed   84

SIX   Noël Coward and Samuel Pepys   105

SEVEN   'What a Perfectly Bloody Play'   129

EIGHT   Wait Until Dark   153

NINE   'The Scenery has Stuck'   176

TEN   Last of the Summer Wine   194

ELEVEN   Where are the Tunes?   212

TWELVE   Wallace and Gromit   220

THIRTEEN   By Way of a Goodbye   232

Index   237

Acknowledgements

I would like to express my thanks to Guy Rose for persuading me to write this book, and to Ian Marshall at Orion for agreeing to publish it. I am also grateful to the latter's colleague Ion Trewin for suggesting that John Miller should help me in putting it together. John had performed a similar service to John Mills with his memoirs for the same reason – our failing sight.

In addition, I would like to record my gratitude for the friendship shown to me by all those named in these pages, who have made my work and my life so rewarding. Too many of them have now made their final exit, but I shall treasure my memories of them all, and I am glad to have had this opportunity of sharing them with you, the reader.

Dedication

For Aidan and Catriona

Foreword

by Roy Clarke

I had the good fortune of having Peter play the lead in my first play for television. This was before *Summer Wine* and a great distance from it in tone and style. And yet – when I began writing the plot for a sitcom featuring three old men – I knew that Peter Sallis was Clegg. How did I know? Because he was in my head running away with the part already. I didn't know who the other two would be – I was happy enough with the characters as they were emerging but they came with no actor attached. Jimmy Gilbert's excellent casting soon took care of that but Peter had cast himself. In something totally unlike the parts I'd seen him play. How did he do that? I still don't know.

Maybe it was magic. Don't think I'm joking. There is magic about certain people where something resonates beyond the sum of the visible parts. With Peter it's a quintessential Englishness. Not just of his own time – God forbid not of this present time – but of a whole stretch of English time. I have no problem visualising Peter in a powdered wig at Doctor Johnson's table in some solidly comfortable tavern. Peter has a sly wit which would have kept Boswell busy. It takes no effort at all to imagine Peter raising an eyebrow at the condition of Nell Gwynne's oranges.

You saw him playing Samuel Pepys. People were thinking it was inspired casting – or was it reincarnation? You might think that's not so fanciful if you saw him in his natural surrounds of the Garrick Club. It fits him like his own good tailoring – that place where it's easy to realise how seamlessly he would have belonged there at any period in its history.

But I can testify not only to his talents and his style. I can bear witness to his steadfastness. I've seen him battling on across draughty Yorkshire moors at a time in his life when he could easily have called quits. And on that note – guess who was cavorting at this year's Hollywood Oscars? Oh yes! Probably still raising an eyebrow at all the fruit on display.

So there we were – my first play – and here we are still. I suppose the moral of this story is: beware of working with Peter Sallis – you'll never get rid of him. And I can promise you, you'll never want to.

There are pleasures which come with Peter above and beyond his professionalism. Peter is very good company. He has a nice line in dry wit. There's a lovely, gentle, slyly funny character called Peter Sallis. I wish I'd written him.

Preface

If you have ever been in any doubt as to whether or not you should publish your memoirs I suppose you could do worse than go to John Lewis's. I was in there one day and all I could think about were mattresses. In the course of five years I have had four mattresses and I wasn't desperate, but I was rather mattress-minded, and a gentleman in that department who clearly worked for John Lewis approached me and said my name. I looked at him and said, 'Yes?'

He said, 'I wonder if you could help me?'

'Oh yes?'

'Well, I'm working here at John Lewis, but I write part-time and I've written three episodes of a *Comedy Playhouse* series.'

By this time my eyes were wandering over either shoulder of his, and I was beginning to think about other things. But he said, 'I just happened to see you and of course I know your name. I know you're in a very successful comedy series, and I wondered if you'd be kind enough to read them and tell me what you think?'

I looked at the floor for a moment and I thought, and then I looked him straight in the eye and said, 'All right, yes, send them to me.' I gave him the address of my agent and we bade each other farewell. He did send the scripts via my agent, I read them and I telephoned him, and he said, 'Thank you very much for reading them.'

I said, 'That's all right, but I don't think I'm going to be much help to you. You've got some very interesting ideas here, but unfortunately in the course of reading all three episodes, which I read fairly conscientiously, I think I smiled once. I certainly didn't laugh at all.'

'Oh yes,' he said.

'If I could give you some advice . . .'

'Oh yes, please,' he said.

I really wasn't going to have any trouble with him, he wasn't going to give me an argument. I said, 'Get a collaborator, you could go through your agency, get somebody who could just write jokes for you.'

'Oh, yes, yes, I see. Well, as a matter of fact I do know somebody who fills that bill.'

'Well, then, that's what I would do if I were you.'

'Thank you,' he said and we parted, and I concentrated my mind again on the mattress. A few days after this I received a telephone call from Guy Rose, who turned out to be the literary agent of the gentleman who had sent me the scripts, and he said, 'Mr Sallis, I hope you won't think it presumptuous of me, but I wonder if you've ever thought of writing your memoirs?'

I should tell you that by now, mattresses aside, I had been involved not only with the latest series of *Last of the Summer Wine*, but also with *The Curse of the Were-Rabbit*, doing the voice of Wallace in the *Wallace and Gromit* series, which had just been nominated for an Oscar, giving me a little bit of publicity and raising my standing a few notches in the public eye. So clearly he felt that I was a subject that might be of interest to some, and talks took place with him and with various publishers, and lo and behold, here we are with my memoirs, and I hope you enjoy them. And I hope also that one day I may find my mattress.

In the meantime, if you are ever in any doubt what to do,

have a wander around Join Lewis's – you never know your luck. I have the feeling that perhaps at the bottom of all this one good turn might deserve another.

ONE

Acting in the RAF

First a dip into the war years: 1943. We were in the thick of it: the Blitz, the Battle of the Atlantic. Only two men stood between us and being overwhelmed by the *Luftwaffe* and the *Wehrmacht*. One was Winston Churchill and the other Adolf Hitler. At the time I formed the opinion that the safest place to be in the United Kingdom was the Royal Air Force Station, Cranwell, in Lincolnshire.

I'd like you to picture the scene, if you would. In such a night as this, Corporal Frank Webb was playing gramophone records to the Cranwell Music Society in hut 300. Knowing Frank, the chances are that he was playing Beethoven's Third Razumovsky Quartet, the one with the pizzicato slow movement, the audience seated with their chins lightly resting on their chests, absorbing the music or possibly even fast asleep, when suddenly, outside the hut, came the most horrendous clattering and banging and Corporal Webb, trained to act on his initiative, leant forward and turned up the volume. After a few seconds, all was peace again except, of course, for the Razumovsky Quartet, but the following day waves of indignation swept through the camp.

Two or three commissioned officers were heard threatening to resign, but of course they couldn't because there was a war on. An American on the camp was heard to say, 'Hey, hey, what do they think they're doing?' Well, what they were doing was that a German bomber, on its way back to the Fatherland, having deposited its bombs elsewhere, had veered off course and, seeing this huge encampment below it, had let loose however many rounds of ammunition it still had in whatever it is you fire ammunition from.

Why am I telling you this? Because I was there. I was a corporal instructor at the number one radio school. I taught the theory of radio, and one day after one of my lessons a young man, a pupil – his name was Peter Bridge – came up to me and asked me if I'd ever done any acting. I said, 'No, no, I've always been interested in the theatre, but I've never actually been on the stage. I wasn't even in the school play.'

'Well,' he said, 'I'm going to put on a production of Nöel Coward's *Hay Fever* at the YWCA for three nights, and I would like you to play the leading man. Will you do it?'

I thought for a second and said, 'Yes,' and I did.

When I went on to the stage and spoke the lines, people laughed. Of course, I wasn't fooling myself, I knew they were laughing at Noël Coward, but nevertheless they had heard what I'd said and I hadn't knocked over any of the furniture. That night, in my bunk, I couldn't sleep. I just lay there going through the play over and over again. I knew everybody's lines, including my own, and after a while I thought to myself, yes, I know what it is: I've got what they call the 'acting bug'. So it turned out, and I determined that after the war, if I survived it, I would become an actor.

Now, if I may, I'd like to take you back a bit. Before the war, in company with others of the same age group, I went to school. The school was situated in a suburb of northern London called, rather inappropriately I thought, Southgate. Two huge iron gates set in a high brick wall opened and a winding drive took you to the fine Queen Anne house, and behind and surrounding the house were the modern buildings: the houses, the gymnasium, the laboratories and classrooms and so on. The school was named Minchenden after an oak tree that stood some half a mile away from the place, such a fine tree that it is mentioned in the Domesday Book. It was a secondary school. It was mixed. There were 200 girls and 200 boys. We all got along fine together. We liked the staff and they taught us well. There was the cane, but it was only administered by the headmaster and it was given without pleasure and received without resentment.

After some five years, the normal length of time, we were required to do our passing-out exams. Nowadays it's called something different, but then it was known as Matriculation, and in company with the others I took my 'Matric' and I didn't do too badly, really: I got a couple of distinctions, as I remember. Then, having completed your exams, you were supposed to leave school, except that I hadn't the foggiest idea what it was that I wanted to do. I had some vague thoughts that I might like to be a journalist. I thought the idea of going out and looking at scenes of accidents and robberies and fires and things, and then going round with my notebook and pencil and asking people about it, that sort of thing, I thought that might be quite fun. I spoke to my father about it. My father was paying four guineas a term for me, so of course he had to be consulted, and I explained to him that there was, in fact, a Sixth Commerce and in this class you could learn shorthand and typing.

'Do you think I could go into Sixth Commerce,' I said, 'and learn shorthand and typing and possibly become a journalist?'

'Well, yes,' he said, 'that's fine by me.' So I did. I went into my sixth year, in Sixth Commerce.

There were roughly a dozen of us, I think, and we were going to learn shorthand and typing. That's what we were going to learn, but the problem was really the shorthand. All those little squiggles and dots and different-shaped and different-sized lines and all that, I just simply couldn't cope with it. And we only had one typewriter. But having said that, the fact of the matter is that I was so happy there. I just loved it and I dreamed. I dreamed. And I dreamed to myself, why can't I just stay here? Well, I mean, there were all these lovely girls. Well, they weren't all lovely, but at least they were girls. I thought, couldn't I just marry one of them and we could settle down behind the bicycle sheds or somewhere and why, we might even raise a family. Yes, I thought, just to be at school.

Of course I didn't tell anybody about my dream and after a few weeks the headmaster, a good man, Mr A. G. Gibbs, sent for me and he said, 'Peter, Peter, you don't seem to be doing anything.'

'No,' I said, 'no, yes, yes, I see what you mean, yes, no, yes.'

'Well, I'm afraid you've got to leave.'

I was horrified. I went to my father and said, 'He wants me to leave.'

My father said, 'Uh-huh.' But I still didn't know what to do. And then my father spoke. First of all I should tell you that he was a bank manager. He spoke thus: 'You could always go into the bank. You go in now, you retire when you are sixty with a pension for life. It's not a bad way of spending your time.'

Well, I have to admit I didn't think very much of it, but I couldn't think what else to do, so I applied and I went into Barclays Bank, Southampton Row, Bloomsbury. As a junior clerk, I was to be paid one pound ten shillings a week. One of the tasks that they asked me to perform was to run the stamp till. Now the stamp till was in fact a tin box and it contained money, and with the money I would go to the post office and buy the stamps, bring them back and put them on the post, the mail of the bank, and post it. As I was only earning one pound ten shillings a week, one or two members of the staff were kind enough to suggest to me that if I made a shilling or two, nobody would mind, I mean, backs would be turned, so to speak.

I thanked them very much but I thought, no, no, no, no. I'm going to do this properly. Goodness gracious me. I'm going to run the stamp till like it's never been run before; and indeed that prophecy in fact came true because week after week, without fail, I was losing money. I was losing two, three, four shillings a week. They were kind enough not to ask me to put the money back out of my own pocket but I thought, oh dear, oh dear, this is terrible. I mean, here I am, in the bank and I can't even run the stamp till.

Then, out of the blue, just like something out of Dickens, an unknown benefactor arrived. When I say unknown, I mean I hadn't actually met him, but obviously his advisers had told him of my plight and he decided to do something about it, and he did.

The next thing I knew, I was in the Royal Air Force. Mind you, I wasn't much better in the Royal Air Force than I'd been in the bank, but at least I was out of the bank. A lot of people have said some very harsh things about the war, and of course I can see their point of view, but I must say it did me a good turn.

This is becoming one step forward and two steps back, but I would like to take you back to my childhood. I was born on 1 February 1921 and, after one or two moves around, my mother and father and I settled into a house in Palmers Green, north London, not far from the school in Southgate. It was a semi-detached house. Quite a pleasant building, really, for its time.

After a few years it began to dawn on me that my mother and father were not happy together. There were no, shall I say, physical outbursts, or anything like that, I just knew instinctively that things were not well between them. I had a little prayer that I used to say: 'Please God, make Mummy and Daddy live happily together.' I'm afraid it had no effect.

I had one great friend. His name was Reg Davis. We were contemporaries. We were both born in February 1921. We went to school together, we played together. His mother and father – he was an only child – were great card fans. They loved to play cards in the evening and I loved to play with them. We would play for money, a halfpenny a thousand or whatever it was. I know that after a while I had to explain to them as carefully as I could that actually it would be cheaper for me to eat out. However, they brushed that aside and I loved them. In fact, I'm ashamed and sorry to say that I had in a way a better life with them than I did with my mother and father, which is not really to denigrate my parents, but it was just that there was a feeling of peace and happiness with the Davises that I didn't get when I was at home.

Reg and I used to put on plays. Now this may have been, of course, a taste of the future, not for Reg because he went on to become a dentist, but we used to tour the plays. We would do them at Reg's house, say, and then we would do them at my house. The one that was the big hit was *The Leopold Pearls Mystery*. I can tell you that when this gripping story came to an end and Reg lifted this tumbler of coloured fluid and drank it saying, 'You'll never catch me alive!' there was a moment in our household. We had a maid called Mary Aither, bless her, and she used to look after us, and at the spectacular close to the play Mary Aither had to get up and be excused because she had wet herself. During my life in the theatre I'm sure that lots of people left during my performance, but I don't think they ever left in order to go to the lavatory.

I had another good friend who lived nearby and also loved the theatre. We built a model theatre of our own and the figures, the little cut-out figures or whatever they were, to go into the scenery. We had one great hit there. That was called *The Secret of the Blue Room*, which ran for all of four and a quarter minutes. With this other friend I had my one and only homosexual experience, or should I say feeling. I remember that he was ill at some time and I went to see him in his bedroom, and when I was with him there I had an almost irresistible urge to get into bed with him. I did resist it and quite what I would have done if I'd got there I don't know. And quite what he would have done I don't know either, but I didn't and the whole effect lasted for only a few days. But it never came back, I'm glad to say, and from that time on I've been what you might call 'normal'.

My father was a good man. Strict, but not very strict. I think he must have become a bank manager quite early on in his life. He kept me back home, except of course for the war years, until I was twenty-seven and actually then became a fully fledged actor.

My mother and I shared many interests. First of all, she used to take me up to the West End with her when I was still only a child. I know that we saw two performances of *Peter Pan*. The early one was with Gladys Cooper and the second with Jean Forbes-Robertson. I found the programme of that the other day and I was astonished to see that Ralph Richardson was Captain Hook when Jean Forbes-Robertson did it. Goodness, he must have been one of the youngest Captain Hooks, I would have thought.

Mother and I used to go up in the bus to the West End and we would go to the theatre. I know we saw *Rose Marie*, but we probably saw other musicals, I imagine, including at least three that starred Jack Buchanan. I also have one special memory of going to the cinema, to the Carlton, Haymarket, where we saw Maurice Chevalier and Jeanette MacDonald in *The Love Parade* and there, where we were sitting in the stalls, up on our right-hand side, sitting in one of the boxes were cut-out figures of Maurice Chevalier and Jeanette MacDonald looking down at themselves on the screen. There were also cinemas in Palmers Green and a theatre, the Intimate at Palmers Green, which was started by John Clements, and for quite a while I used to go there at pretty regular intervals. I think I went mainly by myself, and that was another introductory way of getting to love the delights of theatre.

But I think the interest that my mother and I shared that gave us the most pleasure was listening to the radio, or wireless as it was called in those days. We listened to Christopher Stone, the first disc jockey. At five o'clock in the afternoon, I think it was, he used to play gramophone records of the dance bands and the vocalists that went with them, and so began my introduction to that field of great composers that I refer to elsewhere, the Gershwins, the Porters and the Berlins, Rodgers and Hart and all that. They were marvellous, marvellous times, just soaking in that lovely music.

My father wasn't quite so involved with the music thing as Mother and I were. Nevertheless, he did bring to the family a huge wind-up gramophone in a wooden cabinet, and he was particularly fond of the singers that were a bit of a class above me: Chaliapin, Caruso and others. He had a few of their gramophone records, which we listened to.

We had holidays: we used to go to the seaside, to Bognor and Bournemouth. I remember, only a few years ago, driving through Bournemouth when I was playing there and coming to a place where we stayed as a family. It was called Linga Longa, and it was there that I had my first heterosexual experience. I was five and the young lady was four. I remember that we were devoted to each other. We went everywhere together. We were holding hands always. We used to roll about on the floor together. Oh dear, yes, I was quite a success in those days.

As the years went on, I seem to have become less and less successful, but there we are.

The last holiday that we took together while we were living in Palmers Green was at Leigh-on-Sea, which is on the way to Southend on the Thames estuary. My father had rented a bungalow in Old Leigh. It was called The Dinghy. A pretty, nice bungalow with a large, long, sloping front garden and when you looked out you could see the Thames estuary below you. We used to play something that we called pat-a-ball, where you used ping-pong bats or table-tennis, as I suppose it's called nowadays, and tennis balls, and we had a sort of netting, something strung across the middle of the garden, and I know that I was playing pat-a-ball with my mother one day when she slipped and fell.

She strained or broke something, I never knew exactly at the time. A physician, a doctor, was called and she had to go to hospital, and she was going to be there for some time. Now this meant that my father and I had to go back to Palmers Green, but he couldn't very well look after me; so one of his brothers, who also lived in Palmers Green, very kindly offered to take me in and then it transpired, though at what point I became aware of it I really don't know now, that my mother had fallen in love with her physician.

Now I have to go rather carefully here. I think they obviously were very fond of each other, but I do not for a moment think that anything of a very serious nature took place. However, my mother was emotionally involved, let's put it that way, and I think that my father behaved very magnanimously because he decided, having spoken to her – they talked it over between the two of them – that we would move down to Leigh-on-Sea. I suppose his thinking was probably something along the lines of she's had no love or very little love from or with me. This is her opportunity for some form of fulfilment and I would like to see that she has it. He never explained it or discussed it with me, but obviously I was living with them and it became clear what was going on.

So we were to live at Leigh-on-Sea. By now, my father was manager of Barclays Bank, Harringay, in north London, and I had one more year to go at school. So they talked it over with me and I had a choice. I could either go to a local school at Westcliff or Leigh-on-Sea and finish what you might call my 'Matric' year there, or I could continue to go to Minchenden. But if I went to Minchenden, that, of course, meant going from Leigh-on-Sea to north London, which was a journey of probably something in the order of two hours. How did I feel about it? Well, it didn't take me long to decide. I opted to stay at Minchenden. I knew them there. I knew the staff. I was happy there and I felt that this was the place for me to be.

So what happened was that my father and I used to leave our local railway station, Chalkwell, and travel to Barking, which was a junction, and there we changed on to a local train that took us to Harringay, where my father and I parted company. He walked to his bank and I got on a bus to Southgate, to Minchenden.

The interesting thing, looking back on it, is that I was going to school for a year, and the arrangement had been made so that I would have to miss Assembly, which was just before nine o'clock, but I would be there just after nine for the beginning of the classes proper. And I was never late. The train would come in – the steam train, the tank engine train – would come in to Chalkwell Station and I would get in it with my father; we'd go to Barking and then we'd change and get into the local train, and then we'd both get out at Harringay, and I'd get on a bus and I did that last bit of the journey and I was never late. Looking back on it, I think it's pretty remarkable. The trains were always on time.

We were living this life down at Leigh-on-Sea before the war when my father added to the family entertainment by buying a television set. We were the only people in Grand Parade, Leigh-on-Sea, to have a television set. We knew that because we were the only ones with an 'H' aerial. I remember that every night it was a joy. The evening's entertainment only lasted for a couple of hours, or not much more, and the three of us would sit with our noses not far from a seven-inch Pye television set. Black and white, of course.

I remember two plays in particular. One was *Once in a Life-time* by Moss Hart and George S. Kaufman, which as I write is being played at the National Theatre, and the other was *Richard of Bordeaux*. This was a play by Gordon Daviot that John Gielgud had made his own before the war. It was Andrew Osborn who played the part on television.

After the war, the seven-inch Pye seemed to have died in the cupboard, so we got another one, and I remember the first play that was done on television after the war, *The Silence of the Sea*, which starred Kenneth More, about a German who had been given shelter by a French couple. It was a father and daughter relationship, and the three of them spent their time in hiding really, or at least hiding the German, and when it came to the end of the war they were able to let him go. It sounds pretty simple put like that, but it was a very touching and moving play and years and years later, when I was working with Kenny More, I told him that I had seen it and he could hardly believe it. I think I was the only person, apart from close members of his family, who had ever seen *The Silence of the Sea*.

We were living at Leigh-on-Sea when the war broke out. I was, by now, in Barclays Bank. My father was the manager at Barclays, Harringay, and I was going on a bit further in a different direction to Barclays Bank, Bloomsbury, so I always left before he did. Being the manager he was allowed to be a little on the late side. Being the junior clerk I had to make sure I was there early.

It was the first day of the war when I walked down to Chalkwell; it only took me about four minutes, and when I got on to the platform there were about three passengers waiting there. I thought, oh my God, I mean, is it all over, have we given in already? A few minutes went by and then in came the faithful train: chush-chush, chush-chush, chush-chush. I and the two or three others got in. All the carriages were empty or nearly empty, we set off and when we got just outside Leigh-on-Sea, near Hadleigh Castle – the ruined castle that hangs on a slope over the railway line – the train came to a halt. You could hear it panting quietly to itself as it nibbled the grass either side of the track.

Then I heard in the distance, voom-boom, voom-boom, voom-boom. Even I could tell that that was anti-aircraft fire, so I looked out of the window and I could see the puffs of smoke over the estuary, gunfire smoke, I mean, shells bursting. Then after a few minutes I heard the plane, I couldn't see it, but I could hear it. Just one aeroplane I would have guessed, and they were firing at it. It started slowly to weave and dodge, it was getting closer and closer, and I thought it was time to shut the window, but then it turned away and disappeared. You could hear the sound of it go and the banging of the anti-aircraft fire still went on, but eventually that too died away.

After a minute or two the train pulled itself together and set off again, and we all went on to Fenchurch Street. But when I got to Fenchurch Street there was hardly anybody there. I walked to the Bank tube station and there was nobody there either to speak of, and the tube took me to Holborn, where I got out as usual. I walked along to Barclays, Bloomsbury, where the door was locked, but I was expecting that, so I rang the bell and Jimmy Reynolds, the porter, opened the door. He said, 'What are you doing here?'

I said, 'Well, I've just come from Leigh. I've just come as usual to be here.'

He said, 'Don't you know that there's an air raid on?'

I said, 'No, no, I mean if they blew a hooter or did anything down at Leigh-on-Sea I didn't hear it. Certainly my mother and father who were in the house with me, they didn't hear it. Well, there we are. Still I'm here.'

'Yes,' he said, 'yes, you're here.'

After about another half an hour or so the all-clear went, and later that day it transpired that of course the aeroplane was in fact one of ours.

In 1939 I was eighteen. Now that the war had broken out I was eligible to be called up at the age of twenty. Some of you may remember that the opening months of the war were what we called 'the phoney war'. Nothing seemed to be happening. But then, in 1940, the Germans made their move and swept through north-west France, and we came to the retreat at Dunkirk. The British and the French against the might of the German Army and, as you all know, we survived it, to a large extent thanks to the gallantry of those in the Navy and the Merchant Navy, and some rank amateurs who came to pick up the soldiers and bring them back to England.

While this business of Dunkirk was going on I thought, that's it, I can't stay in the bank any more, I'd better join up. Now I must admit that the idea of being a rifle and bayonet expert and pushing my bayonet into somebody's stomach just didn't feel like me, and I thought, no, if I'm going to be killed, I'd rather be killed sitting down. So I applied for aircrew and after making the necessary enquiries I was told to go to Uxbridge, one of the RAF stations, in order to join up. There was a lady who worked in Barclays Bank as the secretary to the manager, and she had a man friend who actually worked as a civilian in the offices at the RAF at Uxbridge. When she told him that I was going to go along and see them, he said, 'Well, what does he want to do? I mean, he wants to be aircrew?'

'Yes.'

'And which part of the aeroplane?'

She said, 'I've no idea.'

So she asked me and I said, 'Oh, I haven't really given it a great deal of thought.' And then I did think about it. I concentrated and thought, well, no, I think if I'm going to be in aircrew – it's a touch of modesty – I don't really think I'm good enough to be a pilot, but I wouldn't mind being a navigator.

So she reported back to her friend and he said, 'Ah well, if he's going to be a navigator, at the interview, which he will have first before he has his medical, when they ask him what he wants to do he must say "I want to be a navigator" and they will immediately say, "why", and then he must say to them "because I want to be able to steer the ship".' When she said those words I took a gulp – I thought, I just can't bring myself to say something like that, I really don't think so.

I went along to Uxbridge at the appointed time and I had my interview, my viva, as I think it was called. In those days there were an enormous number of officers sitting round the table. There must have been about eight or ten altogether, I think. They asked the usual sort of introductory questions and while they were in the middle of it, the man sitting next to me reached out and touched my collar. I looked round at him and he said, 'Oh, sorry, I'm sorry, I thought that was a spider.' I said nothing. I just looked at him and then I thought to myself, oh, I get it, yes, yes, of course, he wants to know what my reaction will be if I'm attacked by a spider.

We got back to the questioning and they said, 'Mr Sallis, you want to be aircrew, that's good, but what do you want to be, do you want to be the pilot? What do you want to do in the aircraft?'

I said, 'Well, I rather thought I'd like to be the navigator.'

'Oh, why?'

I took a gulp and I could hear myself saying it: 'Because I want to be able to steer the ship.' Well, that did it. They looked at each other and the interview was over. I was in. I was going to be trained to be a navigator for aircrew.

So I went on from the viva and the next thing I did was to have my medical. I passed some urine and did one or two tests, but after a few minutes they beckoned me into the office and a medical officer said, 'Mr Sallis, we want you to take a urine test.'

'Oh yes,' I said.

He said, 'I want you to go home and I want you to have supper as normal, but when you get up in the morning I want you to fast, I don't want you to have any breakfast, I don't want you to drink anything, I want you just to come here, and when you get here you will drink two pints of water and then, after a suitable pause, we will ask you to pass that water.'

I said, 'Yes, that's clear, the only trouble is I live at Leigh-on-Sea and I think by the time I've got back, I don't think I'll get here in time.'

'Ah,' they said, and then I had an idea.

I said, 'No, I think it's going to be all right. I do have some dear friends who live in Pinner,' which was quite close to Uxbridge. 'I could give them a ring and they might be able to put me up for the night.'

'All right,' they said, so that's what happened. I stayed with these dear friends in Pinner and the next day I arrived, not having had any breakfast and not having had anything to drink, and they gave me the two pints of water, which in itself I found pretty heavy going. I mean, I wasn't a beer drinker, I didn't drink anything very much in any quantity and it seemed to take me for ever to get those two pints down.

Eventually I did, and I waited a suitable time, as they asked me to, and then, finally, I went and passed it, or tried to pass it. But my passing wasn't very successful. So they called me back after a short time into the office and they said, 'Mr Sallis, you have albumen in your water.'

I said, 'What's that?' I'd never heard of it, of course.

And they said, 'Oh well, it doesn't really matter about what it is, chemically, the point is what it does, and there's every likelihood that if you fly at about 10,000 feet you will black out, and consequently we cannot accept you for aircrew. Thank you for coming to see us, Mr Sallis, and good luck.'

So I left. And when I left I picked up with a man I'd got to know while we were having our vivas. He struck me as a good RAF type, I must say, and he obviously struck the RAF in the same way, because not only had they accepted him for aircrew, but they'd also recommended him to train for a commission, so he was going to be all right.

The two of us walked out of the place together and when we'd gone through the gates, coming towards us were six WOPAGs (that is, wireless operator airgunner), young, bristling and blue. Their uniforms dazzled and they had their WOPAG badges up, and they were chatting among themselves. They were brim-full of life as they walked past us, and they'd only gone a few yards when this man turned to me and said, 'I wouldn't mind betting they're all dead in six months.' Until he said that it hadn't really come home to me that there was the likelihood of being killed eventually. It was not impossible, of course, far from it, but the idea of only lasting about six months hadn't actually occurred to me.

I thought that I would wait and be called up when I was

twenty, in the normal way. I suppose because I'd volunteered for aircrew, it wasn't very difficult to get into the Air Force as ground crew. I went to a place called Padgate, where I was kitted out.

The first thing they did at Padgate, once we had been kitted out, was to give us a lecture on hygiene or, to put it very simply, how to avoid catching venereal disease, in case they lost more recruits to that than were killed by the Germans.

This talk was delivered by a medical officer to a crowd of us. I must admit, to be fair, that he talked about other elements of looking after yourself, other aspects of hygiene. I should interrupt myself here and say that as a groundling, as the lowest form of life in the Air Force, you didn't get a raincoat. You got a topcoat, a heavy coat, if it was cold, but you didn't get anything to protect you from the rain except a groundsheet. This was literally a square of rubberised material, and sometimes it was known as just a rubber sheet. Now this medical officer, having lectured us, finished his discussion on how to avoid venereal disease by saying, 'If you do have sex with a woman, then make sure that you use a rubber sheet.'

I thought, what? I don't get it?

But I was pretty gullible and I thought, well, if that's what he thinks, fine. But weeks went by and it still rankled at the back of my mind, so I spoke to one of my chums and said, 'Tell me, what did that medical officer say? What did he mean when he said if you're going to have sex with a woman, use a rubber sheet?'

My friend said, 'What? No, no, no. Not a sheet, a rubber sheath!'

'Oh,' I said.

I put this incident into the stage play that Bill Owen and I did on *Last of the Summer Wine*. In the play he and I went to bed one night; we curled up on this large sofa and pulled up the sheets, and I told him this story about how I completely misunderstood what the medical officer had said. In the play Marina wasn't chasing Howard, she was after Clegg, and we had a scene where she was trying to seduce me. After a minute or two I went over to the cupboard under the stairs on the set, pulled out this groundsheet and laid it out for the two of us to sit on, which made the audience laugh.

At Padgate we were interviewed about our training prospects. After looking at my exam results from Matric they said, 'We're going to recommend that you be a wireless mechanic.' I rather liked the idea. Before the war I'd bought myself a Halicrafter – that was the name of the people who made it – a short-wave receiver that I used to listen to when I wasn't using the Super Het that father had bought us. I listened to America, to the dance bands and that sort of thing. So I was into short-wave radio and I thought, yes, I could be a wireless mechanic. That meant that I had first of all to be trained to march and walk properly as an airman, and for this I was sent to Redcar on the north-east coast near Middlesbrough. In civvy billets. Nice people. In fact, I was very lucky in the three civvy billets that I had. The people who looked after me, or rather us, were such decent people, and they wanted to help as much as they could. I guess it was commonplace in those days in time of war.

Like all recruits, we did a lot of square-bashing. We did ours on the sands at Redcar, marching up and down, turning and all that sort of stuff, a bit of drill with a rifle and a bayonet and the like, and it was great. The weather was keen, I remember, with a fine mist. I learnt the phrase 'Scotch mist' up in Redcar, and after a few days of it I began to feel a bit odd and I really couldn't think what it was. I just felt different and then, after another day or two, it dawned on me. I realised that I was feeling fit. For the first time in my life I felt truly fit. So presumably that was what all the square-bashing had been about.

From Redcar I went on to Edinburgh. I was lucky to be there. I was in the initial training college for wireless mechanics and staying in one of those great stone blocks of flats that they built in Edinburgh. Huge, marvellous buildings, with great winding iron staircases. I remember that the bedroom in this particular flat, which was owned by Mr and Mrs Macpherson, took eight cots, so there were eight of us would-be wireless mechanics all staying in the same place. Hard work for the landlady, Mrs Macpherson. A noble city, Edinburgh.

I went to Bolton. Not quite so noble. It smelt more of the war. There was a businesslike look about Bolton, as though they were spitting on their hands and making a lot of guns. I went there for the second leg of my wireless mechanic training. Again, civvy billets. This time to Mr and Mrs Derbyshire. Mrs Derbyshire, bless her, had a way with cooking. She specialised in the entrails, of which there were more available, I suppose, than any other part of the joint, and I remember her blood pudding. I'd never tasted or had anything remotely like it before in my life, but gosh, I liked it!

While I was at Bolton doing the second half of the mechanics course, an officer sent for me and said, 'Sallis, we've got an enormous intake of would-be wireless mechanics, but very few people actually to train them, to teach them, and you are not very good on what I would call the practical side – your soldering and your filing and so on are not up to much – but you are turning in extremely good exam papers, on electricity and physics in particular, and I would like you to prepare a subject, anything you like, on radio, and give a talk on it, and I will attend the lecture with one or two other of my staff, and we will decide whether you can make an instructor to teach radio theory.' I rather jumped at the idea and I prepared a talk on automatic volume control, never mind about what that is. I knew a bit about it, and I gave my talk to the officer and his chaps. I even got a couple of laughs! They said, 'Yes, yes, when you leave here, having passed out from here, you will go to Cranwell, and there you will go on an instructor's course, which will last about six weeks, and then you'll be fully trained to teach others the mysteries of radio.' Great, I thought. So I went to Cranwell. I remember when I arrived there it was snowing. Oh, and while I was at Bolton I had had my twenty-first birthday on 1 February and my mother had sent me a bound volume of the plays of Shakespeare. Was she trying to tell me something? Hmmm.

At Cranwell I became a teacher of telephony, with a class. Cranwell had its own defence system – trenches had been dug around the entire huge perimeter to protect us in the event of an invasion. As a corporal with a class I had virtually a platoon, so every now and then we would march off to man the trenches and go through the drill to save England. One summer day I got my boys together with the other units, and we marched off smartly to our post, down the slope into our trench. When we got into it, we looked out over the top and all we could see was wheat. The wheat was growing fully some five feet off the ground, and it was about three feet away from our noses. I looked around, left, right and centre, and it was all around us. We talked about it among ourselves, and it seemed to me to be as near useless as it could be, so we got up out of the trench and dismissed ourselves.

When I got back to headquarters, I asked to see my sergeant and I explained the situation. I said, 'Look, it's totally useless. I mean, you can't see anything except wheat.'

He said, 'Sonny, if you see them coming, if you see those little white handkerchiefs fluttering down from up in the sky, it won't matter whether you've got a wheat field in front of you or a number thirty-four bus.' So, neither encouraged nor dismayed, I went back to my unit.

Cranwell was a huge place. There were something like a dozen of us in my course and I hit it off immediately with one of them. His name was Mark Robinson and he was a musician, not by profession but he did know his music, and he played the piano. He even travelled with a dummy keyboard, which he would clatter about on, sitting on the edge of his bed, not producing any notes but a bit of a clatter, and practising away. He and I were mates, really, and we talked about music a lot and enjoyed each other's company. And then, as I mentioned before, while I was teaching one of my classes, this man Peter Bridge came up and asked me to be in *Hay Fever*. So that's what I did, and I was teaching hard during the day and playing at night. I don't think for very long – we only did three per-formances of *Hay Fever* – but there were play-reading groups and I loved that. We not only sat down and read the plays, but we also read all the stage directions and that was great fun. Bernard Shaw, I remember in particular, was, I thought, rather more entertaining with his stage directions than he was with the text itself. In the middle of all this, having done *Hay Fever*, I was offered another part: the lead in a play called *The Mocking-bird* by Lionel Hale. I can't remember much about it. I think I played somebody who'd escaped from a lunatic asylum. It was a comedy-thriller and I was only too pleased to do anything! So that was OK by me. Then I met Leslie Sands.

Leslie Sands – those of you who remember him, he's dead now – was a tower of strength at the National Theatre in the eighties, and he also had one notable series on television in which he played a police sergeant, a period piece, because he had a dog and his name was Sergeant Cluff. Leslie was an imposing figure. He was tall, without being over-tall, he was big and he had a big head, which matched his big frame, and a personality to go with it. He was the sort of person you knew straight away was going to brook no nonsense. I liked him enormously. It turned out, as we discovered between us, that he was in fact younger than me, though you would never have thought it to see the two of us together. We formed a company and called ourselves 'The Little Theatre'. To start off with we had two leading ladies. One was a blonde called June Miles and the other was a dark-haired lady called Maureen Shaw. Maureen I know went on, after she was demobbed, to become a professional actress and while we were on the station together I fell in love with her. Well, who wouldn't? Leslie and I had a sort of repertory company, as we were doing plays every two or three months.

The first play we did was by J. B. Priestley, called *I Have Been Here Before*. Leslie and June Miles played a married couple who came to a lonely pub on the Yorkshire moors. Maureen played the landlady, the housekeeper of the pub, and I played Dr Görtler, who was a German mystic / scientist, whose character was based on the works of Ouspensky. This was one of Priestley's bees in his bonnet and made for good theatre. Ouspensky had a theory, which he tried to teach to everyone, that we lived our lives over and over again, and this was the theme behind *I Have Been Here Before*. It was a good play, most interesting and, playing the German who dispenses this theory, I had a lovely part. We did it at the station cinema. I suppose we performed it for three nights, that was the usual time, and a man called Walter Wade, who was the Gas Officer on the station, asked to see me one evening. It turned out that Walter had been a professional. I put it rather crudely: he was a sort of a poor man's Noël Coward. He wrote plays, and he played and sang songs at the piano in a rather Noël Cowardish manner. He and Leslie wrote a play between them, which we did at Cranwell, called *Men of Good Name*. But I digress. Walter said to me, almost straight away after I'd sat down, 'You ought to be one of us,' which was extremely encouraging to hear from a real dyed-in-the-wool professional, and I was grateful to him. He didn't actually tell me what to do or anything, he just spoke in general terms about life in the profession and so on, but it was all encouraging and there's no doubt that he gave me an enormous boost early on.

Leslie had also been a professional before the war. He had been with Harry Hanson's company. Harry Hanson ran a series of repertory theatres and also put plays on tour, and Leslie had toured in one of his plays, if not others. So he had the knowledge and experience to be able to run us, and we were only too glad to be run. Leslie and I had one big clash. I think we'd probably been doing our plays for about a year, and he was taken ill. I've no idea now what it was, but he was in hospital for quite a while. During this time I planned what I thought of as a Shakespeare evening. I had the idea that we might do the clown scenes from *A Midsummer Night's Dream*, that we would open with the clowns Bottom and Quince and co. We would see them meeting for the first time to rehearse the play 'Pyramus and Thisbe' that they were going to do. That would be the first scene of the evening, then I was going to do *Richard III*, the wooing scene with Lady Anne near the beginning of Shakespeare's play. I'd seen Laurence Olivier do *Richard III* in London and of course I was absolutely bowled over by it, and I was going to give my pale imitation of him. Maureen accompanied me as Lady Anne. Then my idea was that Leslie and June Miles should do the dagger scene from *Macbeth* to open the second half, and that we would close the evening with the clowns actually doing their 'Pyramus and Thisbe' play in front of the Duke of Athens.

So, having prepared all this, I went along to tell Leslie about it. He was furious. 'You have no business to put on anything by Shakespeare without . . .' in effect, he didn't quite use these words – in fact, I don't now remember exactly what his words were – but the idea behind his thinking was that I should not have done it without consulting him and we should have done it together. We would have done a whole Shakespeare play and not four chunks, and he didn't approve of this idea at all. When he got better and came out of hospital we did eventually do the evening as I had planned it. He, as usual, put his heart and soul into it, and we got through it and I think it was successful. I didn't take any notes of what the audience said, but I just got the feeling that we were better off doing that than we would have been if we had done, let's say, *Twelfth Night* or another of Shakespeare's lovely plays in its entirety.

The next production was *Pygmalion*, with Leslie as Professor Higgins and Maureen playing Eliza Doolittle, and Leslie took me to one side and said: 'I'm going to punish you. You are going to play the sarcastic bystander in the opening scene of the play, and then you will work the gramophone for the music that's going with the play.'

I said, 'Oh, all right, Leslie, yes, right, I'll do it. Yes, I'll play the sarcastic bystander and I'll do the music,' which is what I did. I think it summed up our two characters: he was the dominating spirit, if you like, and I was, shall we say, the submissive one. Nevertheless, the fact is that I thought it was a bit outrageous to say I'm going to punish you, but there it is, that was Leslie, and nothing changed between us. We did *Pygmalion*, we went on doing plays. We even did *I Have Been Here Before* with Maureen playing the lead, the part that June Miles had played – June had, by now, left the station – and she and Leslie were the married couple, and I played Görtler again. Oh, it was very touching. I remember standing in the wings when Leslie was doing the closing scene of the play with the landlord of the pub and I was in tears. I've only got to think about it to feel they were great days, great days, the three of us together.

TWO

Cranwell to RADA

When I was at Cranwell, it wasn't just acting. Every now and then I would teach somebody, and there was also the station cinema, the same building in which we did the plays, where they used to show two films a week. From Monday to Wednesday they'd show one film, then from Thursday to the end of the week they'd show another. One Monday they were showing a film called *Citizen Kane* and I went to see it. I went to see it again on the Tuesday, and I went to see it again on the Wednesday. I'd never seen anything like it in the cinema before. It's funny, isn't it? You say the name Orson and there's no other name I know that you can put on to it afterwards. Have you ever heard of another Orson? Anyway, if you'd said to me then that in twelve years' time I would not only know the man, but be working with him, well, it would have taken a very large pinch to wake me up. But that's how it turned out.

The Music Society was mainly for playing gramophone records, because of the obvious convenience of the articles, and other people were invited to come and play for us and perform, but mainly it was the gramophone record that kept us going. We were a small group. Flight-Sergeant David Davison supplied many records for us. He was very generous. From the Society, the HMV Society, the Sibelius Society. I would never have got to know Sibelius as quickly as I did if it hadn't been for Davy

Davison. There was Norman Hecht, who used to look after the technical side; he'd wire things up for me. There were Frank Pears and Frank Webb, whose gallant performance against the *Luftwaffe* I've already mentioned. Then there was David Reed. There may be one or two others that I can't recall now, but we were a happy bunch, and we used to take it in turns to play gramophone records. But we also had access to the world outside and musical agents like, for instance, Ibbs & Tillett would provide us with the names of artists who would come and perform for us. The artists had to be paid, of course, but that came out of the station funds, which were allotted to keeping the Music Society going.

Among those who came to play for us, I remember the name of Ida Haendel, who must have been in her teens then, Pouishnoff the pianist, and a lady with a foreign name. It was spelt F-U-C-H-S-O-V-A and I was appointed to announce her. We had a conference and it was decided that I would introduce her as Madame Fushova, which I did, and nobody turned a hair. Then we also had artists who were already in the RAF, and the two sets of performers that I remember most were the Griller String Quartet, who fulfilled all my wishes about listening to string quartet music, and then there was Denis Matthews. Denis was a charmer. He was not only clearly talented and intelligent, all those obvious qualities that you need to have, but he was also a great demonstrator, and after he'd given a recital we would trot off to one of our huts that had got a piano in it and Denis would play for us. Not only would he play just for us, but he would invent little things like the way Toscanini would approach, let us say, Brahms's First Symphony, and the way Beecham would conduct it, if he ever conducted it. Little items like that, which we found fascinating.

I became quite friendly with Denis, in the sense that I used to look after him and provide him with a bunk in the hut where we all were – that sort of thing. Years and years later – it was in the seventies, because that's the nearest I can get – he was playing as a recital pianist. One of my friends at Cranwell at the time, who was also very interested in music but wasn't actually with the Music Society, was Reg Lascelles. Reg worked for Professor Lovell at Jodrell Bank, and one day Reg phoned me and said that they had arranged a recital for Denis Matthews and Peggy Ashcroft to perform in. Denis was to play the piano, of course, and Peggy Ashcroft was going to recite poetry, taking it in turns. It was to be done in the planetarium at Jodrell Bank, but Peggy Ashcroft had to pull out at the last minute and, in a slight state of desperation, Reg phoned me and asked if I could come and do it instead. I said, 'Can I read the poetry?'

He said, 'Oh yes, yes, you can read it all right, you don't have to learn it.'

So I said, 'Right, OK, I'll be there.'

And there I was, in the planetarium of Jodrell Bank, that great old building. The doors were open and there straight outside, looking across the grass, you could see the big dish. I can't think of anything, really, more scientific or more romantic at the same time. Denis played and when he stopped playing I read some poetry, and so we alternated throughout the evening. It was magical to be with *him* on the concert platform. Well, blow me. I remember Leon Goossens there among the audience, and Denis introduced me to him. Leon said to Denis that he'd never heard him play Beethoven's Opus III Sonata better. I'm not surprised, really. It would have made anybody play better. Denis went on with his career but eventually it was obvious that he didn't really go for the big concert platform, the Rachmaninov IIIs were not for him. It wasn't just the quality of the music or the power needed to play it, although Denis had got an infinitely light touch, I just don't think he wanted that circuit of playing, going round the country. Then he was given the job that was just made for him, the Chair of Music at Newcastle University, and I think he was there until he died. Dear Denis.

One day the BBC came to Cranwell. They were doing a tour of the country, visiting all the big stations and camps that had music societies like ours, and that was where I got to meet Alec Robertson. Those of you who are roughly the same age as me will remember that Alec Robertson used to write regularly for the *Gramophone*. He wrote books on music, he was a scholar and a gentleman, and he knew how to communicate; just as Denis knew how to communicate music, so Alec could, but in his own way. We became friends. I even took him to the theatre once, to see Ralph Richardson in *Henry IV, Part One*, and by then I'd pretty well made up my mind that I was going to be an actor. I told Alec and he said, 'Oh dear, oh dear, you don't want to be an actor!' Well, when I presented him with the alternative of going back to the bank he softened a bit. For a short time he was a great friend.

When the BBC came to Cranwell they went through the different aspects of the Music Society and among other things we were invited to say a few words, and the reason I'm telling you all this is because I was interviewed. So there I was on the wireless, but we were unable to listen to the transmission for some reason or another. Later on he sent me a recording. I listened to it, and it was then that I realised I had what can only be described as a suburban cockney accent. I didn't know it. I knew I wasn't talking posh, but I didn't know that I was actually talking with flattened vowels and that sort of thing. Actually, it's rather difficult for me to do it now. But more of that later, when I got to RADA and they came to my rescue.

It was at Cranwell that I met another man. His name was Peter Gough. Peter taught the apprentices. Now the apprentices at Cranwell were the equivalent of the cadet force in the Army and they were trained and educated to become officers in the future and to fly – that was their main objective. For this they required a higher standard of education than people like myself, ordinary chaps who were just going to be wireless mechanics for the course of the war. Peter was a qualified physics master. He'd taught at Brighton College before the war and he was pretty brainy, I can tell you. He was not only brainy, but he was also married to a lovely lady, Daphne Banks as she was before she married him, and Daphne was one of the three daughters of Leslie Banks, the English actor. If you don't all remember Leslie Banks, you might if I go on to say that he played Chorus in Olivier's film of *Henry V*. He was a fine British actor in the theatre and in films

Daphne, Peter and I were talking about the possibility of my becoming a professional actor, and Daphne said, 'Well, I'll write to father. He's in the West End at the moment, he's with John Gielgud in a season of plays at the Haymarket Theatre. I'm sure if I write to him he'll see you after the play, whatever it is he's doing, and he may be able to give you some advice.' I thanked her very much indeed, I couldn't think of anything more likely to be helpful. So she wrote the letter and her father asked me to go and see him. I booked at the theatre and went to a matinée of *A Midsummer Night's Dream* in which Mr Banks was playing Bottom. When the play was all over I went round, knocked on his door and thought to myself, poor man; I mean, what on earth is he going to say to me? Yes, he's got his daughter's word for it that I'm, in her opinion, fit for the theatre, but what could he say, apart from that? Well, as it turned out he said two things and they were both enormously helpful.

'First of all,' he said, 'you want, if you can, to get into the Royal Academy of Dramatic Art,' to learn my trade, in other words. He also said, 'You should read Stanislavsky's *An Actor*

Prepares. It will give you a very good insight into one way of going about your job as an actor.' So I thanked him very much, left him there in his dressing room and went straight out down Charing Cross Road to Foyles and bought myself *An Actor Prepares* by Stanislavsky. I took it back to Cranwell and then I started to make enquiries of RADA as to whether there was any chance of my getting in.

It was obvious straight away from the various pamphlets and communications that they sent me that I would never be able to afford to go there unless I got some form of scholarship. My father, who had been very generous to me – as generous as he could be in keeping me, apart from the war years – was then going to have to go on keeping me if I went on to RADA. They didn't have a scholarship that covered living expenses. But there was one scholarship it seemed to me for which I would be in with a chance. It was given by Sir Alexander Korda, the maker of great British films – *The Private Life of Henry VIII*, with Charles Laughton, is the most obvious one – and Sir Alex had very kindly and generously offered to give ten scholarships for ex-service personnel to go to RADA. In other words, you would have to pay your own keep, but the fees would be paid by Korda.

So I wrote in and was offered the opportunity of auditioning. I would go to RADA, having learnt three pieces that they wanted me to do, and I would then do an audition in front of Sir Kenneth Barnes, who was the principal, and other members of staff, and if I was good enough I would be accepted. So after a week I'd learnt my pieces and went to RADA, and when I got there I had to go downstairs. The whole building had been hit by a bomb during the war and the centre of the building, which covered numbers 62 and 64 Gower Street in Bloomsbury, had a hole in it.

When that bomb dropped on RADA, one of the students at

the time was Richard Attenborough, and he and the other students got to work, doing what they could to help clear up the mess. Not much they could do with a hole that size, but they tried. What concerned them most was the fact that this meant RADA must close. They couldn't believe that it could survive something like this, but later on that morning, while they were still sweeping up the rubble, Bernard Shaw arrived. He was a patron and leading figure in the running of RADA, and his energy and generosity were unsparing. He came down the steps, waving his hat at them, chuckling away and saying, 'Don't worry, children, we're not going to close.' At a RADA centenary celebration in 2005, Richard Attenborough published his reminiscences of that bombing incident, which were read out by Martin Jarvis. I believe that Richard has carried on the tradition of Bernard Shaw and I cannot think of anybody who has done more to help RADA, not only to survive, but to grow in strength over the time he has been on the council, as Chairman, President, or whatever he is now – congratulations, Richard, you've done a marvellous job for RADA.

I didn't know all this at the time, but that was the situation, so the theatre, such as it was, was really a sort of a cellar. It was actually underneath the road and it is still there, being used as a theatre, but there's a beautiful new theatre there now, a real one, where the bombsite was. I went down the steps into this cellar. I could see that there were a few rows of seats, and then there was a box at the end, where obviously Sir Kenneth Barnes and his fellow teachers were sitting and waiting for us to do our stuff. In the wings of this little theatre, there was a couch and I sat on it with a man who was clearly very young and, shall I say, just a touch effete? He turned to me and said, 'Are you nervous?'

I said, 'Well, no, I'm not really nervous. In fact, I'm quite looking forward to it.'

'Ah,' he said, 'well, take my advice, breathe deeply.' I listened to what he said but I didn't think about breathing, actually, I just went on the stage and did it.

I finished my three pieces and Sir Kenneth said, 'Thank you, Corporal Sallis, can you find your own way out?'

I said, 'Yes, I think so,' and I left. As I walked down Gower Street on my way to the station to go back to Cranwell, for the first time in my life I felt determined. I thought, if I don't get in here, if I don't get into RADA, I'm going to go round the reps. If I have to go round on a bicycle, I'll knock on their doors and see if I can get auditions or whatever, or even just get a job sweeping the stage. So that was my attitude of mind when I went back to Cranwell. Well, I've still got the telegram. They sent me a telegram that afternoon to say that I'd been awarded the scholarship, so I was in RADA.

Eventually it was time for me to be demobbed. You will have gathered by now why I wrote that opening little sentence at the beginning of this memoir, that I reckon Cranwell was the safest place to be during the war in the United Kingdom. I had been there for four and a quarter years when it was time for me to be demobbed, and I had to go and present myself to be signed out by my commanding officer, who was much younger than me. I won't say he was half my age, but he was certainly younger than me, and he had his wings up, and he had so many medals that as he sat facing me he leant slightly over to the left. He looked at my papers and said, 'How long have you been here, Sallis?'

I said, 'Four and a quarter years, sir.'

He said, 'Good Christ Almighty!' So I left Cranwell and it was a great chunk of my life. I was just very, very lucky. I did enjoy the years of the war, if you can say that about a war.

So now I was off to the Royal Academy of Dramatic Art. I was due really to start the next term, but Sir Kenneth said that if I wished I could begin in the middle of the term that they were in then, and I jumped at the chance. I had a bit of demob leave, which I spent in the Lake District, and then I went to RADA. I've just explained to you the sort of hero I was during the war, but as far as the RADA pupils were concerned, especially the young ladies, anybody who'd been anywhere, even if he was only a corporal, and even if it was only at Cranwell, was by way of being something a hero.

I didn't let this go to my head, nor to any other part of me, for that matter. I thought, well, I'm just going to be very cool, and whatever you do, Sallis, do not in any way attempt to show off. Just play it very cool. Which I think I did. Of course, there were some people who'd really been in the war, like Robert Urquhart. He'd also got a Korda scholarship. Bless his heart. He's dead now. I think Robert was in the Merchant Navy.

But there we were and we started our lessons, and straight away I realised what the effect of being at RADA was, because we had two men who taught us voice. One was Clifford Turner, who was quite famous (I didn't know that at the time) in the West End as a coach for actors. I believe even Sir John Gielgud had been 'helped' by Clifford Turner. There was another man, Freddie Ranelow, who taught voice production. In other words, how to fill your lungs and get the stuff out to the other side of Trafalgar Square if necessary. So one was, shall I say, dealing with the actual spoken word for its own sake, and the other was talking about projecting that word, and within weeks they'd helped me. Especially Clifford, because in fact, as I've explained, I didn't know I had a suburban cockney accent, but he did straight away, and he gave me things to do, passages to learn, and he was so precise in telling you how actually to produce it. I mean, I can't do it. If I could I'd be out teaching people myself. But if you did the vowel sounds in exactly the way that Clifford told you and hung on to each half-vowel, if you'd like to put it that way, just the right length of time, eventually your voice would improve, and you would be able to listen to yourself.

Now in those days there were no tape recorders or things like that to listen to yourself on – if there had been I'm sure they would have been mammoth machines and very expensive – but with his help and listening to other people around me, and the other teachers, gradually it became clear to me. So that was the first big step.

The other big step, of course, was the teachers themselves. Most of them were in the theatre. In other words they were not just actors, they were working in the theatre, they were in the West End, to put it rather simply, and they would come and work at RADA during the day, then trot off in the evening and do their play. Some of them were more helpful than others, but there wasn't one of them who didn't help in some way or another.

However, slightly going off at a right angle, one of the lessons that we had were what they called movement classes, and they were run by a man called Theo Constable. Now I don't know whether I can describe this to you, so you'll have to be patient and use your imagination, but the dress for movement classes was that the men would wear a singlet and shorts, and some sort of plimsolls on their feet. The girls would be in a top and a little skirt, and dressed their feet in the same way.

But I hadn't got any shorts. All I'd got were underpants. There was still rationing and my mother and father and I hadn't any coupons, so my mother took an old shirt of mine with two flattened used tails, she cut them horizontally across, so that she just had the two tails, and she sewed them up the middle, then attached them at each side at the top. So it was like two 'U' shapes joined up the middle. Now in the class if you looked at me head on, straight on, I was perfectly safe and so were you, but if you went round the side, the curtains parted and nearly all was revealed, and this caused hysteria, not to say quite a lot of curiosity. We hadn't even got through the first lesson when Theo took me to one side and said, 'Peter, Peter, we don't want to lose you, but those have got to go!'

If you think that RADA should be accused of male chauvinism or something like that, I should say that Sir Alex in his awards of scholarships had given them to women as well as men. I can't remember what the proportion was, I know that there were more men than women, but at least women were given the opportunity. We were also helped by, if possible, getting us work in the RADA holidays. I was given a job by Colin Chandler, one of the teachers there at the academy, who was going to produce a play of Sheridan's, *The Scheming Lieutenant*, at the Arts Theatre in Great Newport Street. He invited me to play a couple of parts in it, a soldier and a sort of a footman-cum-valet, nothing very spectacular, but my goodness, there I was, actually in the West End. The fringe of the West End, yes, but never mind, and it was a marvellous beginning for me.

Apart from anything else, it got me introduced to British Actors Equity. One day in the dressing room that I shared with others at the Arts Theatre, there was a knock on the door and this man put his head round the corner and said, 'Peter Sallis?'

I said, 'Yes.'

And he said, 'I'm from British Actors Equity and I understand you've just started at RADA?'

I said, 'Yes, I have.'

'Well,' he said, 'I've come to ask you if you would like to join Equity.' Then he explained a little bit about the organisation and what the fees were. I think in those days they were six guineas a year. But I said I'd like to join and so I did.

It's interesting, of course, that later on it became compulsory to join Equity and not everybody wanted to do so. Then we came to the situation where we had a closed shop, so there were different what you might call political undertones to all this, but never mind. I felt good about being a member of British Actors Equity, although I'd only done one little job in the West End.

Another play that I was offered was given to me by Ronnie Kerr, who had connections with the Guildford Repertory Theatre where one Christmas they were going to do a play by the two Farjeons, Herbert and Eleanor. The play, *The Rose and the Ring*, was half-pantomime, half-play, and I managed to set Guildford alight by giving them my imitation of Laurence Olivier's interpretation of *Richard III*.

But then, out of left-field, as the Americans say, I got my first television job. Television in 1947–8 was black and white, of course – it came from Alexandra Palace and the cameras were huge. They were wheeled about on perambulators. The medium was in its infancy, but somehow or other either Sir Kenneth from RADA or Michael Barry, who was the Head of Drama at the BBC, managed to persuade each other that they should do scenes from Shakespeare using pupils of the Royal Academy of Dramatic Art. The director and producer of the shows would be Robert Atkins, who was running the Open Air Theatre in Regent's Park, and apart from being a startling character in his own way, he was also an extremely gifted man of the theatre and kept that outdoor theatre running for years.

I'm going to digress for a moment and say that I had been to Regent's Park just after I'd left RADA, to see *A Midsummer Night's Dream*. Robert Atkins was playing Bottom, I can't remember any of the rest of the cast, but for once in a while it was a glorious English summer evening. As the sun went down and the lights came up on that theatre – the shrubbery, the trees, the natural setting – I sat there and I thought I'm never going to come back here. I'm never going to see anything else here. This is perfection. And I didn't.

Three groups of students were chosen from the Academy by Sir Kenneth and I was lucky enough to be one of them. We were going to do scenes from *Twelfth Night*, and I was going to be playing Sir Toby Belch, watched under the keen but friendly eye of Robert Atkins, who had made Sir Toby Belch one of the principal characters he played. It went out live, of course, and I suspect it's just possible, because I know that she had a television set, that my mother would have watched it. I can't remember telling her that I was doing it, but obviously I did. That was in 1948 and it was a little while before I did my next television, but not really all that long.

There's one teacher that I'd like to talk about at RADA and that was Fabia Drake. Fabia Drake had been a well-known leading lady in her own right. The only thing I can remember that she did was *As You Like It* with Robert Donat, but she was a leading Shakespearean actress in her time, and a very strong-minded woman. I mean, you got that impression immediately, she knew what she was talking about and she wanted you to take in what she was talking about. She was the only person there, or the only person I've ever come across in that small field of the acting profession, with just a couple of exceptions, who made you feel that she could actually teach you to act.

When you finished a lesson with Fabia you came away thinking, yes, I think I've got it. Now I must be fair to all concerned and say that acting is entirely a matter of instinct. To put it very simply, you've either got it or you haven't, and I'm really not showing off about this, but that's why, when Peter Bridge saw me do my lecture at Cranwell about wireless, he could tell that I could act.

You get the same sort of thing in the law, with people like

John Mortimer. Lawyers – or barristers, perhaps I should say more correctly – are most of them actors. They need to be. They don't take their work into the field of actually being paid for the acting they do, but rather for the results they get. But the same sort of feeling, the instinct, is there of persuading the audience about things that they might not otherwise have believed in, and Fabia could teach you to act.

We did have one or two little, shall I say, exchanges of views. She insisted, when you were doing a play, that you went on the stage carrying the book, the script, and that you kept on working with the script, working with it until you had learnt it by actually doing it. She didn't believe in the business of taking it home and learning it quickly, and then coming on and doing it. Of course, this didn't really work in repertory, where you jolly well *did* have to learn the thing as quickly as you possibly could; nor, of course, does it work in the film world.

You can't turn up at a film studio with the script in your hand, having been given the part to play. They want to turn over. They want to shoot it straight away. You are given the moves and told where to sit and all that, but you're not expected then to start rehearsing it with your opposite number. There is one glorious perfect example of this in the film *JFK*. Donald Sutherland has this scene right bang in the middle of the film, where he is seated on a bench in Washington, talking to the lawyer who is trying to find out who really did shoot Kennedy. The film was mostly written and directed by Oliver Stone. Donald Sutherland learnt that part before he even arrived in the park in Washington, and it is a beautiful bit of acting. He is telling the lawyer man what he knows about the background to the shooting of Kennedy, so it is narrative and there are connecting passages. In other words, to put it really simply, it's all roughly on the same note, but boy, is it marvellous. The length of the shot and the way he holds it all together, and yet shifts the emphasis every now and then. Anybody who wants to be a film actor should see *JFK* and watch that scene and think to himself, could I do that? And if the answer is yes, fine, jolly good.

Fabia was a fine woman, a great lady, and a good teacher. I think probably she smoked more Turkish cigarettes in one day than even the sultan, and possibly she liked a drop of gin at the end of the day's work too, but my goodness you came away from her lessons thinking, yes, it's beginning to work, I can feel it. Something like that.

Now we come to a little bit of RADA history, which I think is probably known to only a few. The principal in the scene was probably the Principal of RADA, that is to say Sir Kenneth Barnes. He sent for three of us, three men. Robert Urquhart, Harold Goodwin and myself, and he sat us down in his study and said, 'What I have to tell you is in the strictest confidence. You must not discuss what I'm going to discuss with you with anybody. Have I got your word?'

'Yes,' we said.

'I have to tell you that in the men's lavatory the other day was discovered a rubber sheath.' Of course, the moment he said the words my mind went back to Cranwell, but I fought it off and paid attention. He said, 'It was given to the police, and it was subjected to chemical analysis, whatever you'd like to call it, and it was found to have been used on a male. It was found in the male lavatory and it had been used on a male.' Now, I didn't know much about sex yet, in the sense that I couldn't have given a lecture on it. But I thought that was a bit odd. I mean, this is years before AIDS and HIV positive and all that, and I couldn't understand why the person who'd used it had gone to the trouble of using a rubber sheath, a French letter, in other words.

But I kept it to myself, and he went on talking and said, 'If this became public, it would be the ruin of RADA. Parents would not send their children here if they thought that they were going to be subjected to that sort of sexual encounter. So I want you three, I have trust in you, to tell me if you know of anybody in this school that you even suspect of being a homosexual. You don't have to offer me any proof, all you have to do is to come back to me and say a name and then leave the room, and that person will be dismissed immediately. I do not have to give any reason for dismissing anybody from this school. I have the power to do so. And there'll be no inquiry, no board of inquiry, nothing. They will simply leave because, I repeat myself now, I dare not keep them on, it would be disastrous for parents to think that they were going to send their child to a school where this sort of happening took place. Thank you.'

So we left, and we stood outside in the corridor, and we looked at each other, the three of us. Robert and Harold and me, and we all took it in turns, but the answer really was – no chance, Sir Kenneth, no way, sorry. But even as we spoke, we each of us had faint ideas. I had only one person in mind who I felt sure might be a homosexual, and that was really because – can I put it this way? – of his overt sexual behaviour. He was just, well, we'd call them nowadays just a bit queer.

But there was no way I was going to tell Sir Kenneth that and even now I don't know what the outcome was. I hope that nobody was ever dismissed for those reasons.

When I left RADA I was offered work almost immediately and I was grateful, but it took ages before I realised how valuable RADA had been, and it had been valuable for two main reasons. It taught me how to speak properly, and it found me an agent. Towards the end of my first year I was in a class that contained an American lady, Leora Dana. She was already a professional actress. She had worked on Broadway, she had come over to England as a sort of finishing school, and she was going to spend a year with us. We were in the same class and we did a play called *The Matriarch*. Then I got a letter from a man by the name of Kenneth Carten, who was with the agency of Myron Selznick, probably the biggest agency in London at the time. He asked me to go and see him and I did, and he said, 'Well, I'm the agent of Leora Dana. As you know, you've just done *The Matriarch* with her, and I went to see it and I would like to represent you. We won't have a contract, we'll just trust each other, and if you want to leave me you may, and if I want to dismiss you I can. But I would like to represent you. I saw your performance the other day and I couldn't take my eyes off you.'

It's conceited of me to include that passage, but the fact is that it meant so much and any actor will tell you the same thing. So I said, 'Thank you, yes, I would like to be looked after by you,' and thus it turned out. I've been in this profession for sixty years, roughly, and I have been represented by two agents, one was Kenneth Carten and the second was Jonathan Altaras, who was, for a time, Kenneth's assistant. When Kenneth retired, Jonathan took over his clients and it's been like that ever since. I think I've been lucky to have been represented by two excellent agents, and never had to think about changing.

So we come to the end of term. The end of one's time at RADA when there is the public show. This is held in a public theatre. In our case it was the St James's Theatre, and what happens is that you are divided up into groups of pupils who are leaving that term. Each of you does a part of a play, you don't do the whole play, or probably, even, one act, but just a section of it, and it's watched by parents and members of the family, but it's also watched by the press and by agents. Then they had judges, and the judges decided who was going to get which award for what. There was an award for voice, and an award for movement, and diction, and that sort of thing. Then there would be three medals: a gold, a silver and a bronze, and as it happened with us, an old mate of mine, who is sadly dead now, Brewster Mason, won the gold medal, Leora Dana won the silver medal, and Peter Sallis won the bronze medal. So Kenneth had got two out of three which, if you think such things are important, wasn't a bad start.

I should say I believe that those awards have now been done away with. I think they still have the public show, but not in a way that means you get a medal at the end of it, or do *not* get a medal at the end of it, which is even more disappointing. Much better off without them, and now you can be seen at RADA all the year round.

The theatres in the building are open to the public. You can be on a mailing list and you can see some smashing things there. The other day I watched Stephen Sondheim's musical *The Assassins* – it could have been done in the West End. The Vanbrugh Theatre, which occupies the centre of the building, is the best theatre I've ever been in anywhere. Of course, the concentration is mainly on the stage. The seating accommodation will only hold about 200, but you can do what you like with the stage, you can move it about, you can raise it, lower it, and the acoustic is marvellous. I'd love to do a play at the Vanbrugh Theatre. Well, let's say for one night.

When I left RADA Kenneth Carten was approached by one of the judges of that public show, Basil Dean. Basil Dean had been a great figure in the British theatre before the war, and he had many fascinating and interesting productions that he offered the public, not the least of which by any means was *Hassan* by James Elroy Flecker, with music by Delius. After the war he continued to produce and in 1948 he put on *The School for Scandal* to open the first post-war Bath Festival. He had an interesting cast. It was headed on the male side by Leon Quartermaine. and it contained several distinguished actors: George Curzon, William Fox and others. The cast on the female side was led by Evelyn Laye, known as 'Boo' Laye. Before the war 'Boo' had been one of the queens of the British theatre. She was so attractive, so glamorous, and I suppose her most important production was *Bitter Sweet*, the Noël Coward musical.

She had a lovely voice, and I think that probably Basil Dean had managed to persuade her to play Lady Teazle in *The School for Scandal* by suggesting that she sing 'Sweet Lass of Richmond Hill' during the course of the play. I'm quite certain it did nothing to disturb the box office, quite the reverse. Another lady in the play was Lally Bowers. I didn't know Lally Bowers at all before I did this play, but I learnt about her. I learnt about her with my own eyes and ears. She was a mistress of the spoken word and the last time we worked together was in 1980, when she was good enough to do a play that I had adapted for the Chichester Festival Theatre. It was called *Old Heads and Young Hearts,* and Lally played . . . well, I can only describe it as the leading character actress in that play. In *The School for Scandal*, Basil Dean's production, she played Mrs Candour. She could speak the words better than anybody I knew, ever, on the female side of the curtain, better than anybody except Edith Evans. I had the privilege of working with Edith Evans, and I know that she was the greatest and I know that Lally was the second best.

The School for Scandal duly opened the Bath Festival in 1948 and then we toured. It was going to come in to the West End, but for reasons which I don't know about and didn't know about – whether they were political, or whether they were literally that it was considered not good enough (I can't believe that!) – at any rate it was not brought in. Never mind. During that time I had the privilege of working at close quarters with those two ladies, apart from the rest, a fine cast.

I played two characters, one was Snake, who opens the play with Lady Sneerwell, and the second Careless, who runs a sort of auction. I was learning as much as I could, and as fast as I could. One day Lally Bowers asked if I knew the story about Lady Sneerwell and Snake. I said no, and she said, well, it goes like this, and she told me. I haven't heard that story since and I thought it might be fun to drop it in here.

Snake is a local journalist who pops items of interest into the local papers, the scandal sheets as they were known. Items such as 'Is it true that Lord Popitoff is seeing too much of Lady Touchit?' those sorts of paragraphs. The actual opening lines of the scene are:

Lady Sneerwell says to Snake: 'The paragraphs you say, Mr Snake, have all been inserted?'

Snake: 'Yes, madam.' And the scene then proceeds.

Lally explained that in this particular incident the play was being done probably in a weekly rep or something like that where they don't have much time to rehearse, and it is a fairly long and difficult play to do, but the curtain goes up on the first night and Lady Sneerwell, who's only just sat down behind the curtain, takes a deep breath and looks at Snake and says, 'The snakes have all been inserted, Mr Paragraph?' Snake looks at her, takes a deep breath and says, 'Yes, your majesty,' whereupon both parties collapse and the curtain comes down, and they have to wait some minutes and then take it up and begin the scene again. Well, no such mishap happened with us. Lady Sneerwell and Snake managed it all right this time.

After *The School for Scandal* I would spend three years working in three repertory companies, with roughly a year in each.

THREE

Fortnightly Rep

After the closure of *The School for Scandal* I spent three profitable years, from an acting point of view, with three good-quality repertory companies. All of them were what we called 'fortnightly rep' as opposed to weekly, and the first one was Guildford, where I had given my spellbinding performance as Laurence Olivier being *Richard III* one Christmas.

Now I'm going to digress for a moment – well, quite a long moment, actually – and say that some actors, in fact, most actors, can say that they have gone through their careers without ever having been in William Congreve's *The Way of the World*. In my case I had the misfortune to be in it twice: first at Guildford and the second time with John Gielgud in his season of plays at the Lyric Hammersmith. This is not to cast any slur on William Congreve, he was a great playwright, but he wrote English prose and verse in such a density of verbiage that it was the greatest difficulty to keep up with him. Let me give you an example: in the production that I was in with John Gielgud we sat down and read the play for the first time at our initial meeting. There are two leading parts: one is Mirabell, who is in love with Millamant, and Millamant is a woman who knows exactly how to deal with Mirabell at every turn of the way. At the end of the first read-through, John Gielgud put the script down and said, to no one in particular, 'It's not a very good part, is it?' Well, what he could have said, and perhaps should have said, is that Mirabell is not as good a part as Millamant, nothing like. Congreve had put all his energies and all his wicked thoughts into Millamant, and during the course of the play, from a verbal point of view, she wipes the floor with him. Pamela Brown was playing Millamant this time, opposite John Gielgud.

But let's go back now to Guildford. I was in the company and Lally Bowers was engaged to play Millamant. What I wasn't expecting was that they were going to ask me to play Mirabell, and the reason wasn't at all clear; in fact, at the time I wondered why on earth we were doing the play at all. Later I thought about it some more, and I supposed it was the fact that they had engaged Lally to play Millamant, since she was such an obvious choice, but they hadn't really thought very deeply about who was going to play Mirabell, and we hadn't got what I would call an ordinary straightforward up-and-down leading man. We hadn't got anybody, say, over about five foot ten for a start, or even reasonably good-looking, so it got landed on me.

We rehearsed it for two weeks, I suppose it was, and I struggled to keep up with Lally as best I could, but it was a hopeless task. On the Saturday morning of the weekend, before we opened the play on the Monday, the director phoned me and said, 'Look, Peter, I'd like you to do the prologue.'

I said, 'What prologue?'

He said, 'The prologue of the play, *The Way of the World*, look at the script.'

'Oh, all right.' I grabbed the book and had a quick look at it, a whole page of iambic pentameters and I didn't, of course, read it then, being young and eager, I just said, 'Oh, righto, yes.'

He said, 'Right, fine, good, see you on Monday,' and put down the phone.

And then I read the prologue. Well, it typified dear William Congreve – the density of the writing. I reckon that if you took *The Way of the World* and made a compendium, or whatever you'd like to call it, of all the words there, you would have nearly as many words as there are in the English dictionary. It is full of stuff that most of us have never read or seen before. But I learnt it.

Guildford Theatre, Monday night, *The Way of the World*, two seats for the price of one, that's a billing; and I'm sure that a lot of people coming to the theatre that night, encouraged by the two-for-one procedure, wouldn't have had the faintest idea what *The Way of the World* was all about. Never mind who wrote it! I think they may have thought it was a travelogue, I don't know.

I was dressed for the part of Mirabell, I had the full regalia: a large wide, broad-brimmed hat with a feather in it, a full-length wig that dropped on to my shoulders, a brocade coat, and the coat landed just below the knees, a pair of white stockings, and a pair of buckled shoes – silver-buckled shoes – and nobody could find a pair that fitted me. They were, well, at least half a size too big, and then I was covered round the neck and fingers with rings and things. I had a cane with a knob on the end and I was, as you might say, ready for action.

Now the curtains at the Guildford Theatre opened sideways, they didn't go up and down, and in charge of them was Glyn Houston, brother of Donald Houston, both of them very good Welshmen, and he was going to pull the curtain at the end of my prologue. I would deliver the prologue, he would open the curtains, I would then bow to the audience and go through the opening in the curtains on to the stage, where the rest of the cast were ready to receive me, and the play would begin without a pause. Fine. So there we were, I went through the curtains. Fortunately nobody actually laughed and I got stuck into it. I

went on and I went on, and I kept going, and I was beginning
to think to myself, go on, Pete, keep going, keep going, until I
came to the last couplet which is as follows:

Who to you judgement yields all resignation
So save or damn after your own . . .

and I couldn't remember the last word of the last line. Glyn
Houston was waiting for me to say it, so that he could pull the
curtains and the play could begin, and I stared at the audience
and I said, 'I'm terribly sorry, I've dried.'

And a chap in the front row says, 'Inclination?'

I said, 'That'll do, inclination,' so I've said it, and Glyn, who
didn't know what the last word was anyway, just pulled the
curtains, I turned round and I began the play with my fellow
actors. Then all I had to do was to get through two hours, or
about fourteen rounds with Lally Bowers.

The notice from the *Surrey Advertiser* was quite a lengthy
one, and about a third of the way through it said something
like this: 'The part of Mirabell requires that the actor should
be handsome, tall, virile, loquacious, witty', so it went on, and
on, and on, there was adjective after adjective and at the end it
said, 'Unfortunately, Mr Sallis has none of these qualities.' A
few years ago I was in Guildford again at the Yvonne Arnaud
Theatre, and I sought out the critic who had written this notice.
I had made enquiries and tracked him down, and I said to him,
I can't remember his name now, but I knew it then, 'Could you
go through the archives, could you see if you can find that
notice of 1948, because it's a real humdinger and I would love
to have it.'

He went away and when he came back, maybe it was just to
save my face or maybe he really genuinely couldn't find it, but
he said, 'I'm terribly sorry, we do destroy quite a lot of our

back numbers because we simply haven't got the space for them.' Well, I regarded that as a great pity; I would love to be able to read that notice again now.

Staying with *The Way of the World*, only very recently I had the pleasure of meeting again with Pauline Jameson. Pauline was with the Tennent management at roughly the same time that I was. She was one of their regular supporting actresses, and she had been in *The Way of the World* playing Mrs Marwood. In the play as it is written, Millamant makes her first entrance with Mrs Marwood, and I told Pauline this story about me at Guildford, and reminded her about what John Gielgud had said. She said, 'Well, that's very strange, because do you know, Pam Brown and I used to go on together, it was our first entrance, and every night that we did it she would hold my hand in a grip of iron, and she wouldn't release me until we actually got on to the stage and she had to speak.' So there you are, it looks as though William Congreve had worked his magic, or whatever it is, on Millamant in this case.

I don't think he had the same luck with Lally Bowers, but that's not a reflection on Pamela Brown, who was a great actress. You only had to look at her work with Gielgud in *The Lady's Not for Burning*, you don't have to turn anywhere else. Once or twice we worked together in different things and she was a charmer. I am now really digressing (and I don't care!), but she was discovered originally by the critic James Agate. She was playing with one of the universities, either Oxford or Cambridge, when he went to see her in *Hedda Gabler*, and he wrote a whole notice in the *Sunday Times* about her, which resulted in Pam coming to the West End. Good for you, James Agate.

Now that I've drifted off course I'm going to stay off there for a bit, and again take you backstage to the John Gielgud company, where we were doing *The Way of the World* and

Richard II. Gielgud would wander the corridors and I used to bump into him – well, we all did for that matter – and while we were doing *Richard II* he was there, pacing about and doing the crossword and that sort of thing, and if he bumped into me he would usually say, 'Do you think you can do it?' Meaning, of course, Waitwell in *The Way of the World*.

By now I was beginning to feel my feet a bit more, so I said, 'Oh yes, yes, Mr Gielgud, yes. If you don't mind my mentioning it, I once played Mirabell.'

'Oh, did you?' he said.

Later on, while we were actually playing *The Way of the World*, once again we bumped into each other, and he sort of half congratulated me on my Waitwell. Something to the effect that I wasn't doing too badly, which cheered me up and, encouraged by this, I said it again. I thought he would have forgotten. I said, 'Do you remember I told you I once played Mirabell?'

'Oh yes,' he said, 'oh yes, hm. I'm sure you were better than I am.'

Another little thing that amused me, a couple of things really, that amused us all. He was a great crossword addict, he could carry *The Times* crossword about in his hand while he was still playing the part, although not on the stage of course. We were doing *The Way of the World* and there were three or four of us together in the dressing room somewhere, we were all doing the puzzle as well, and he came in and said, 'Ah, ah.' He looked around and said, 'Have you got one across?' and nobody had got one across. 'Ah,' he said, 'ah ha ha ha. I have!'

'What is it, Mr Gielgud?'

'Diddemans.'

'Diddemans?'

'Yes, yes, diddemans, D-I-D-D-E-M-A-N-S. Diddemans.'

'Mr Gielgud, there's no such word.'

'Oh, oh. Oh,' and he left.

There was another bit in rehearsals when Geoffrey Bayldon, a dear friend of mine, was playing a servant, and he had about half a page of speech of Congreve, which I remember began with the phrase 'There's such coupling at St Pancras'. Then it went on to list what all the different people were up to, and when Geoffrey was rehearsing it Mr Gielgud finally stopped him and said, 'Oh Geoffrey, Geoffrey, dear, dear Geoffrey, do be funny!' Those are the sort of notes that you really love to duck and weave under if you're an actor.

The next repertory company that I joined after about a year with Guildford was Chesterfield. Chesterfield is a lovely town in the centre of Derbyshire. It is, of course, famous for the crooked spire of its church. It should also be famous for its inhabitants because they were a typical bunch of people that you find in that part of the world, warmed in one way and chilled in other ways by the Derbyshire Dales. They had not got a repertory company at all, and it was formed through and by the energies of the amateur actors in the town. They converted a building next door to the town library, maybe it had been the town hall, into a theatre with proper seating accommodation and proper stage equipment, and they engaged two companies each to do fortnightly rep.

So, in effect, you had a large company, which played for half the month each. Then there would be a break, and then the amateurs would come in for a week, or it might have been two weeks. The company was managed by a gentleman – I hope I've got his name right – Ian Vogler, and there was a committee, so in a sense it was run by a committee of amateurs. I'm not going to say anything detrimental about amateurs, but I think that they did overload the theatre a bit. The idea of trying to have two companies was really too much, they couldn't possibly have afforded to keep half the company not working for two weeks. Nevertheless, they produced some good work, as far as I can remember.

I found a programme the other day for a Christmas show that we did called *When Knights Were Bold*, and I ran down the cast list and blow me, yes, I thought I'd find it, among the extras was the name Harold Pinter. With Harold, whom I got to know slightly in later years, I probably went the whole of that Christmas show without speaking to him once. But I'm sure that he was doing what other people who work in the theatre have done (Guthrie is an obvious example, who worked for some time as an actor in order to prepare for his work as a director) and was preparing for his work as a writer. Maybe he was actually writing then, I really don't know, but I think you need that feeling of being in the theatre *with* the theatre, even if you haven't got much to do, and Harold, in my opinion, epitomised that attitude. It certainly did no harm to his play-writing.

Towards the end of my year with Chesterfield I received a phone call from Geoffrey Ost. Geoffrey was the manager and director of the Sheffield Repertory Company, the Sheffield Playhouse as it was known, and I went to see him and he said, 'We really shouldn't be having this conversation, I shouldn't really make an approach to you in this way, but nevertheless, the fact is that I think I could say to you that if you were to approach me, I would be delighted to take you into the company.' It was something like that. I'm making this up, of course, but it was diplomacy stretched to breaking point, and I thanked him very much and went away, and waited a decent forty-eight hours before I phoned him and asked him if I could come and work for him, and he said yes. So that's how I joined the Sheffield Rep, for dear, dear, Geoffrey.

Geoffrey Ost *was* the Sheffield Playhouse. He was in the tradition of the classic managers. (The only other person I met in my life who was in the same category was Hal Prince, but more of him later.) It was a small theatre, it didn't seat very many and the stage was small, but Geoffrey designed all the sets and helped to create them. He placed the furniture as best he could to fit that particular production, and he did the entrances and the exits, and altogether he ran a very tight ship.

When I was leaving the Sheffield Rep I was sorry to go in a way, but it seemed to be the right thing to do. I said, 'Geoffrey, you know, you're absolutely marvellous at getting us on and off and arranging all these things for us, so that we have the least possible trouble or problems on the stage, but you never actually tell us how to do it. You never really give us any acting notes at all.'

'Oh,' he said, 'that's not my place, oh no, no, no. That's what you're here for. You're here to learn how to do it.' Well, I still don't think that he's altogether right about that, but never mind, he was a lovely man. A saint to work for. Among the cast, you might like to know, were the following people when I was there: Patrick McGoohan, Paul Eddington, Peter Barkworth, Alan MacNaughtan, John Rutland. Not a bad line-up.

I mentioned Peter Barkworth in that cast list. Peter and I were at RADA together. As he was younger than I, and had not been in the war, he had to do his National Service, and he worked for a short time with a repertory company in the south of England before he was called up. When he came out after two years, he had planned to go back to Eastbourne, or wherever it was. When he told me about this I said, 'Look, Peter, Eastbourne [or wherever it was], sorry to have to say so, is not quite in the same class as Sheffield in the league table of repertory companies. I'm absolutely certain that if I spoke to Geoffrey Ost, I could get you in.' The main reason for this was that Johnny Rutland, who'd been with us all this time at Sheffield, was leaving to come to London to do, was it *The*

Boyfriend?, one of those early musicals, early in the sense that they were just around that period after the war. So I said, 'Look, don't forget about Eastbourne, but I mean if you write to them and say that you've had this offer, they cannot refuse you and there's no reason on earth why you should feel bad about it. That, to put it rather simply, is showbusiness.' Fortunately, he did eventually give in to my request, so he came to Sheffield.

Now he, too, was with Kenneth Carten, who had a good friend, a colleague who worked for Tennent, a lady called Daphne Rye. Daphne was the principal casting agent for H. M. Tennent, under the leadership of Hugh 'Binkie' Beaumont, and she was very conscientious about her job. Every year she would make a tour of the principal repertory companies, maybe a half a dozen, maybe even more than that, talent spotting, and Kenneth Carten used to go with her. Of course there was a joint interest, that is to say if they saw somebody that they both thought was worth giving a contract to or engaging for a production, Kenneth would benefit by it, but nevertheless he wouldn't speak just to make Daphne happy. He had a mind of his own.

By now Peter and I were in the Sheffield Rep, and we were working away there, happy as sandboys, when one day we both got a letter from Kenneth to say that he and Daphne were coming to see next week's production at Sheffield. We looked at each other and, without making any motions at all, really, we just quietly shook hands. The week went by, but when the notice went up to say that the next production was a play called *Bonaventure*, we also saw that neither of us was in it.

So we crept away to the nearest hostelry, neither of us was a very heavy drinker, in fact we don't even drink much at all, but we did have a couple of pints each that night, and it was gloom and despair. Oh dear, oh dear, oh dear, was the opening line, and we went on oh dearing. I mean, there we were, both of us with Kenneth Carten, and he was going to come and see the play at the Sheffield Repertory Company and we were not going to be in it.

'Well,' I said after a bit, 'you know, Peter, we've got to socialise. On the night that they come, we've got to meet them, we can get some drinks ready in the bar, and meet them in the interval when they come and just socialise. I've read about it, about people going to a party, and there's a famous film director there, and the next thing they know is they've got the leading part in his new picture. We've just got to charm them. We've got to charm them right into the ground,' and Peter didn't disagree, so we prepared for the visit.

The day arrived and Peter and I were ready for them. We'd got gins and tonics set up in the bar, and a couple of glasses of ale for us, and we waited until the interval, then we ran round to the bar to get there first and in they came. Now I should say that Daphne Ray was a handsome, one might almost say glamorous, woman. She was, to put it lightly, extremely well-built and all her life, I think, she was aware of this attraction she had for men. So we all shook hands and said hello, and we were all being very jolly, chatting away, and every now and then somebody would crack a joke and we'd laugh. At one point Peter, who was a great giggler anyway, found something particularly funny and it tickled him, and he got more and more hilarious, and finally he threw his head back, and as his head went back his glass went forward, and the contents of this pale-ale glass went all over Daphne's front!

So it was handkerchiefs out, and it was patting away as delicately as we possibly could. Kenneth looked scarlet, and we mumbled our apologies and all that sort of thing, and Daphne made as light of it as she could. Finally we dried her out as well as possible, the interval bell rang and we went back to our seats. We sat out the rest of the play, and then we went back to our hostelry and ordered something to drink. We were crestfallen, we were suicidal. Oh dear, oh dear, oh dear. What have we done? How many years will go by before they come back to Sheffield Rep or anywhere where we are? I didn't blame Peter, it could have happened to either of us, but it had happened and there it was. We were sunk – hook, line and sinker. Months went by, weeks certainly went by, and I received a telegram from H. M. Tennent Ltd. It was to invite me to go to London to be in their production of *Three Sisters*, which was to be the one Tennents were staging for the Festival of Britain.

Not a mention of Peter. I left for London but only a couple of months went by before he too received a telegram from Tennents, from Daphne obviously, saying that he was invited to come to London to have a Tennants contract, which meant, in plain English, that he would work with them for at least a year, and be paid X pounds a week to play as cast. So there we were, within a few months both of us were in the West End with H. M. Tennent. I should say that one other member of the company, somebody that they really had seen on the stage, was Ella Adkinson. And she had turned down their offer because, in fact, she had family problems. She lived in Sheffield and I think it was her mother who was poorly, so she didn't come, but Peter and I did. So you see, it pays to socialise.

FOUR

'He Might be Green'

The year was 1951, that of the Festival of Britain. There was an exhibition called 'Britain Can Make It'. I went round this exhibition and came away with the slightly unhappy feeling that Britain could not make it, but that was purely personal. Everywhere around you there was a feeling of optimism, that the war really was all over. There I was, employed by H. M. Tennent Ltd, under the leadership of Hugh 'Binkie' Beaumont.

I would like to say something about Binkie. I was never on intimate terms with him, I never called him Binkie, to me he was always Mr Beaumont. The number of times that we had a face-to-face interview was not very many, and certainly I was never really introduced to him at the beginning of this staging of Chekhov's *Three Sisters*. But he had a reputation. He led Tennents for four decades, 1933–73, and under his leadership they just blossomed. They were the biggest producing company of theatrical plays in Britain, possibly even in the world. So to work for them was not only prestigious in a sense, but it was almost like getting an honour, and I was well aware of that.

It has just occurred to me, while I was putting this down, that there was somebody else in the world of art that you could compare Binkie with: Walter Legge. Legge was the man who did more for the recording business of opera and classical music, orchestral music and so on, than, I think, any other person, certainly in Britain. What he and Binkie had in common was consummate taste, and they wouldn't be put off, they wouldn't be side-tracked. Second-best would never do for either of them, which rather implies that I was first-best, well, I didn't really mean to put it like that.

The cast that Mr Beaumont had assembled for *Three Sisters* was made up of the following (not the complete cast, but these were the leading members): Ralph Richardson, Celia Johnson, Margaret Leighton, Diana Churchill and Renée Asherson, not bad for starters, eh! I was cast as Fedotik, and as soon as I knew this my thoughts went back to before the war, not that I had seen the production, but John Gielgud had more than one season of plays at the Queen's Theatre in London and he employed Alec Guinness. The first part that Alec Guinness played for John Gielgud was Fedotik, so I had to watch my step.

But it was a fun part, there's no doubt about that. In the play he is a jolly, romantic distraction from the heavier goings-on in the Vershinin world. He is devoted to Irina, the youngest of the three sisters, he brings her presents, a large spinning top and things like that – 'Listen to this, listen to this' – and I seem to remember that he also took a lot of photographs, or was that Rodé, the other soldier who went around with him? But it was a good part, and I had an entrance in the fire scene, when the town has caught alight, where he comes bursting in on the family and says, shrieking with laughter, 'I've been burnt out, I've been burnt out, everything's gone!' I remember that I had to come on in this scene when Margaret Leighton was having rather a heavy time with Ralph Richardson. I was standing there, she was in the middle of the stage, and she gave me the cue to come on, but before she delivered the cue, she turned to the director and said, 'He won't be late, will he?' I heard this, of course, I was meant to hear it, and I thought, no, no, Miss

Leighton, no, I won't be late. Whatever else I am, I won't be late, and so it turned out.

At the first read-through of the play we sat round in a semi-circle and Mr Beaumont was there, and the director was there, and as we read the play I ran my eye over that semicircle of people, and after a minute or so I thought the most nervous person there was, in fact, the director. I could just sense it and I think I was right, and the effect of this was that he never really quite had control of what he would have liked to have done, as opposed to what the players let him do.

This is not meant as a sour remark, it is meant as the thought of a young man who had just come from repertory and was dealing with the higher echelons for the first time. But I think I was right, and when we opened the play at the Aldwych Theatre in London it got those sorts of notices, and it is now, of course, quite a long time ago that this happened, but I have the feeling that Mr Beaumont had concentrated too much on getting the best stars that he could for this production, whereas a really good production of *Three Sisters* doesn't need stars at all. It wants people who can work together and really do their stuff together, and not worry quite so much about who they are as what they are playing. This is an unkind reflection on these great people. It isn't meant like that, it's just really a reflection of the notices we had.

Ralph Richardson was nearly fifty when we were doing *Three Sisters*, still a relatively young man, but his memory was already a bit shaky. I used to find his cribs, which he left about all over the set. He was also tone-deaf. He and Margaret Leighton, playing Masha, had their signature tune, the waltz from *Eugene Onegin*, and she could sing it, but he couldn't. So he used to do his bit from the wings, and Eric Porter would stand beside him and do the singing.

But I had previously watched him cope with his struggle for

the lines in the television version of *Witness for the Prosecution*. He had to reel off a whole list of solicitors, about eight pairs of names, and after they said, 'Turn over, and ... Action,' he got up and said, 'Send for Nelson, Rodney, Frobisher, Drake ...', listing all these English admirals instead. I thought he would never stop, he couldn't remember any of the solicitors, but he was very good on admirals. I played his valet in the film, and after I had done my final shot, he turned to me and said, 'Very good, very good, you just breathed on it. It was good, good.' Of course he couldn't have said anything nicer, I just curled up in a corner and never wanted to speak to anybody ever again in my life.

It took me back to his Falstaff, and the most effective thing he did in that Old Vic production. After the Gadshill mob attacked him in disguise, and Falstaff pretends he knew it was them all the time, he turned his back on them, saying, 'By the Lord, I knew ye as well as he that made ye.' He did it almost in a stage whisper and I remembered how he just breathed on it. He was so perfectly cast, he was an English gentleman, and yet he had one foot in the cow pasture. A lovely man.

In 1952 I made my first motion picture. Now, the verb to *make* a film is one used by actors only in relation to movies. An actor never *makes* a play, or *makes* a television, they *do* plays and they *do* television, but for some reason or other, which I've never followed, you *made* pictures. The reason for telling you this, however, is in order to be able to introduce the Buckstone Club. I never knew what Buckstone's Christian name was, but he had been an actor-manager of some note. I know nothing about his history, but it was after him that the place was named. It was in a basement opposite the stage door of the Haymarket Theatre.

It was begun shortly after the war by Oscar Quitak, and it was first called the Under 30 Club. The inference was obvious, it was to give young actors in the London area a chance to get together, and to be able to drink and eat at moderate prices. If you were a big star you went for a slightly more selective type of club, let me put it that way. In fact, it didn't actually last very long as the Under 30 Club, the main reason being that it wasn't populated by enough people. So it was decided that the age limit should be made limitless, and therefore it pulled in a few more bodies to be members. Nevertheless the implication was that you were going to be meeting chaps of your own age and standing in the profession. Every now and then you would bump into a star like Eli Wallach, or somebody like that, but it was mainly for us starters. While I was visiting there one night, Oscar Quitak had by then really left it in the hands of Gerry Campion, whom some of you may remember. He had made his name in television by playing Billy Bunter in the Greyfriars School series on television; he was a round-faced, jovial man, and he ran that club very efficiently and in a very friendly way. One day I was in there having a drink and he said, 'Are you doing anything at the moment?' I said no, and he said, 'Well, look, I think I may have a part for you. I've been cast in a film and I'm due to start any minute now and something's come up.' He had some serious reason for not being able to do the film, and he said, 'If you go along, or get in touch with your agent, they may take you on to play my part.'

I thought that was very nice of him, and very kind, and I must have reported back to Kenneth Carten, because before I knew where I was, I was cast in this film. It was called *Child's Play*, and the essence of the story was that there was a bunch of children, six or seven of them, who had discovered the secret of atomic energy, and they had concentrated their efforts on making popcorn. The popcorn had to be delivered and the young man who drove the van with the popcorn in the back was to be played by Peter Sallis.

If you think that sounds a pretty daft idea for a film, well, so would I in the normal way, but if you look in your Halliwell you will find that it gets a very good notice, considering the type of film that it was. I presented myself on the day of shooting, which was quite quickly after I'd had the conversation with Gerry Campion, and Hal Mason was the producer, Margaret Thomson was the lady director, who had also partly written the script.

Hal Mason regarded me with suspicion right from the word go. What little he had heard about me led him to believe that I was a theatre actor, and that my experience of films was very limited, and he was absolutely right. His main concern was that as a theatre actor I would be waving my arms about and bellowing, and generally carrying on in order to be heard at the back of the stalls. Well even I, beginner as I was, knew well enough to avoid that trap. My real problem was being cast as the young man who owned the van, and who drove the children and their popcorn about. But I couldn't drive.

I had never driven in my life, I had once had a children's bicycle, but that was about as far as I had got. Nobody thought to ask me this when they were casting me, but there I was on the set, and here was the van, and they expected me to leap into it and drive off. They were not going to recast it at that stage, the timing was too important, so they managed it somehow, they got somebody to lie, crouch or sit behind me, somehow or other, and work the controls. I knew enough about driving that if you wanted to go right you turned the wheel in a right direction, if you wanted to go left you turned it to the left, and somehow we overcame that obstacle. As I say, the film had quite a nice reception. I actually saw it and I thought it was quite charming.

In 1952, in addition to making my first film, I established a toehold in television. Naomi Capon, that was the name. She was an American by birth and had married an Englishman, Kenneth Capon, who was an architect, and had built the family a home in Hampstead. As the years went by, I became a friend of Naomi's. She had lots of friends and I was one of them. She did stories for children written specially for television, and usually they had more than one episode. They illustrated certain aspects of British history, the background of kings and queens, etc, and very often we were peasants. We might be marching peasants, as in *The March of the Peasants*, or we were revolting peasants, as in *The Revolt of the Peasants*.

Naomi had built up her own repertory company. I didn't think of it like that at the time, but that's really what it was. She had about six, seven or eight of us, whom she seemed to use regularly to man these various stories. The truth is, at least for the men, that we were a group. The only one of those people that I can remember now, really with any certainty, was Timothy Bateson, but there we were. Naomi was a good friend to me, as well as being a great help in terms of casting.

Later in the same year, 1952, Tennents came up with another play that they asked me to be in. What happened really was that I auditioned for a part. The play was *Summer and Smoke* by Tennessee Williams. It was an early work of his and the leading lady was played in our production by Margaret Johnson, a fine actress who became a friend. The character that she portrayed was really the forerunner of Blanche Dubois in *A Streetcar Named Desire*. In the final scene of *Summer and Smoke* you see this woman who has been treated badly by the leading man of the play, in our case William Sylvester. He is a bit of a swine and he lets her down, and at the end of the play she wanders off on to a little side set where there is a fountain. In fact, it's been there all the evening, and she picks up a young American boy and they go off together, and we are to assume that that leads her to a life of prostitution.

I was invited to audition for the part of the young man that she picks up. At the same time others auditioned and among them was Harry Towb, who became another friend, and still is, thank goodness. Harry auditioned and got that part, and I was cast as the young man who saw himself as the boyfriend of the leading lady:

'How did it go, Miss Alma?'

'How did what go?'

'My solo on the French horn?'

So there we were, doing *Summer and Smoke*, and Tennessee Williams attended all the rehearsals. I particularly remember one day with great affection. In the play there was an episode between the louche, rather over-masculine leading man that was Bill Sylvester and a young girl, played by Sheila Shand-Gibbs, and they had a little scene together. He is a doctor, and she goes to see him in his surgery. He is teasing her, and generally speaking playing around a bit, and she doesn't say anything.

Peter Glenville, our director, turned to Tennessee at one point in the middle of this scene and said, 'Tennessee, she doesn't say anything. I mean, I think she should have something, you know.'

And Tennessee said, 'Oh, oh, well,' and he began to move down the aisle of the theatre, and those of us who had been listening and watching crept nearer, because we were thinking, it's Tennessee Williams, we're going to hear him create.

My mind went back to William Shakespeare and I could hear somebody saying, 'Well, Will, look, we need a few more lines here, you know.'

'Oh, what do you want? Do you want eight?'

'Well, twelve will be good.'

'OK, I'll give you twelve.' Well, I don't suppose he actually said 'OK', but you get the drift, and we thought, well, this is it.

This is Tennessee Williams and he's going to create. We shall get something about the silver pearly raindrops falling on the railway line, something on those lines.

By this time Tennessee had got up on to the stage. He said, 'Has she got a purse?'

'Oh yes, she's got a purse, that's fine, that's fine. Well, she could put her hand in the purse and take out this little paper bag and offer it up to him and say, "Sweet?"'

'Oh. Oh yeah. Oh, yes, of course, of course, yes, yes, yes,' and we crept back to our places, and Tennessee Williams, having made his offering, went back and sat down and the rehearsal continued. Of course, what was interesting about it was that Tennessee had got it right, it was the perfect little something for her to say and to do. *Summer and Smoke* came in to London at the Duchess Theatre and we had a fair run.

Incidentally, another man in the company I became friends with was Gaylord Cavallaro. An American as you might imagine from his name, and he was over here picking up odd parts in plays. I remember one night we were in Brighton playing the Theatre Royal, and we were both of us going back to our digs after the show and just chatting away, and Gaylord said to me, 'Peter, you know, I do miss home. There was this big garden and at the bottom of it there was this huge tree, and I wish I was there now so that I could practise my knife throwing.'

Then I was offered an audition. I was asked if I would go to the Old Vic and audition there. Just a general audition, they were holding things like this all the time, it wasn't for any specific part. So I went along and at that time the Old Vic Theatre was run by Tyrone Guthrie, probably the greatest stage director of his time, certainly in this country. They were doing *Timon of Athens* by Shakespeare, and the leading part was going to be played by Donald Wolfit, but he and Guthrie didn't see eye to eye over something or other, and the result was that Wolfit left the company and André Morell was asked to come in and fill the role of *Timon*.

I like to think, although of course it's complete nonsense, that that meant that everybody moved up one, and there was a hole at the bottom. I went along and did this audition, and I was successful up to a point because Guthrie asked to see me, so I went to meet the great man. I can't describe his character, you just had to be with him and the character enveloped you, but I can't describe it well enough. He was a great man, and his knowledge and taste in the theatre were outstanding. Later he created the Stratford Ontario Theatre in Canada, where they produced Shakespeare. He and the designer Tanya Moiseiwitsch went over to Canada to build the theatre. Not going off at too much of a tangent here, but they more or less invented what we now know as the thrust stage, of which in Britain the Chichester Theatre is a typical example, the way that the seating is arranged so that it's like a shell, and the stage is in the centre of the bottom of the shell. Fine in the sense that you've got a full house, or you can get a full house, at the minimum cost, because you don't have a proscenium arch.

But in my opinion that is a disaster. I think that the theatre in the round, of which the Royal Exchange Theatre in Manchester is the most obvious example in this country, is a disaster too, but we will come to that later.

Tyrone Guthrie was directing *Timon of Athens* and I was invited to join the cast. When I went to see him he offered me three parts, which naturally I grabbed with both hands. The first was in the opening moments, and then I had a scene as a messenger with the Senator. I had to hand the Senator a scroll, and there was a little bit of dialogue between the two of us before he walked off with it.

When we arrived at this scene in rehearsal, Guthrie came up on to the stage with the scroll in his hand and gave it to me and said, 'Look, I want you to come on, and I want you to just take the stage. I'll give you two minutes before I send on anybody else, you've got the stage for all that time to yourself,' and he went back down into the stalls. I thought, blow me, oh, yes, OK, all right. I haven't the faintest idea what I did now, but I know one thing: it didn't last for two minutes. Two minutes is an eternity in the theatre. No. What Guthrie was doing demonstrated what I'd heard of his personality as a director, and why among the younger members like myself he was such a name.

Guthrie had a reputation for not being all that kind to his leading players. I do not mean that he didn't treat them well, I'm just saying that he rather left them to their own devices and didn't direct them, if you'd like to put it that way. And why, indeed, should he if they're great players? But when it came to the younger members of the cast – and this I'd heard before joining his company – he was more helpful, to say the least of it, and here he was helping me. He was giving me time on the stage to do something.

I wish to goodness I could remember what I did. I have a feeling I may have put the scroll up to my eye as if it were a telescope, something like that. But at any rate it certainly didn't last two minutes and the actor who was playing the Senator came on and we continued with the scene, but of course I would have given my heart and soul for Tyrone Guthrie. I did work for him in a play a few years later, but more of that anon.

We came to the end of our run of *Timon of Athens* at the Old Vic, before going to Zurich, where we presented the play for a week. Thus I left these shores for the first time in my life. I was going to fly and I know that I didn't give it much of a thought, but since then I've thought about it. Of course, in those days there weren't jets. It was a propeller-driven aeroplane, what I think was probably then called a Viscount, and this aeroplane didn't fly above 10,000 feet. If it had it would have been interesting to know whether I would have blacked out or not, but I never had a chance to find out.

I realised that even though we were performing in what was to the audience a foreign language, by some instinct or other most of them knew what we were talking about. My other memory of Zurich, a beautiful city, was that Lee Montague took me boating on Lake Zurich and I had my first Campari soda. The aeroplane got me back and I still hadn't blacked out, and I got the call to go to the Mermaid Theatre in St John's Wood.

The Mermaid Theatre was built, with some assistance from others, by Bernard Miles. An eccentric of the theatre, he was a man who certainly left his mark, and he, of course, was also responsible later for building the much bigger Mermaid Theatre at Puddle Dock in the City. Years after I had done my short season with him at the Mermaid Theatre in St John's Wood we did a broadcast together and there were just the two of us, so we spent some time drinking coffee and chatting, and he told me how he had succeeded in raising the money to build the theatre at Puddle Dock.

The Mermaid was already well established at St John's Wood and doing, for the size of the theatre, very well. It never lacked an audience, but Bernard was ambitious and he wanted to transfer it if he could. He needed to raise money in the City and he knew that the way to do this was to get some money from the Governor of the Bank of England. If you could establish that you had raised even five shillings from the Governor of the Bank of England, you were 'in' the City, and people would start investing in your project.

So he wrote to the Governor and didn't even get a reply. But it wasn't very long afterwards that he had a letter from the wife of the Governor. To raise money for one of her charities she was going to have a garden fête where they lived, and she asked Bernard if he would go along and do his act. In this he played a rustic with a straw sticking out of his mouth and a floppy hat, leaning over a gate in a fence and talking to you. In other words it was a comic monologue, which he did in his country style in a country voice.

After he had done his turn he got a message that the Governor would like to see him. Back in the main house the Governor showed him round, and during the course of their tour of the house they came across pictures of former Governors of the Bank of England, and then a contemporary picture of this one. They looked at it together and the Governor said, 'What do you think of that, Mr Miles?'

And Bernard said, 'Well, sir, he looks like a fellow you'd have great difficulty in getting any money out of.' That was more or less the end of their conversation that day and Bernard went home. Within twenty-four hours the post arrived and in it was a cheque from the Governor of the Bank of England. I cannot remember, or Bernard didn't tell me, how much it was for, but it got him started and with that he was able to raise the money through the City to build the theatre in Puddle Dock.

In 1952 Bernard, once again showing the way that he could win friends and influence people, had persuaded the Swedish soprano Kirsten Flagstad to sing for him, or for the audience, rather, at the Mermaid Theatre. She was to do *Dido and Aeneas*, and on the nights that she sang, or for the matinées that she sang, she would be rewarded with a bottle of stout. That was her wage. It was fun to be in the same house while we were doing our plays, and hearing in the distance Kirsten Flagstad practising. A lovely thought.

One of our two plays was *A Trick to Catch the Old One* by Thomas Middleton. Now Thomas Middleton was early seventeenth century, and he was better known for two plays that were published posthumously, *The Changeling* and *Women Beware Women*. Our play was to be directed by Joan Swinstead, who had taught me at RADA, and she was also a client of Kenneth Carten. Eric Chitty and I played two old men who were at loggerheads throughout the play – I can't remember any of the details at all, but it was watched by the critics, among them Kenneth Tynan. By then Tynan was flavour of the month among the critics. In other words if you wanted to find out how your play was going to do, the first person you read was Ken Tynan and at the Mermaid he gave me a marvellous notice.

I wish I'd got it now. I would flaunt it in front of you if I could. All I remember about it is something that I didn't understand at that time and I don't understand now. I just remember the phrase that Kenneth used, which was: 'Mr Sallis plays [whatever his name was] from his own point of view.' Well, there we are. But I think I can say it was the best notice that I've ever received for anything, and it must have attracted the attention of my old friend Daphne Rye, because she came to see the play, and the next thing I knew was that I was awarded a Tennents contract.

It meant that I was to work for Tennents for twelve months, that I would be paid twelve pounds a week, and I'd play as cast. To my surprise and delight, the first job they asked me to do was to be a member of Mr John Gielgud's company in a season of plays that he was to do at the Lyric Theatre Hammersmith. Mr Gielgud, as he then was, was to produce three plays. He was going to direct *Richard II* by Shakespeare, with Paul Scofield playing the King, next he would direct as well as play in *The Way of the World* by William Congreve, and finally he would do

Venice Preserv'd by Thomas Otway in a production by Peter Brook, where he shared the two male leads with Paul Scofield.

I was invited to go along to the Globe Theatre and meet the great man, together with other actors and actresses who, like me, had been told that they would be in the season but, also like me, had not yet been cast. I went along and Mr Gielgud was seated on the stage at a table with two stalwarts of Tennents, Kitty Black and John Perry, and eventually it was my turn. When I went up on to the stage, he rose graciously to greet me, shook me by the hand, bade me sit down and then, speaking very rapidly but with perfect precision, he told me exactly how he intended to produce *Richard II*. He talked about the sets and costumes by Loudon Sainthill. He talked about the King's relationship with Bolingbroke, about the King's relationship with his three toadies, Bushy, Bagot and Green, and finally he rattled to a stop, looked me straight in the eye and said, 'Do you agree?'

Well, I hadn't come all the way from St John's Wood to muck it up at this stage, so I said, 'Oh yes, oh goodness me, yes.'

'Oh good,' he said and, somewhat reassured, turned round to Kitty Black and John Perry and said, 'He might be Green, he might be Green.' Then he turned back to me and said, 'You see, we have two men playing Bushy and Bagot, very beautiful. You might make a good contrast.'

Well, I wasn't cast as Green. I was cast as Lord Willoughby and we had the first read-through. We sat in three rows, with Paul sitting in the middle of the front row, of course, with Joy Parker, his wife, who was playing the Queen, Veronica Turley, my old mate Brewster Mason was there, and an old withered character actor, built like a beanpole, the darling Herbert Lomas. Herbert 'Tiny' Lomas was probably the gauntest Gaunt who has ever graced the English stage. Then there was the second row, and that was made up of the not quite so eminent members of the cast, and finally in the third row there were Lord Willoughby and his kind.

We read the play and at the end of it Mr Gielgud congratulated Joy and Paul and Tiny Lomas, and then he worked his way through the second row, and finally he came to the third row, where he had a few general notes. He was shuffling his papers together and we thought he'd finished, and then he said, 'Ah, ah, there's only one voice that is wrong and that is Peter Sallis.' I put up my hand. 'Ah,' he said, 'what are you playing?'

'Lord Willoughby, Mr Gielgud.'

'Aahhh,' he said, 'ah. How would you like to play the servant to the Duke of York?'

Well, this story so far is absolutely true, but now I'm going to invent a bit. I see Mr Gielgud going into that little lift up at the Globe Theatre to see his friend Mr Beaumont, Binkie Beaumont, and they discuss their hopes for the future, for the production, and finally they finish what they have to say, and Mr Gielgud moves to the door and opens it and then he pauses to say, 'Oh, this young man, Peter Sallis, he's not up to this sort of thing. I've given him the servant to the Duke of York.' He is just about to close the door behind him when he hears Mr Beaumont scream, and he comes back, 'Yes?'

'Peter Sallis,' says Mr Beaumont, 'Peter Sallis. We've just put that young man under contract. We're paying him twelve pounds a week! We could get anybody off the street to play the servant to the Duke of York for a fiver!'

'Ah,' says Mr Gielgud, and he goes.

So the rehearsals began. Well, as you can imagine, as I was playing the servant to the Duke of York I hadn't got a great deal to do, so I sat in the stalls and watched, and I watched a masterclass in how to direct Shakespeare, particularly *Richard II*. Mr Gielgud was on the stage most of the time. He never looked at the script, he knew every word. He positioned the actors and told them why they were standing where they were, where they were looking, what their thoughts might be, but generally speaking he was marshalling them, and he was doing it inch by inch, line by line, and then going back and redoing it. As I watched this process, I sat there thinking to myself, this is great, and to think I'm being paid twelve pounds a week to watch this.

Eventually it was the turn of the servant to the Duke of York. At last I was going to do the scene with the Duke of York, who was played by Richard Wordsworth – a direct descendant of the poet, by the way. I was in the wings waiting to go on and when it was my turn I went on and I knelt a lot, and I shuffled a lot and I bowed a lot, and I got up to Richard Wordsworth, and I said my little speech as the servant to the Duke of York.

Basil Henson, who was in the company, talking about it later said that he thought that I had not perhaps the *only* funny line in the play, but certainly *the* funniest line in the play, and the speech went like this: 'My Lord, an hour before I came, the Duchess died,' and then I went on for a little bit more, finished, bowed, scraped, backed off into the wings, and Mr Gielgud, who knew my name by now, called out, 'Peter, Peter.'

And I came back. 'Yes, Mr Gielgud.'

'Is that all you do?'

'Yes, Mr Gielgud.'

'Oh Christ.'

The run of *Richard II* ended and we came to do *The Way of the World*. I've written about that earlier when I was at Guildford Rep, so I needn't say any more about *The Way of the World* here. But then we came to the last of our three plays, which brings me to a different sort of triumvirate. In 1947 we had Ralph Richardson, Laurence Olivier and John Gielgud. They were the great triumvirate and early in 1947 they knighted Ralph

Richardson. The first thing he did was to send a telegram to his friend Laurence Olivier saying, 'They've given it to the wrong one.' Well, they made up for it and later that year they knighted Laurence Olivier. Then we all waited for John Gielgud, and we waited, and we waited, and we waited, and the years went by.

So we came into the 1950s and we were still waiting, and then in 1953, when we were doing *Venice Preserv'd*, the last play of this season, we either read in our papers or heard on the news that morning that Mr Gielgud was to be knighted in the Coronation Honours. I think that day we all arrived early at the theatre. We queued up outside his dressing-room door to go in and congratulate him. I've never felt such a happy feeling anywhere and he was standing there in the dressing room with tears running down his cheeks. I've never seen anybody look so happy. One by one we went in, and we either shook him by the hand or were given a hug or a kiss, depending, I suppose, a bit on your billing, and his telegrams were stacked high on the table. Mac, dear old Mac, his dresser, hadn't had a chance to open them. They were just stacked up there in piles.

The feeling in the theatre was of enormous relief and excitement and pleasure. When we got up to our dressing room, one of us, I think it might have been Geoffrey Bayldon, said, 'You know, we ought to be in the wings when he comes on.'

And we all said, 'Oh, good gracious, yes, of course we must be in the wings.' So we got dressed, hurriedly, and we got down into the wings and we waited, the usual wait that precedes the lifting of any curtain in the theatre. The house, we learnt, was packed, you couldn't get a seat anywhere and they were standing where they couldn't sit, and the feeling was one of intense excitement.

I should tell you how the play opened. If Thomas Otway had known about this occasion he could not have written anything better than he did. The curtain goes up and off stage you hear two men quarrelling. One is an old man and the other a not so old man, and eventually the old man comes on and says his first line, then there's a brief pause and the second man comes on and says his first line.

We were standing waiting in the wings and the curtain went up, and off stage we heard the voices. The older man was played by Tiny Lomas and the younger man by John Gielgud. Tiny Lomas came on first and said, 'Out of my sight, knave, begone, I will not hear you!' There was the briefest of pauses and then the audience saw John Gielgud's foot come round the corner of the stage, and they were on their feet, clapping and cheering and whistling, and we in the wings were clapping and stamping our feet and whistling. It was hubbub! The rest of his body followed his foot, and he entered and stood in the centre of the stage.

I can see him now, his head is back, the tears are cascading down his face, his smile is radiant. Well, I thought he looked happy in the dressing room, but this, he is just radiating happiness and he stands there and he stands there, and he laps it all up and the cheers go on and on, and the clapping and the stamping. They won't let it stop. But it does stop, eventually, and he says his first line, which is 'My lord, you shall hear me, I am not that arrant knave you think me!' And they all erupted again.

Eventually the play continued on its way. As the days went by our nerves settled and we got used to the idea of Sir John Gielgud. Then, apparently, he had a message from the government of Rhodesia. The Rhodesian government were to give a festival to celebrate the centenary of the birth of Rhodesia by Rhodes, the explorer, and Sir John was invited to take a company there and do a production. They were running a festival of some three to four weeks, in Bulawayo, not in

Salisbury the capital as it was called then. So he accepted the invitation and the obvious thing to do was to take *Richard II*. He must have spoken to Paul Scofield, and Paul obviously agreed, so Sir John was going to play Richard II, and we were going to rehearse it with him, not that it needed much rehearsal, because, of course, he had produced the play and he knew it, I'm tempted to say, backwards.

The man who had been playing the gardener in *Richard II* had a job elsewhere, so he left before we were due to go to Bulawayo and Sir John asked me to play the part instead. As it happens, it was the part that I would have chosen to do, had I had a free hand, but it was already cast when I first went to see him.

But something happened that was rather sweet, and because of all that had gone before I'm going to tell you. We had been rehearsing it for a couple of days, and I had been doing the gardener and so on, and one day as we came to the end of rehearsal we were all streaming off the stage, and going through the little pass door to take us back to our dressing rooms when Sir John stopped at the top of the steps. Looking over the crowd of us, he found me with his eyes and said, 'Oh, Peter, Peter, you're so good as the gardener, so good,' and he disappeared. I thought, ah well, that's marvellous. It made up for everything. Lovely.

So off we went to Bulawayo, and needless to say he didn't get through his visit to Bulawayo without committing at least one faux pas. At a coffee morning or something like that, he made a little speech of thanks and prefaced it by saying, 'We've all been working like blacks!' You wouldn't have expected anything else from him, actually.

I was still under contract with Tennents, who announced that they were going to do Christopher Fry's latest play, *The Dark Is Light Enough*. Christopher Fry had prefaced the writing of what became known as his four seasonal plays by saying that he wished to do a spring play, a summer play, an autumn play and a winter play. *The Lady's Not for Burning* was the spring play; the summer play, *A Yard of Sun*, had yet to be written; the autumn play was *Venus Observed*; and *The Dark Is Light Enough* was the winter play.

Edith Evans was to play the lead. James Donald was to be her supporting male actor. My old friends Maggie Johnson and Peter Barkworth were in it. I was asked to be a soldier in a second-act scene that contained three or four soldiers.

The sets were by Oliver Messel. Now I have spoken elsewhere, and will probably speak again, about the habit that they have these days, that when you go into the theatre to see whatever it is you're going to see the curtain is already up. I have never understood this. I have never seen the point of it. That you should sit, let's say, for fifteen or twenty minutes, thumbing through your programme and looking at the set that you are going to be watching for the first act, and possibly two acts. Why the management, why the directors, do it goodness knows. There was no way that Oliver Messel was going to let the audience come in and see his set before they were settled, and they were ready for it and he was ready for them. The sets, when we saw them, were magnificent. They had a hugeness about them.

We did it at the Aldwych, but we toured beforehand, of course. The first set had a great sweeping staircase, that is all I really remember of it. The second set was this stable scene with straw, and the third act was another interior. What Oliver Messel needed, though, in the first set, the one with the great staircase, was a small occasional table, but he didn't want it to affect the opening setting that he had already planned. So somebody had to bring that table on before the action began and I was given the job. I was going to play an old retainer who was to come on from the audience left, walk across the stage carrying this ormolu table, set it down and then continue on my way and go off. After a suitable pause, the play would begin, and the characters would come on.

So I was given another part, and it was decided that I was to be Old Tenky. Why they bothered to give me a name at all I don't know, but I was very proud of it and was a bit miffed when the programme was published for the opening night and I wasn't in it. No mention of Old Tenky – Peter Sallis. Never mind, I got ready. I had a long coat, a dark suit, typical sort of footman, if you like. I was also given a whitish wig. We had several dress rehearsals and before the first one, which also included a dress and make-up parade, I prepared myself with a lot of Leichner No. 5, if you know what No. 5 is, there was a lot of lake, giving me age lines, and there was a lot of white stuff too. In other words my face was beginning to resemble Charing Cross on a snowy day.

Eventually, I was ready to go on and show myself to the producer, and I walked on to the stage and my old friend Daphne Rye was there, and she said, 'Who's that?'

I said, 'It's me, Daphne.'

'Who do you think you are?'

'Well, I'm Old Tenky, I'm going to bring the table on.'

'Not looking like that!' she said. 'Off you go and take it all off, put a little bit of powder on and that's it. Right?'

'Yes, Daphne.' So off I trotted and got ready.

The producer was Peter Brook. Christopher Fry was there throughout the rehearsals and we opened in Newcastle. The first night came and went, and Peter Brook called a rehearsal on the stage the following day for the full company, including Edith Evans. He came on to the stage, with Christopher Fry following him, and addressing us all said, 'Well, we've done the play Christopher's way, and now we're going to do it our way.'

I felt he could have put that rather better, although of course I didn't say anything, but there was something obviously wrong somewhere and Peter Brook was determined to put it right, as he should have done and did.

So we went off on tour – and I'm only telling you this because it's a bit personal – Christopher came with us and he used to watch the play from the front. Then he'd wander around the dressing rooms and pop his head round the door, and I'd got with me a copy of his play *The Firstborn*. I had done this play in Chesterfield Rep, and I played the Pharaoh in it. I had found it pretty heavy going in places and one day I had the script open on the make-up table beside me when Christopher came in.

I said, 'Christopher, come and have a look at this,' and I pointed to this page in *The Firstborn*. 'I played the Pharaoh, could you tell me what this passage of mine' – it was all in blank verse – 'could you tell me what this passage that I say here means?'

There must have been about a dozen lines or more, and Christopher obediently read through it and said, 'No, I'm sorry, Peter, I haven't the faintest idea what I'm talking about there.'

'OK, Christopher, I just wanted your confirmation that it's not easy.'

'No, no, it certainly isn't,' he said.

Leaving *The Firstborn* to one side, what a master of the English language he was. Thinking back to my old friend William Congreve and *The Way of the World*, this stuff was lighter, this was frothy, and *The Lady's Not for Burning* in particular was so funny, and I was lucky enough to do it in rep. We did it at Sheffield and it was gorgeous stuff.

I think Christopher was seduced by the cinema. After he wrote the screenplay for *Ben-Hur* he was called upon to do a biblical film, directed by John Huston, called *The Bible*, and if you can imagine trying to compress the Bible into something like two and a half hours, that is what they asked him to do. I'm sure the money was good, but Christopher, I think, suffered by it.

FIVE

Moby Dick Rehearsed

While *The Dark Is Light Enough* was still being produced and playing at the Aldwych Theatre, Guthrie asked if he could have me in the next play that he was going to do, and obviously Mr Beaumont agreed, so I left the cast of *The Dark Is Light Enough* and entered the cast of *The Matchmaker*, by Thornton Wilder, which was to star Ruth Gordon. For any actor, never mind me, to move from a play starring Edith Evans to a play starring Ruth Gordon was an extraordinary shift. You could not imagine two leading ladies in the theatre more different, not only in the way that they worked, but of course in the material that they did.

I had barely heard of Ruth Gordon, and yet when I began to get to know her I realised that she and her husband, Garson Kanin, had written three great movies for Katharine Hepburn and Spencer Tracy. The first was the best, *Adam's Rib*, then there was *Pat and Mike*, and the third was *Desk Set*. They were a pretty formidable couple, Ruth and Garson Kanin. They wrote some dazzling material and here she was playing the lead in *The Matchmaker*. In case you think you're not going to be told this, I have to say straight away that of course *The Matchmaker* finally turned into being *Hello Dolly!*.

Ruth was diminutive in size, but she went about the stage like a buzzing hornet, popping into corners and digging into people and generally scurrying about, busy as a bee. Edith Evans, when she played Millamant, never made an entrance. She was always discovered – in a large high-backed chair, seated and with a fan, and what Edith Evans could do with a fan was, well, nobody's business.

I am now going to use a word that I expect is only going to be used once in this memoir, and I'm doing that because there is no other word in the English language that quite makes its point as this one does in this context. Laurence Olivier, Vivien Leigh, Garson Kanin, Ruth Gordon, Spencer Tracy and Katharine Hepburn were all having supper together in one of their houses in Hollywood, and they were talking, as actors tend to do, about acting, and they were coming down to the crunch, what is the secret, what is the real core to being an actor, being a good actor?

One by one they gave their opinion, and finally it was left to Spencer Tracy who was sitting there moodily looking into the fire, and Katharine Hepburn said to him, 'Come on, Spence, come on, what do you think is the essence of acting?'

And Spencer Tracy looked at them and said, 'Learning your fucking lines!' and this I have found to be absolutely true. I knew it by instinct before I met Ruth Gordon, but Ruth made it abundantly clear what Spencer Tracy meant.

It is that ability by an actor to be able to so absorb the lines that they are completely second nature to him or her. Of course, it happens if you're in a very long run anyway, but Ruth had it from the word go, and later in conversations with her and with Garson I knew that this was the secret (well, not a secret exactly) of the way in which she mastered the art of comedy as she knew it. Every day – and I wasn't there every day, but I did go to her dressing room quite often – you would see her making up in front of the mirror, and while she was making up she was going through the lines of her part of the play. Then she moved into position in the wings and got ready for, let us say, her first entrance. While she was there, you could see her lips moving and she was going through the lines. It wasn't because she was a bit shaky on them, it was simply because she was going to make sure they came first and nothing else when she was actually on the stage. When she got on to the stage, after a suitable time really to absorb what she was doing, she would start to improvise.

Now I don't mean by that that she changed the meaning of the lines or anything like that, but let me give you an example. If she was in the middle of a speech with Horace Vandergelder, in the script as written by Thornton Wilder she says 'Would you like some more toast, Mr Vandergelder?'; well Ruth would say that one night, and then the next night she might say, 'Mr Vandergelder, you ain't got no toast, let me get you some more toast,' simple little examples like that, which she used for her own benefit throughout the run of the play. She never failed to give you the cue. She never tried to improvise on the actual cue, but in the centre of the speeches that she had, and she had quite a few, this was her way of keeping the mind fresh and alive.

She was a strong advocate of holding the line together. Most jokes come at the end of the line, the rest is just a build-up. If you have a line that ends in a joke, then don't let the inflection fall in the middle of the line, so that there's a chance that the audience will laugh before you want them to, before you get to the end of the line: 'That wasn't a lady you saw me with last night, that was my wife,' keep it going, keep it up. In a way Ruth was giving a lesson in how to play comedy every night, and I spent a lot of time in the wings watching her and absorbing her. She was great.

The part that Guthrie had in mind for me was listed in the programme as 'A Musician'. Well, that's one way of putting it,

I suppose. I was dressed as a gypsy. I had the full golden earrings and a bandeau round my head and a lot of red make-up, and I leered a great deal. Ruth and Eileen Kirby, who was playing her friend in the play, and Arthur Hill and Alec McCowen, were at a restaurant. They sang 'East Side West Side all around the Town', there was some dialogue and then they were interrupted by the entrance of a musician, and I came on playing 'The Skater's Waltz' with one finger of each hand. I leered a lot and went round them two or three times, finally I went off, and that was my second part of the evening accomplished.

Guthrie took me by the scruff of the neck and led me to Leslie Bridgewater who was the music director for most of the Tennent shows. He had me in one hand and the concertina in the other, and he said to Leslie Bridgewater. 'Teach him to play "The Skater's Waltz" with one finger of each hand,' and he gave me a little friendly shove in the back and went off and left us to it. For the first week of the tour, he was kind enough to let me have a musical backing, in other words Leslie Bridgewater recorded 'The Skater's Waltz', and it was played on a sound-track while I just went through the motions on the stage.

But on the Monday night of the second week of the run, wherever we were, Guthrie came into the dressing room and with a leer, one of my leers, said to me, 'You're on your own tonight, chum, I'm cutting the music, you do it without the backing.' So I took a deep breath and went on and did it without the backing, and it was a pleasant little interlude in the play, not a great soul-seeking experience for anybody, but it was quite sweet.

There was a feeling of success at the Haymarket Theatre about *The Matchmaker* even before it opened. This sort of thing happens in the theatre, there is a certain amount of word of mouth, it is just a feeling that the audience get that this is going to be all right, and so it turned out. Even me – after my first appearance as the barber with Sam Levine – when I went off at the end of it I got a round of applause. Now I think it was the only time I'd got a round on that exit, and I'm quite sure that it was due to the bubbly feeling in the audience, they just wanted to enjoy everything. When I got to the pass door and I bumped into Guthrie, he said, 'Is your mother in front?'

Garson Kanin was in the theatre every night with his wife, and at matinées too. He used to wander around, pop his head round the corner of the dressing room and say, 'Can I come in?' Of course the answer was always yes. There were four of us in one dressing room and Garson came in very often, just for a chat, and talking about anything under the sun.

After a bit, he came in one day with a suitcase, and he put the suitcase on the ground and said, 'Listen, fellers, I've just been doing a little shopping in Jermyn Street, and I've got these rags that I'm not using any more. Dip into them. If there's anything you fancy just take it. I'll come back for the case later.' Well, this happened more than once and there was quite a grand selection of clothing, and indeed I collected two light-weight suits. I had never had a lightweight suit before. This, of course, was an American cut, but Garson and I were about the same size and they fitted me perfectly. As the years went by the little tummy became a big tummy and I couldn't get the trousers on any more. But that was typical of Garson, he just really wanted an excuse for a chat.

He always referred to Ruth as 'my wife, Ruth Gordon, the actress'. He never said 'Ruth' or 'Miss Gordon'. One day – I can't remember how long we'd been running but it would have been a matter of months – one day I came in to the theatre and there was a note waiting for me from Garson and it said, 'Dear Peter, knock on the door marked "Ruth Gordon, the actress", I'd like a word or two with you, maybe three, Garson.' So I knocked on the door and I went in, and there she was, making up, going through her lines by the mirror, and Garson said, 'Pete, I'm bored. I've got nothing to do, or at least I didn't have anything to do until just now. I've got a play, it's written by a friend of mine called Chester Erskine and it's called *Into Thin Air*. I offered it to John Mills and he turned it down, and really I don't know how to cast it, but Ruth has suggested that I audition you. So I'd like you to take the play away and read it, and I've marked the scene that I'd like you to audition. I'd like you to learn it, if you would, please, and do it for me, let's say in a few days' time.'

So I said, 'Right, yes, right,' and I took it away and read it. I have to be as fair as I can about this, I didn't think *Into Thin Air* was a bad play, I didn't think it was a great play. It was a comedy and the central point about it was that it was a young New Yorker in conflict with some gangsters; for some reason or other he gets mixed up with them, and he has a habit, which is that when he's nervous he sneezes, and when he sneezes he becomes invisible. I'll just let that sink in for a minute before I go on.

I thought, I'll be working with Garson Kanin. I mean the man had written *Born Yesterday*, and all those lovely films with his wife. The thought of just working with him, even if we never opened, seemed to me to be marvellous, plus the fact that I might possibly finish up in the West End playing the lead. There was no question that the part, Virgil Penny, was the out-and-out lead in the play. So I said, 'Right, OK,' and I went away and learnt it, and I auditioned for him. I didn't know it at the time, but Ruth was there in the theatre to see me when I auditioned, to watch me, and he gave me the part. So I then had to prepare for leaving *The Matchmaker* and start to rehearse with Garson.

In order to do this, of course, I had to abandon my two parts in the play, and Mr Beaumont, I think, was a little bit unfair but he said, 'Well, if you're going to leave the play, you'll have to find somebody to take your place.' Now I don't think that was quite the right thing for Mr Beaumont to do, but I had such respect for him, and I thought, well, that's a small price to pay.

I was a little bit worried about whom I was going to think of to ask to play this part, and whether they would accept, but after a short time my mind settled on a friend of mine called James Bree, and he very kindly said yes. So he took it over and I taught him how to play the concertina with one finger of each hand.

I can only remember two members of the cast of *Into Thin Air* now, one was Jill Melford who played my wife, and the other was Hartley Power who played the heavy, the man who was, in a sense, against me in the course of the play. Hartley Power had been in *Born Yesterday* with Yolande Donlan, which Olivier had directed a few years before.

We rehearsed and Garson insisted that we all know our lines before we began rehearsing, but that seemed OK by me, and Ruth came to any number of the rehearsals. I can't really remember much about it now, but thank goodness I still have in my possession the scribbled notes that she would leave me after coming to see a rehearsal. All of them were encouraging, not too overblown, but just 'you're doing great' and those sorts of things, in a way to keep me going.

One day the note said, 'Binkie was there at rehearsals today and I sat next to him,' then in inverted commas she put, '"He's very good," said Binkie, and I said, "Well, why don't you tell him so?" and Binkie said "Oh that's not my place,"' which indeed he regarded as *not* his place, and quite right too. He was there simply to supervise the overall play, not any individual performances.

There was nothing special about the play, there was nothing

to turn anybody's head, really. But of course as far as I was concerned there I was, playing a leading part, and being directed by one of the masters of comedy, and I tried to take advantage of it, or at least as much advantage as I could. On the tour, Garson was great. He would take Jill and me and one or two of the others out for supper from time to time. He would regale us with his stories of the theatre and altogether he was having a good time, and we eventually came to the week before we were due to open.

The theatre had already been chosen, it was to be the Globe Theatre, now the Gielgud Theatre, and the week before we opened we were at Brighton, and Binkie came down to see the play towards the end of the week. I think it was on the Thursday that he came and what happened I don't know. That is to say, what happened between him and Garson I don't know, but it transpired that he had said to Garson, 'I am not bringing this in, it simply isn't good enough.'

Garson said, 'Well, Binkie, I've promised these kids that they will have a West End opening.' What happened after that I never knew, but the rumour was that that night Garson had got drunk. In fact, I know that was true because he told me, and he also said that the day after he had got drunk he swore never to drink again, which I believe is also true. But we did open and I believe – and this really is mostly rumour – I believe that Garson undertook the expense of bringing the play in himself and Binkie allowed him to do it.

We opened on the Thursday at the Globe, the notice went up on Friday morning. We did the Friday night, we did the Saturday matinée and we did the Saturday night, and that was the end of Virgil Penny. He went, as you might say, *'Into Thin Air'*.

A couple of days after we closed, Garson took me to lunch and he said, 'Well, I'm sorry about that, Pete.'

And I said, 'Goodness gracious, it's just been such a pleasure and a thrill and a lesson working with you.' I said, I think, all the right things and they were all true.

I particularly remember one typical Garson Kanin gesture. On the first night of the play he came to my dressing room, and he had what was obviously a suit or something on a hanger, it was in one of those zip-up covers, and he said, 'Pete, Ruth Gordon, the actress, has given me a first night present, it's a new tuxedo,' which, in case you don't speak American, is a dinner jacket. 'So I'm going to give you my old one. I hope you don't think that's rude of me, but you might like it.'

I said, 'Oh, gosh, yes, thank you very much, Garson.' When his back was turned I tried it on and it fitted me and I kept it. As the years went by I had it converted from a double-breasted to a single-breasted, which is what it is now, and I still have it, and I was wearing it the other day at the Oscars. Dear Garson.

Ruth died in 1985, and Garson followed about fourteen years later. They were a great couple, they epitomised the American way of life: Broadway, Hollywood. They glistened, but they were very human. Can you be very human? Well, I think they were. Why they found somebody like me to, shall I say, nurture for a while I don't know, but I was very, very lucky and I mourned their passing.

The days of being a contract artist with H. M. Tennent had ended when I started work on *Into Thin Air*. Mr Beaumont was paying me thirty pounds a week for that, and a promise of more if it made a successful entry into the West End. He needn't have worried about that, but we didn't know it at the time, of course. So now in 1955 I was suddenly an unemployed actor.

I had had lunch with Garson and his last words to me were, 'Keep in touch.' After a couple of days at home I got a telephone call from Kenneth Carten, who said, 'Orson Welles is in town and is running auditions, and I've put you up for it.'

I said, 'Oh, great,' and then I thought, well, why not? So I phoned Garson and said, 'I'm going to do an audition for Orson Welles, believe it or not.'

'But I know Orson,' he said, 'I'll give him a ring.' Well, I wasn't going to say no and I let it go at that.

So I was to audition for Orson Welles. Auditions are grim affairs. In fact the only ones I ever remember doing that I actually enjoyed, I suppose, was the one for RADA, and then later for Garson Kanin. Let's face it, the participants, that is to say the people who are actually doing the auditions, are all out of work, otherwise they wouldn't be auditioning, and the people who are watching them perform, well, it's their money, and if they make a wrong decision it's possible that in the long run it will affect their income. So everybody is pretty well on edge.

I went to the Duke of York's Theatre, where the auditions were to be held. I went to the stage door and made my way in, and when I reached the stage area I heard laughter. Laughter and chuckles, and I went up to the curtains and peeked through, and sure enough, there he was, he was unmistakable, a big figure of a man, wearing the customary clothes that we have got used to seeing in photographs – a long jacket, a black suit with a Sandeman's Port cape over the top. He was holding in his hand a large tumbler full of some amber fluid; I had no idea what it was. He was chuckling and talking to the three or four people sitting in the stalls, probably either the management or his stage management, and there was a man on the stage, who had obviously just been auditioning. He was chuckling too, they exchanged a couple of jokes and the man went away, and the next man came on. I had been given a sheet of paper – in fact, we all had – with the words of the particular bit that Orson wanted us to audition for, a section of the play with a part printed on it.

Eventually it was my turn. I went up on to the stage, he came down to the footlights, put out his hand and grabbed mine and said, 'I'm Orson Welles,' and as if to make sure that I'd got it right and that he'd got it right, he took a swig of this amber fluid.

I said, 'Do you mind if I move about a bit?'

'No, no, no, do what you like, do you want a chair? You can sit down if you like.'

'No, it's all right,' I said, 'as long as I can just move.'

'Sure, sure, just do it.' So I just did it, and as it turned out I got a part in the play. The name of the play was *Moby Dick Rehearsed*. It had been adapted by Orson from the book by Herman Melville, which tells of the captain of a whaling vessel, the *Pequod*. The captain's name is Ahab and he is in search of the white whale. The white whale is called Moby Dick and he has devoured one of Ahab's legs, so Ahab has a wooden leg.

In his first night notice of the play Kenneth Tynan wrote, 'At this stage of his career, it would be surprising if Mr Welles presented us with anything but the surprising,' and so it turned out. When the audience came into the theatre, the Duke of York's, what was going to happen was that the curtain would already be up. Now I've said elsewhere that this is a habit in the West End nowadays that I cannot understand, especially as so many of the West End theatres have absolutely beautiful curtains, which were made especially for that purpose: to guard or protect the stage area from the eyes of the audience until the time is right.

But in this particular case Orson had a reason. The curtain was already up and what Orson was saying to the audience was, 'Ladies and gentlemen, I am going to magic you tonight. What you see, first of all, is that I have nothing up my sleeve,' and it was true, because the stage area was completely bare. Well, almost completely. You could see right to the back of the stage where there was this large brick wall, and in the brick wall were two doors, which let you through to the dressing-room area. A couple of packing cases, a coil of rope and that's about all there was on the stage.

Then, as the play began, so the stage was built up before you, and Orson was saying to you, 'What you are going to see, ladies and gentlemen, is a port on the eastern coast of North America, Nantucket. You are going to see the whaling vessel, the *Pequod*; you are going to see that vessel at rest in the port; you are going to see it at sea in calm, and at sea in a storm; and then you are going to see the white whale; and you are going to see the *Pequod* hunt the white whale down. You are going to see Ahab go into the whaler, the rowing boat that is going to row him out nearer and nearer to the whale. He will then hurl his harpoon into the whale and the whale will drown, gushing blood. That, ladies and gentlemen, is what you are going to see. You may not really see it, but I'm going to magic you so that you think you have seen it.'

The house lights slowly go down, the stage lights come up, the period is about 1890, and through the doors at the back come the cast. One or two of them might be smoking pipes, others are reading newspapers. They are talking casually among themselves, and then, after a few minutes of this desultory conversation, the guv'nor strides in. He is, of course, Orson Welles, and he is to play Ahab. The play is *Moby Dick*. He too joins in the conversation until he gives a nod to the stage manager (that was the part that I was playing) and the stage manager calls the company to order and begins issuing certain simple stage instructions.

The idea of this is not so much to tell the actors what to do as to inform the audience, who haven't quite caught on yet maybe, what is going on, where we are and what is about to happen. The first part of the play is given over to the sermon by Father Mapple before the launching of the *Pequod*. This was the part that Orson had played in the Gregory Peck movie, which had been made a couple of years before. In the film, Orson had to do this sermon, which is quite a long one, in one day and he benefited to some extent from the fact that he was given a large bottle of brandy to keep him going while he was doing it.

There is no such brandy in this particular play, or certainly not at this stage of the proceedings. He finishes his sermon, then the *Pequod* leaves the port, and it travels first through calm waters, then a great storm comes up, and after the storm comes, in our case, the interval. After the interval you see the *Pequod* and Ahab and all pursuing the white whale and the ending as already described.

The opening scenes are fairly straightforward from a theatrical point of view. There are dialogue scenes between Pip, the cabin boy, and Ahab. There are the beginnings of the rumblings between Starbuck, the first mate, and Ahab about the wisdom of undertaking such a voyage at all. Starbuck is against this hunting down of the white whale. There is something he regards as blasphemous about it. Then we come to this great storm at sea and this is when we have to say goodbye, for the time being, to our Ahab, because Orson goes down into the stalls and he spends days there: day after day after day with William Chappell, a director of the theatre and a fine one at that. Billy was there to help him to orchestrate the movement and the sound and all the effects of this tremendous storm scene. It meant that Orson separated himself from the rest of us and spent days barking instructions at us. First of all the ropes were lowered, and they represented the rigging of the ship. Then a huge lantern with a soft orange glow, about the size of a large dustbin, Anthony Collins's storm music began, and then the storm itself, the thunder, the lightning, and we, the cast, were grabbing hold of the ropes, partly having conversations among ourselves and partly issuing orders to each other, and generally carrying on with that frantic bustle that takes place when you are in the hands of a storm.

Eventually we did get some sense into the proceedings, and Orson relaxed a bit and came up on to the deck and the act ended. In the interval, when we hoped the audience would go to the bar, the cast, except, of course, for Orson, built the walkway down the centre of the aisle of the Duke of York's. This consisted of trestles and planks, which would be the whaling boat that casts off from the *Pequod* when the white whale is sighted, along which Orson will move as Ahab, getting nearer and nearer to the back of the theatre until he delivers the *coup de grâce* to the whale. We, not all the cast, but quite a lot of us, are going to be down in the aisle with our backs to the audience rowing away, straining at these imaginary oars, and continuing conversations with Ahab, and also a kind of running commentary, which is delivered by the man playing Ishmael.

At this stage it might not be a bad idea to have a little break from the story and tell you about the cast. An historic note, first of all: Joan Plowright played Pip, the cabin boy. It was her first part in the West End. Gordon Jackson played Ishmael, the narrator, the 'I am Ishmael' of the story; Patrick McGoohan was Starbuck, the first mate; Kenneth Williams would play anything he could get his hands on. Altogether, it was a pretty strong cast. But it did seem to some of us that we were getting perilously near to the end of the play, which clearly was going to be the most difficult part to stage, the actual harpooning of the whale and the final scenes, the final gasps of the play, and we were running out of time.

Actually, what happened was that we came to the last two days, which were both going to be given over to dress rehearsals, and then the audience was going to come in on the third day for the opening night. There would be no previews or anything like that. We would dress rehearse it twice, then the audience would come in and we would do the play.

So we have got to the bit where the interval has come and gone, the trestles and the planks and everything else were laid, and the whale is sighted and then the stage lights begin to go down, and one single spotlight lights up the head of Ahab, as he moves up the plankway towards the whale and the con-versation – you can hardly call it that, we were all yelling at each other – takes over.

He gets nearer and nearer to the whale. Now Orson hadn't even trodden these boards with some lights on, and the first time he attempts to do it in this first dress rehearsal, the only thing that is lighting the theatre at all is this single spotlight on his face. It takes only seconds before he and the rest of us realise that he can't see where he is, so the dialogue is interspersed with great yells of, 'Jesus, Jesus, I can't see, I can't see, what's the line? Give me a line somebody,' and usually it would be Gordon who knows what to feed him with, so he'd pick up the cue and go on a bit, and then it would be, 'Oh no, oh no, it's this goddamn light,' and one or two of us would think to ourselves, well, Orson, sorry chum, but it's your light.

We reached the end of the first dress rehearsal in those circumstances and we were a bit worried, but there was another dress rehearsal to come the following day, and we thought that Orson was bound to have a trial run on his own, or something like that – no such thing, as far as we could tell. We came to the second dress rehearsal and exactly the same thing hap-pened. The cries for help, the mutterings and the expletives as he groped his way along this walkway, and we were sitting there with our backs to an imaginary audience, rowing away, and feeding him the lines and Gordon was carrying on some sort of a dialogue with him. But still it was not very good. It was pretty chaotic, and that was the end of our second dress rehearsal.

We all said goodnight, and there were some heads being shaken and mutterings were going on, oh dear, oh dear, was the general undertone of the remarks made, and we came to the day of the first performance.

We were in the theatre getting ready, but no more rehearsing, just straight in to the audience. We took it in turns to go down and wish him good luck, and when it was my turn I went in and he was sitting there with the glass of amber fluid within easy reach. 'Ah,' he said, 'good luck, Peter.'

And I said, 'Good luck, Orson.'

He said, 'Do you want a drink?'

'No, thank you, Orson, no, thank you.' I thought to myself, I'm not a good enough actor to drink stuff like that on a night like this.

So there we are. The audience is assembled. They have had a good look at this empty stage and then the lights change. The house lights go down, and the lights on the stage come up to full and the play begins. There are jokes in it. There are different changes of mood, and the story is pretty easy to follow and we get the smell of it. We get that smell that you get sometimes on a first night, and we think, this is going all right. It really is. He does the Mapple speech, and it's not exactly greeted with applause, but it's terribly well done. He thunders it out and then he has the scene with Pip, the cabin boy. This is a sort of Cordelia–Lear scene, at least that's how Orson interprets Melville's words – Lear and Cordelia.

Then the beginning of the troubles between Starbuck and Ahab. The fact that Starbuck thinks that this whole thing should be abandoned – tension there. Towards the end of the first act we get this storm scene. There is total blackout. There's a flash of lightning. Anthony Collins's storm music rolls out and it is drowned by the thunderclaps of the backstage artillery. The ropes are already down and we're hanging on to them. The great lantern, the great orange lantern, is swaying to and fro, and then the lighting. (I swear to you that even while we were doing it I could never tell where the lights were coming from. They were coming roughly horizontally across the stage, and Orson and Billy Chappell had timed it so that every time one of us spoke or a group of us spoke, we were picked out in these lights, and then somebody else spoke and the lights would change over to them. It was a great piece of staging.)

When we reached the end of the storm and the curtain came down for the first time there was an enormous round of applause from the audience and we were greatly heartened by that.

We come back after the interval, and then it isn't very long before the white whale is sighted. Well, then we begin to get a little bit worried. We've already made the walkway with the trestles and everything in the interval, and then comes Ahab with his imagined, but clearly seen by the audience, harpoon. He strides up the planks, and we've got our backs to him most of the time because we're just rowing, but my goodness he seems not to put a foot wrong. The words are coming out strong and clear, and with Gordon as Ishmael they are playing a tennis match between them with Melville's lines.

The theatre, just to remind you, is in almost complete darkness except for this one light on Ahab's face, and we get nearer and nearer and nearer to the whale, and finally he launches the harpoon and it strikes the whale, and the whale leaps into the air and then thunders down, gushing blood, but the rope that is attached to the harpoon that is now stuck into the whale, the rope catches itself on something on the whaler. It then twines itself round Ahab's leg, and Ahab is dragged into the water after the whale, and they both go down together and the rest of the whaler crew are all drowned. The only one left is Ishmael, and Gordon goes on describing the scene in the words of Ishmael as the lights gradually go down until the entire auditorium, the whole stage, is in darkness.

There is a long silent pause, then the stage lights begin to come up again. Up and up and up they come, and there is the guv'nor. He's no longer Ahab, he's the guvnor. He takes out a cigar and lights it. He walks over to the prompter's corner and he takes the book, the script of the play, and he closes it, and he turns back to one of the stagehands and says, 'You can bring down the curtain.' It comes down, and as it touches the floor the audience stand and they are shouting and they are clapping and they are cheering, our audience that Orson, by sheer will-power I would say, has won over. He's had a bit of help from others in the cast, of course, but it begins to dawn on us all that this is Orson's night. It's the first time we've actually seen him or heard him get it right and it's magical. We line up for our curtain call, and we're just in one line with Orson in the middle, and although we don't turn inwards, I think mentally we all do, and we all bow invisibly to Orson. It is his night.

Within the next two days the house was sold out for every performance for the three weeks; you couldn't get a seat and then at the end of the three weeks we closed. Orson gathered us all together and he said, 'Don't worry, fellas, I'll be back,' and he was.

There are some incidents in an actor's life which are imperishable and they're usually to do with something going wrong, and this was certainly no exception. Let me digress just for a moment to say that Kenneth Tynan, again, in his first night notice, went off on to a branch line in the middle of the notice, when he wrote about Laurence Olivier talking to the press about his film version of *Hamlet*. Olivier had described Hamlet as a man who could not make up his mind, and Kenneth said in his notice about *Moby Dick* that in this particular case Ahab was, in fact, a man who could not make up his nose.

What Kenneth had witnessed, which not many of us in the cast did, was that during the first night performance, when Orson was doing his Ahab, Kenneth was fascinated to see that the top part of this nose that Orson had built on to his own nose was peeling away, and the wax or the plasticine, or whatever it was that he was using, came away, forming a curl. It was rather like a question mark the other way round, and clearly Orson was aware of it, but there was nothing he could do about it. So he went away and when he came back later he'd managed to fix it.

It wasn't on the opening night that Patrick McGoohan and I and some of the cast were treated to another diversion, but it did happen after we'd only been doing the play for three or four nights. For Ahab's first entrance he came from the back of the set, against this great brick wall, and he had between him and the audience the line of packing cases, parallel with the footlights, which represented the bridge of the *Pequod*. There was a small ladder attached to the upstage side of it and Orson, as Ahab, was going to make his first appearance in front of the audience by climbing up this ladder. On the other side of the packing cases and nearer the audience Starbuck and Flask, the two mates, were waiting for him. Starbuck was played by Patrick McGoohan and Flask by Peter Sallis.

We heard the approach of Ahab – tap tap, tap tap, tap tap – that was Orson's walking stick, which was taking the place of Ahab's wooden leg. As you will remember, the original leg is in the tummy of the whale. Tap tap, tap tap, tap tap. Then he had to come up the back of the packing cases to make his first appearance. So far in the play Orson had been wearing what I still refer to as his Sandeman's Port get-up, but he was also clean-shaven and, on this particular night, we heard the tap tap,

tap tap, and then above the packing cases there emerged this huge white mop of a wig. It reached down to his shoulders and it was followed, or paralleled, by two enormous shaggy eyebrows, and they in turn were followed by a huge white moustache and beard, which stretched all the way down to his navel. He looked like Father Christmas coming up the chimney.

Finally he was in full view of all of us, resplendent in this white 'wiggery' and he said his first lines, which were: 'There are whales hereabouts, I smell 'em. Keep your eyes peeled and if you sight a white one, split your lungs for him.' Then he turned round and returned the way he came – tap tap, tap tap, tap tap – and I had to turn to McGoohan and say the next line.

I was frightened and thought that the world was about to come to an end, and I stared down at the floor and I said as best I could, 'What do you make of that, Mr Starbuck, ain't there something a bit queer about that?' and McGoohan, who has a stronger mind than I have, looked me straight in the forehead and said, 'I fear me you are right, Ahab has that which is bloody on his mind.' How we got through that little passage I don't know, but it was greatly to our credit.

Now, the interesting thing is that, having done that show for us, Orson then continued to play Ahab for another two or three scenes with all this white stuff on him and then, it was unbelievable, he came back after another break from the acting and he'd taken it all off. It was as though he'd gone down to the ship's barber and said, give me a short back and sides. He only tried it for that one night but it was worth it, in its own strange way, it was worth every penny.

A short postscript to the first night. I went to the Buckstone by myself after the show to have something to eat, and not long after I'd got there Ken Tynan arrived, having presumably written his first night notice. He said, 'Just the man I want to see, come along, I'll buy you supper,' and he wanted to know all about it. 'Tell me, what was it really like working with him?' all that sort of thing.

I was happy to oblige, very happy, but I said, 'You know, all that stuff with the ropes and the pulleys and the swinging to and fro and the lantern and all that, we went on doing that for day after day after day. I think he must have taken two of the three weeks' rehearsal just doing that, but it was very boring. I mean, it became boring, and after a while, you know, we just wished he would come upstairs and just be Ahab.'

Ken said, 'Well, I must admit it was worth every penny. It's a long time since I've seen anything as exciting as this show was tonight.' So his first night notice came out and I was delighted to hear it from what you might call the horse's mouth.

SIX

Noël Coward and
Samuel Pepys

Orson had said he would be back, and he did come back in three or four weeks, and only Orson would have reassembled the cast at the Hackney Empire. This great Edwardian Matcham theatre seated, in those days, about two thousand. It has recently been renovated and I am very glad to hear it. It's good to know that there are some great theatres like that still in existence. I think it was a variety hall when it was first built, but we were going to use it to film *Moby Dick Rehearsed*.

Orson had raised some money from Columbia Pictures, and he had also got some from someone called Margolis, who ran a chain of milk bars. We were going to film it, presumably for television in black and white, and it would probably have made a fine movie. It was a good idea, and it wouldn't have competed with Gregory Peck's mammoth colour movie that had been made a couple of years before. We were to shoot it, all out of order, of course, but principally he wanted to get the storm scene and the rope scene out of the way first, so that's what we worked on: the swinging ropes, the crew doing their shuffling backwards and forwards and saying their lines in time with the beat etc., etc. We were working quite hard on all of that.

I had brought my wireless set into the theatre, because it was a hot, dry summer in 1955, when we were playing the South Africans, and I managed to sneak off every now and then to listen to *Test Match Special*. Those were the days.

We were filming away, and one day one of the engineers – I was surprised he hadn't thought of it before – asked Orson as we were breaking for lunch if he could open the roof, what you might call the sunshine roof. Orson said, 'Why sure, sure, let some air in,' so the engineer went away and pressed the button, and this circular hole appeared in the roof of the Hackney Empire.

The effect was startling. It was Wagnerian. This great shaft of incandescent light shining down from this circular hole in the roof on to the stalls below. It was as if somebody had turned a searchlight on its head. Orson stopped. He stopped everybody, and without issuing any instructions or any particular note, he started to go round grabbing up wooden chairs and tables and things, and placing them in the centre of this beam of light, right over the stalls. It was clear what he was up to, and we all helped him and finally built this kind of trestle table, and then he got Gordon Jackson and me to go through both our parts in this shaft of light. Gordon, playing Ishmael, had the bulk of the lines. In fact, he had a great many, but we had been doing it in the theatre, so he knew it all right and he was able to do it fairly quickly, and then I followed suit, doing my stage directions bit.

Between the two of us we managed it. Gordon was a very good-looking man and I would say that in this light, with his head thrown back and the light shining full on him, he looked almost godlike. I don't think I quite matched that, but at least I was well lit. While all this was going on, I thought back to what Orson had told us in one of the breaks about a moment of improvisation when he was making *Citizen Kane*.

If you saw the movie, you may remember that Kane is married to this woman who fancies herself as a bit of a soprano, an operatic diva, and there is a scene where she is actually singing in the opera house, she is lying on a couch and warbling away. The camera was going and in the middle of all this the continuity girl turned to Orson and said, 'I wonder what it would look like up there?' meaning up in the flies. Orson got to the end of the shot, then he got the camera rigged on to a sling, and they reshot the scene with the woman still warbling, but the camera this time was going up, up, up, up into the flies. It travelled up, looking down at the woman, until eventually it came level in the flies with these two flymen who are looking down at this woman making a fool of herself, and they turn and they look at each other and they shake their heads.

It is one of those moments that you remember and I have never forgotten it. But Orson said that it was improvised, that the continuity girl had just said I wonder what it would look like, etc. and Orson pounced on it. And I thought, this is really rather similar, it's a different shot entirely, of course, but it's a straightforward case of improvisation. There was no mention of Wagner and searchlights and things in the script.

We went on filming and I would think we had done perhaps a couple of weeks, or something like that, when the word filtered through that Orson had used up all of Columbia's money. I don't think he made a public announcement, but the grapevine picked it up and we came to one rather gloomy lunch break when we were sitting around on the stage, including Orson, having our sandwiches. All of a sudden he cried out, 'For Christ's sake, Margolis, sell another milk bar!' Well, Margolis had better things to do with his money and he didn't sell another milk bar, so the filming came to an end and we went home, and that was that.

It was years later that Patrick McGoohan told me that that was not the end of the filming. Orson, apparently, had got enough material to patch together a movie. But what he hadn't got was his own stuff, his own soliloquies, and the scenes he did with McGoohan as Starbuck, so one day Patrick got a message from Turin where Orson was, saying, 'Come to the studio here immediately,' and then he asked, no I think in Orson's case, *told* McGoohan to bring some special equipment, lighting or camera or something like that. He told him to check into this hotel, he gave him the name, and wait there until he sent for him: 'Don't come to the studio until I send for you.'

So Patrick made his way to Turin with the equipment. He booked into the hotel, but Patrick, too, had a mind of his own, and the following day he thought, oh no, no, I'm not going to sit around like this waiting for him to call me, so he made his way to the studios, he enquired about Mr Welles and they told him where to find him. He made his way to a studio in the studio block. He squeezed the door open and then he heard the familiar voice growling away. He looked through the door and he saw what he thought was the Hotel Negresco in Nice, and he shifted his gaze and there were what looked like the Rocky Mountains. He went on a bit further and there was a palm beach somewhere and then, following the sound with his eyes, he saw him, or rather he saw the camera crews' backs.

Then he saw Orson talking into the microphone and into the camera, perched outside what he took to be Monte Carlo. Orson was talking about Monte Carlo, and what he was doing was filming *Around the World with Orson Welles*. The whole studio was taken up with miniature sets of these various places around the world. I saw that film without knowing anything about this; I saw *Around the World with Orson Welles* and it never occurred to me for one moment that he wasn't really there. I thought that he was just sitting there in Monte Carlo or wherever it might be. Yes, that was Orson, he wasn't going to waste his money. But it was the end of *Moby Dick Rehearsed*.

★

In 1955 I found myself in another West End play. It was called *The Count of Clerambard*. It was directed by Murray MacDonald and it starred a great figure of the English theatre and film world, Clive Brook. I don't remember very much about Clive Brook, except working with him on this occasion, but I remembered him while we were working as a man who was constantly in the West End, and constantly making movies. He was a very strong character, and he was joined in this production by Valerie Taylor, Mai Zetterling, Helen Haye and some fellows filling in near the bottom, Alec McCowen and Peter Sallis.

Helen Haye was a great lady of the English theatre. A diminutive figure but with enormous strength and great poise. She was, in other words, an English lady, and she had gone through her career, which was a very strong career, without any reward, without any titular reward, let's put it that way. But British Actors Equity did something quite extraordinary. They had a whip-round and when she reached a certain age, and I've now forgotten what it was, they presented her with an Austin Mini motor car.

Helen had a companion, a lady who went around with her and looked after her, and this lady could drive, and so when we were on tour, they used to take Alec McCowen and me around with them, which was great fun, and we explored all sorts of interesting places: Chester, I remember in particular, a great city, and the surrounding countryside. We had a lovely time, the four of us, as well as doing the play, before we came in to the Garrick eventually. It wasn't an enormous success, but it did reasonably well.

After *The Count of Clerambard* closed, I followed it with Sheridan again. This time it was *The Rivals*; John Clements and his lovely attractive wife, Kay Hammond, were to star in it, and lending them support, if that's the right word, was the great Athene Seyler who was one of the theatrical loves of my life.

The play was produced and directed by William Chappell, who had helped Orson with *Moby Dick Rehearsed*, and I think that it was probably Billy who asked me to play Fag.

Fag is not a great part, but he does pop up throughout the play, and Billy coached me in the part. He gave me steps almost to dance to, I had a lovely little cap, which he showed me how to use, and altogether I managed to follow his directions and produce something that I think was probably quite charming. I have never really been famous for my charm, but I think that Fag was an attractive little figure on the stage.

However, unfortunately, while we were doing the play, and not for very long either, Kay Hammond fell ill. It was a wasting disease of some kind, I don't know what it was, and she never appeared in the theatre again, although she lived for quite a few years after that.

In 1956 H. M. Tennent, under the leadership of Binkie Beaumont, announced that they were going to produce Noël Coward's latest comedy *Nude with Violin*. It was to be directed by Sir John Gielgud and he would also be playing the leading part. The title refers to the name of a painting, which is the last work to come from the studio of Paul Sorodin, an avant-garde painter of worldwide renown who had died a few days before the curtain goes up. He had left his studio apartment in the charge of Sebastian, his faithful manservant. This was the part to be played by Sir John, and into the play come the members of the late painter's family.

This was where the play proper began, but Noël Coward had written a sort of prologue, an interview scene between the manservant, Sebastian, and a young reporter from *Life* magazine, who had come over from America especially to talk to him. It opened the play and by means of this prologue Noël Coward was able to tell the audience about the background of the painter, and also, if all went well, to get a few laughs.

I was asked to go and audition for the part of Clinton Preminger Jr. I was given a script, which I read, and I went to the Globe Theatre to meet Sir John. When I got there, there were three chums of mine already in the wings, waiting. They were going to audition for the same part. There were Alec McCowen, Lee Montague and Donald Churchill. We chatted among ourselves and a few minutes went by, then on to the stage came Sir John with Alison Colville, his stage director. She gave him a sheet of paper and he looked at it and it was fairly obvious that he was looking at the names of the four contenders.

After a few oohs and ahs of surprise and delight, he suddenly said, 'Ahhhh, Peter Sallis, no, he's quite wrong for this part.'

He hadn't intended us to overhear, but we did, and I got up to leave but Alec grabbed me by the sleeve and pulled me down, and said, 'Don't be a fool, you'll get the part.' We started to audition and I was the last on, so I got myself lost somewhere backstage, so as not to eavesdrop on the others, and eventually it was my turn and I went on to the stage.

I could have wished that Sir John would have been a little bit more enthusiastic, but there it was. 'Ahhh,' he said, 'you've read the play?'

'Yes, I've read the play.'

'We're going to read this opening scene.'

'Yes, Sir John, yes.'

'It's the part of Otto Preminger.'

'Well, actually it's Clinton Preminger Jr.'

'Ah, hmm.' We sat down on the stage facing each other and we began the scene. It lasted about ten minutes. It was quite a lengthy scene and we went on into it, and after a couple of minutes or so Sir John got up and began to pace the stage. He then started to project, so I did too, still sitting down where I was, and eventually we were going at it hammer and tongs.

Then it dawned on me. I thought, he's not auditioning me, he's auditioning him. He's trying to find out what it's like to be Sebastian. Eventually we came to the end of the scene, and he sat down again facing me and said, 'Can you do an American accent?'

I said, 'I've just done it. That was it.'

'Ahhh,' he said, 'ahhh.' Well, Alec was right. I got the part and we started to rehearse.

Because the scene opened the play, Sir John suggested that we work on it for a couple of days before he let the rest of the cast in and I couldn't see anything wrong with that. He explained the set to me and then he said, 'Have you seen *Present Laughter?*'

Present Laughter, in case you don't know, is an earlier play of Noël Coward's, and I said, 'Yes, I've seen it.'

He said, 'You remember the part of Roland Maul?'

'Yes.'

'Well, I think you ought to play this like Roland Maul.' Now Roland Maul was a sofa hopper. You put a sofa anywhere near Roland Maul and he would hop on it, he would straddle it, he would kneel on it, he might even walk on it and there was a sofa on the set of *Nude with Violin*, so I started hopping. Well, this went on for a couple of hours and then he said, 'No, no, I'm wrong. I'm wrong about Roland Maul, no, no, no, no. I think you'd better play it like Marlon Brando.'

We opened it Dublin. We opened in Dublin because it was essential that Noël Coward see the play. This was the first work for the theatre that he had ever written where he had not directed the first performance himself. But he was living in the Caribbean and if we had done it anywhere in the United Kingdom it is possible, thanks to his problems with the Inland Revenue, that it would have been cheaper for him if we had done it on the moon. So we were to open at the Olympia

Theatre in Dublin on the Monday, and we were to have the presence of Mr Coward in the audience on the Wednesday.

So there we were, Monday night, the Olympia Theatre, Dublin. Sir John and I were to open the play. I thought to myself about first night nerves and I thought, well, this is the first time – and it hadn't really occurred to me before – this is the first time I will ever have been alone with a great actor. I thought, never mind about my first night nerves, what about his first night nerves? Well, I needn't have worried. They were so pleased to see him; when the curtain went up and he came on they applauded, and they were so happy. I don't know at this time if that was the first time he'd ever played Dublin, but there he was, and I was to have the pleasure of being there with him.

We started the scene, and straight away it began to get laughs. Noël Coward had written some very funny stuff. It was mainly, of course, his stuff for Sebastian, and I bowled him the lines and he would stroke them through the covers, and then a bit later he'd slip them round to leg, and every now and then he'd go down the wicket and hit them full toss, straight into the pavilion. It was heady stuff.

In the course of rehearsals I had lit a cigarette at the beginning, and it had just about lasted the length of the scene. My initial indication of how we were doing on that first night was that I lit and smoked two cigarettes. Eventually we came to the end of it and I made my exit, and on to the stage came Joyce Carey, David Horne, Basil Henson and Ann Castle, all dressed in full-length mourning, and the temperature of the theatre certainly dropped a bit. But they got it back and we received some pretty good notices. They were not exactly raves, but they were good. We didn't feel smug about it, but at the same time we didn't feel disappointed.

Mr Coward came to see the play on the Wednesday and on

the Thursday he called a full rehearsal in the morning, including Sir John. He addressed us all and it was pretty clear that he wasn't altogether happy with what he had seen. We were standing pretty well in a row, with him facing us, and it seemed to me that his eyes came back to me more than anybody else. Later that day he took me to one side and spoke quietly but firmly, with just a hint of steel in what he said, and I remember at one point I attempted to jolly things along by saying, 'Yes, well, perhaps I'm just trying to be funny,' and he said, 'Yes, well you know that can be fatal.'

I had done the evening performance the following day, the Friday, and I went and sat in the stalls while they carried on rehearsing. After I had been there for a bit, I realised that a few rows in front of me was my understudy, John Sterland, a Canadian, and a good actor. A few more minutes went by, and then through the pass door came Noël Coward, and he went and sat next to my understudy. I know that Coward had no idea that I was sitting there behind them, and eventually he turned to him and I heard him say quite clearly, 'Do you think you can do it?'

So I got up, left the theatre, and found the nearest phone box. I called my agent Kenneth Carten in London and said, 'I am going to get the sack.'

I went back to the theatre and that Friday night I did the performance, and at the Saturday matinée I did the performance. Nothing was said at all, but towards the end of the Saturday matinée I received a note from Sir John and it read as follows: 'Dear Peter, David Horne and I are going tomorrow, Sunday, for a little run around County Wicklow to shake the dust of the theatre off our feet, and we would be so pleased if you could join us.'

I thought, what a lovely note. What a lovely man. He knows I am going to get the push. There is nothing he can do about it, so he is going to give me a treat. I wrote back immediately and thanked him, and said that I would be happy to join them on the following day. We went for a little run around County Wicklow. I must make it clear, of course, that we were not on foot. We were in David Horne's chauffeur-driven Rolls-Royce, which did nothing to spoil the day. We chatted among ourselves and we laughed a lot. Not a word was said about the goings-on at the Olympia Theatre.

We had lunch and Sir John told us the story of how Noël Coward had originally written *Nude with Violin* with the part of Sebastian, the male manservant, written for a woman, and it was going to be played by Yvonne Arnaud. That kept us going for a bit. We came back to Dublin and I thanked them both very warmly, especially Sir John.

The following day, the Monday, I did the evening performance and during it I got another note. This time it was to say that Mr Beaumont would like to see me after the performance in the manager's office. Well, I knew quite well what that meant and I went along, and Binkie was very kind. He gave me a cigarette and the first thing he said was, 'How did you know you were going to get the sack?'

Well, I wasn't going to tell him that I had heard the author ask my understudy if he thought he could do it, I just said, 'Well, Mr Coward obviously doesn't like what I'm doing.'

And Binkie said, 'No, I'm afraid you're right, he doesn't. Well, you've given your last performance. Do you play golf?'

I went downstairs and knocked on Sir John's door. He was in tears. 'It's all my fault,' he said.

'No, no, no,' I said, 'no, it's not your fault. He just doesn't like what I'm doing.'

We wished each other well. We shook hands and I left, and I came back home, and the first thing I did when I got back home was to read *Hay Fever*. I just wanted to renew my faith in

Noël Coward, if you see what I mean. I needn't have worried about *Nude with Violin*. John Sterland took over from me and they opened in London, and the play ran for three years. John Gielgud played it for about a year. He handed over to Michael Wilding, who played it for about a year, then he in turn handed it over to Robert Helpmann, who also did it for about a year. So you see, Mr Coward knew what he was talking about. I did go and see it, and do you know, it's an awful thing to say, but I don't really remember very much about it. I do remember going to see Sir John after I had seen the performance, just to say hello and wish him well, and all that sort of thing, but I really don't remember it, and I don't remember John Sterland doing my part at all, but then of course it is rather a long time ago.

I had to find some work on my return to London, and I wrote to two or three managers that I knew of, and one of them was Mr Basil Dean, who wrote back to me and asked me to go and see him. He said he had got a play with a part for me in it, and he gave me the script to read. It wasn't going to be produced for a little while, but in the meantime I was also fortunate enough to be asked to go and see Mr Beaumont.

This is where Mr Beaumont showed how well he knew how to run a company and people, because he had a television company. I think it was just called H. M. Tennent Television, something like that, and I knew the man who was running it because I'd worked for him in the theatre as a company manager. In the space of almost no time at all I had done three Tennent Television productions, and Mr Beaumont had done what he could to help. I thought that man was great, I really did, and as I've indicated before, he just had a way of running a company, he really knew how to do it.

The play that Basil Dean asked me to be in was called *Who Cares?*. It was a political comedy written by Leo Lehmann, who was a wartime émigré, I believe he was Polish. He had made his home in England, he was working successfully as a writer in various fields and this was a play that he had written. Basil Dean had elected to do it, and it was to be done at the Fortune Theatre, that little theatre tucked away near Drury Lane. Alec Clunes was to play the leading part, with Valerie Taylor, Denholm Elliott, Kathleen Ferrer, and me. It was not a great play, but it was an interesting one and perhaps if it had not been tucked away at the Fortune, we might have run a little bit longer than we did, nevertheless it was certainly not a failure.

While we were doing it, Kenneth Carten had conversations with Googie Withers and John McCallum. They were to do a play together called *Janus*. It was virtually a three-hander. Googie and John, who were married in real life, were to play man and wife on the stage, and there was another man who was quite different in character and in every aspect from the one played by John McCallum, and this second man is having an affair with Googie Withers. Kenneth Carten suggested to Googie that she might like to go along and see me in this play at the Fortune, so she did and decided, having watched me, that I would be right for the part.

As it happened, *Who Cares?* didn't last very much longer, and I was free to do *Janus* with Googie and John McCallum. I think you can probably imagine my feelings. There I was, playing the lover of perhaps one of the most attractive women in the English theatre, one of the most attractive women there has ever *been* in the English theatre, and my opponent in the play was dear John McCallum. I say dear John McCallum, because he became very dear to me and we used to play golf together, I very badly and he very well. But I took my clubs off on tour with us, we used to spend the days playing golf and then in the evening we would do the show.

This whole venture, this whole doing of *Janus*, taught me

one enormous lesson which I'd like to pass on to you. We opened in Manchester at the Opera House. We were an instant and immediate success. Boy, did they love it in Manchester. Then we took it on tour, following Manchester, and everywhere we went we got marvellous audiences and attracted excellent notices. I felt so good about it, I enjoyed playing with the two of them enormously, and Googie in particular; I don't mean to take sides, but Googie was just terrific to work with.

We came to the London first night at the Aldwych and, from the moment that the curtain went up, even I could tell that we weren't doing so well. The drop in the atmosphere, the drop in the general reactions of the audience to the little laughs and the big laughs, was quite different from what we had experienced on tour. There was a single interval, and when I got back to my dressing room at the end of Act One I was soaked with sweat. I had to change my underwear and shirt, and I was about as scared as you can get, really. Scared in theatrical terms. But I did admire Googie and somehow or other I managed to keep going. Although I think I failed to handle the situation as well as I should, I don't think that in itself was responsible for the play's not succeeding, but it didn't get very good notices. We ran for only a short time, but I came away thinking great thoughts of Googie Withers and learning something of a lesson, which is: do not take any notice of what they think of you in what we call the provinces, it is in London that it counts and in London you're going to go through a much stiffer examination than you get in the provinces.

Googie Withers had come to see me in *Who Cares?* and somebody else came to see *Who Cares?*, another lady, only this time she was a television director/producer. Her name was Chloe Gibson and she was going to have a look at *Who Cares?* with a view to doing it on television. This happened quite

Zoo Story 1950
'Edward Albee is in a world of his own.'

Name up in lights for *Wait Until Dark* 1966
'What are you doing at the moment?'

With Honor Blackman in *Wait Until Dark*
'Did you get the scream?'

Painting in the studio.

The Cowardly Lion in *Oz* with Tessa Wyatt, Geoffrey Bayldon and Christopher Beeny at Eastbourne 1983.

Bobard in *Rhinoceros* 1960
'What a perfectly bloody play.'

Oscar Wilde in *Wilde West* for BBC TV, with Jessie Evans and director Hal Burton.

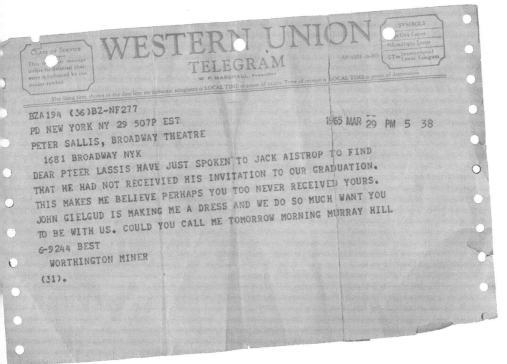

A charmingly garbled message from Western Union.

Ivanov 1989
'Not a very successful Chekhov.'

frequently in those days, maybe it still does, the plays that haven't been a total success in the West End, or even in the provinces for that matter, might very well fill a slot on television.

It sounds a bit denigrating to say that about *Who Cares?* but I think there was an element of that, and I think also that Chloe was interested in the nature of the story, which is why she came to see it. Then she sent for me and said that she was going to do it on television, and she would like me to play the part that I had played on the stage. Obviously she made the same offer to the other members of the cast, and Denholm Elliott agreed to do it again.

What I learnt about Chloe was that she was scrupulous in her casting. She would leave no stone unturned to make sure that the person she was casting was absolutely right for the part, and in that connection I would like you to imagine a scene where, let us just pretend, Chloe is casting for a production of *A Midsummer Night's Dream*, which she is going to put on. She is interviewing children and young people for the parts of the fairies, and one day a little girl comes into her office. She is about seven or eight, she is blonde and pretty, and she is wearing a nice little dress, and sticking out from the small of her back are two wings. Chloe questions her about her experiences and she says, 'What would you like to play?'

And the little girl says, 'Peasblossom.'

'Very good,' says Chloe, 'I see you have wings.'

'Yes, Miss Gibson.'

'I see. Well, would you like to fly for me?'

'Yes, Miss Gibson.'

So the little girl flaps her wings, goes up to the ceiling and bangs her head on it, and Chloe says, 'Very good, my dear, very good, we'll let you know.'

★

We did *Who Cares?* on television, and a while later Chloe sent for me and she explained. Michael Barry was still the Head of Television Drama. You may remember that he was in that job when I did my very first television when I was still at RADA, doing those scenes with Robert Atkins. Michael Barry had decided that the BBC were to do *The Diary of Samuel Pepys*. At the time this was a very big undertaking for the BBC. They had never done anything before on this scale.

It meant that they would be doing thirteen half-hour episodes that would go out live – still live television in those days – every Friday evening for thirteen weeks, and Chloe was put in full charge of the production, which she spent, as you might imagine, some time in casting. But, for reasons best known to herself she had decided that I would be Samuel Pepys and that was really what we were talking about. I was not exactly bowled over, because I don't think at the time I quite realised what it entailed. This length of programme, this scale of programme, with the sets and the costumes and so on, meant very little to me then. It did, as we got stuck into it, I can tell you, but while she was talking about it my mind didn't really reach all that far.

It was to be done in Studio D at Lime Grove, a building which has now been turned into flats. The scripts were to be written by Colonel A. R. Rawlinson. I didn't know his name at the time, but it turned out that he had written a number of film scripts. I would like just to say something about A. R. Rawlinson, and that is that if you were examine the editions of *Pepys's Diary*, you would realise that it is a mammoth work. Maybe he volunteered for it, maybe it was Rawlinson who suggested it in the first place, but to reduce that size of diary down to thirteen half-hour episodes was in itself an accomplishment and a half.

The studio was a rectangular one, and the sets were put round the perimeter facing inwards. In the centre of the studio were the cameras. As far as I can remember, we never had more than four cameras and in those days they were pretty huge. They knocked each other about if they weren't careful. Then you had to get the booms in for the sound, and then you had to light the sets. So altogether, technically, it was a huge undertaking, particularly in view of the fact that it was live, so you couldn't blow a whistle and stop in the middle of it or at any part of it, for that matter, because the action had to be continuous.

Chloe was in sole charge of ensuring that the cameras were where she wanted them, that the sound was where she wanted it, that the lighting was correct at any one moment and that the actors were there. Which brings me to another point – as it was my diary I therefore had not only to be in every scene, but to be in virtually the entire part of every scene. I mean, otherwise, how could I know what to write about? This introduced what we called the 'do but' scenes. Brief little episodes where somebody would say, 'I do but wonder what is keeping Sam?' and of course we all knew what was keeping Sam, he was running like a ferret from one set to the next.

I adopted one or two ploys. One was the gay laugh, the sort of ha, ha, ha. This was to give the impression that I was enjoying it, and also that, with a wave of the hand and the accompanying ha, ha, ha I could give the impression of panache. There were a few chums in it: Paul Eddington was playing Sir William Coventry, Alan Rowe played Will, my faithful servant, who went all the way through the Diary with me – a great chum – a great Will too, he was marvellous in the part; Don Wilson was there, oh, I can't go through them all, there were so many who either were mates or became mates.

But there was one incident in particular that I remember, and that was when Paul, as Sir William Coventry, and I were in the King's palace gardens, being entertained by the King.

Charles II was played by Douglas Wilmer, and we had to go from the King's palace gardens round to a church across the other side of the studio. We had to go up the back of the church and I was going to throw the doors open and the scene would begin. So we finished with the King's gardens. We ran like the proverbial ferrets, we leapt up the stairs, I pushed the doors open and went 'ha, ha, ha', and Paul hissed, 'You know it's a funeral!'

Looking back on it since, it has dawned on me what a huge undertaking it was for Chloe and for everybody on the technical side. The only people who got off fairly lightly were the actors, and the reason was that we were going to do one half-hour programme a week and most of us had been in weekly rep, where you do the play every evening and where you might rehearse for a week and then do the play, but you're going to do the same play for the next six nights. This meant that by the time you'd rehearsed it and got into it, you pretty well knew, even in weekly rep, where you were, and with this it was pretty much the same.

We only had to do one show a week, and we had to get it dead right, and I like to think, to our credit, that we did. Nobody, I believe, ever got in the way of a camera, or did anything unfortunate like that. It did run pretty well and I must admit that I wangled out of the BBC, a few years ago, a couple of recordings of episodes, which I watched with great pleasure and a big smile on my face. It wasn't bad. It really wasn't bad.

Why did she choose me? Well, if you look at prints of Pepys with his long wig and costume, he's got a pretty nondescript sort of face. He was, of course, as we know, a womaniser, which featured as much as they dared in the television programme, but womanisers don't have to be Clark Gables; they can look just like me and do. As far as the rest of him is concerned, he was a brain. He wrote those diaries, as you also probably know, in a code that he had invented and he had a brilliant mind.

He was known as perhaps not the 'Father of the Navy', but the 'Creator of the present-day Navy'. Not so much in an actual fighting capacity, but how to man the ships, how to provide the food and the quantity of ammunition, and how they should be apportioned for any particular voyage that the fleet or fleets were making and, generally speaking, to make the whole thing run in a more businesslike way. He couldn't tell the Nelson to come how to fight a battle, but he could tell him how to man it and how to prepare for it, and this, I believe, was why he was considered to be, in a sense, the 'Father of the Navy'.

Some years after I had done it – and now I'm jumping my attempt to keep this in chronological order – I think it was early in the eighties, I was approached by the National Trust to take part in an evening's entertainment based around Pepys, and because of that I was invited by a man called Robert Latham to go to Magdalene College Cambridge and to meet him. Now Robert Latham was *the* authority on Pepys. I didn't even know his name when we were doing the Diary on television. The version of the Diary that I bought was, I think, a Cambridge edition, but it had been published roughly round about the turn of the century and although there was nothing actually wrong with it, I never got to read it.

By the time I even contemplated reading it we had finished the series and really there wasn't very much point in a way. I used to dip into it, but I couldn't be said to be a Pepys scholar. Robert Latham was going to be the centrepiece, in a way with me, of this evening show that the National Trust were planning, so he invited me to Magdalene College to meet him and his wife, Lynette. He had a collaborator when they were doing their version of the Diary, who had sadly died before it was actually published. Robert was a scholar – well, he had to be, didn't he? – and he took me across the road to Magdalene and showed me Pepys's room, where Pepys, I suppose, had spent a lot of his time. He showed me the bookcases, and what was charming about the bookcases was that Pepys had bought the books first and assembled them, and then had the cases made to fit the books. So although the cases were all of exactly the same dimensions on the outside, on the inside the shelves varied in height and width to accommodate that number of books that made up the set. Then, running down the centre of the room were the showcases with pages, well volumes, of Pepys's Diary on show, heavily protected against the sun and quite unintelligible as far as I was concerned, because of the code. But it was fascinating to reach out, not a hand but an eye, and look at these things. Because the chap, by then, meant a great deal to me.

In the show that we were going to do, Robert was to sit at one side of the stage and read the prose passages from the Diary, selected scenes and incidents, and I as Pepys in full costume was to read my own dialogue. We also had Trevor Pinnock, the great Trevor Pinnock with his harpsichord, or he might even have been playing harpsichord and piano for this occasion, and he had two singers who sang for the audience in between the passages of dialogue. We did it at the Bluecoat School, in Petty France in London. A lovely evening, which brought back great memories.

For years now I have been trying to persuade the BBC from time to time to do the Diaries again. I'm not offering myself up as the Pepys, good gracious no, but I think they ought to do it, I really do. It is a great piece of writing, a great piece of history and just think what a show they could make of it now, with all their technical abilities, perhaps with Alan Bennett to do the script? Come on, Alan. As long as they don't get a tall, handsome man to play Pepys.

My face and figure were on the front of the *Radio Times*,

dressed as Pepys, and I had attracted a certain amount of interest; even nowadays people say, like the man did by the river bank, 'Weren't you Samuel Pepys?'

'Er, yes.'

After *Pepys* I accepted the first job that was offered me. It was a nice one, and I thoroughly enjoyed doing it. Val May phoned me from the Nottingham Playhouse. He was running the Repertory Company there and he had a play called *Lucky Day*, in which he offered me one of the leading parts, and I accepted straight away. I went to Nottingham and we ran it for two weeks. It was a nice little play, but I have to say it was only a little play, and I came back to London and waited again for the telephone to ring.

When it did ring, I was invited to be in a play with Jane Baxter and Dennis Price. I think you could say that they were two of the most charming people that I've ever worked with. Jane was bright and funny, and Dennis was suave and a gentleman. He and I played crooks, I think, and she was our victim, not that we got the better of her, of course. Jane had an uncle who was a famous surgeon. He did operations on people to change what you might laughingly call their way of life, and she told us the story about how she was discussing it with him one day and he said, 'Oh no, my dear, no, no, no, it's perfectly simple, you just take a little snip here and a little snip there and Bob's your auntie!'

The play was called *Be My Guest*. We ran it at the old Winter Garden Theatre, and like several of the plays that I have been in, it was nice, it was good, but it wasn't quite good enough. The Winter Garden Theatre was a little bit like the Fortune in that, although a much bigger theatre, it was rather tucked away. But then, in 1959, there came – if I dare say it, with all due respect to the previous play – something much more interesting.

They called themselves the 59 Theatre Company. It was headed by Casper Wrede, James Maxwell and Michael Elliott and others – Richard Negri for instance, who did the sets, and Richard Pilbrow who did the lighting. They were planning to do a season of plays at the Lyric Hammersmith, *Danton's Death*, a story of the French Revolution, then a double bill, *Creditors* by Strindberg and *The Cheats of Scapin*, a period piece, and, finally, *Brand* by Ibsen.

I am going to concentrate, for obvious reasons, on *Brand*. When I knew that we were going to do it and that I was going to be in it, I went to the library and got out a copy of the play. I think the translation was by William Archer, and it was a great tome, it went on for page after page after page and, keen and anxious to please as I was, and like to think I still am, I ploughed through it. I don't know how long it took me to read it but I thought, we'll never make an evening out of this. What do the chaps think they're up to? Well, what the chaps had not informed me, of course, was that that was not the translation we were going to use. No. They had brought in a man who had already translated the major works of Ibsen.

I didn't know his name, but it was Michael Meyer, and Michael produced a two-hour version of the play written with all the strength that he could muster to represent the text of Ibsen, but in a much shortened version. So they had the text, they had the cast, a great many of them, and of course they had Brand. They had, in Patrick McGoohan, probably the only man in the country who could have played that part. Single-minded, physically of the right strength – I'm tempted to say when he was on full throttle, he was the best actor we had.

The BBC had said that they would televise all three productions that we had in hand and this, of course, was a great encouragement; it also provided more money for the productions and it gave one a little added incentive, naturally. The

DVD of the production of *Brand* is available, or it was until recently, and this will give you an idea of what the production was like. It will also give you an idea of what Patrick's performance was like. But nothing can give you really a proper insight into what it was like actually to work with him every night in the theatre.

His effect on the cast, well certainly on me, was magnetic, and I had two scenes with him: I played a doctor who climbs up the mountain to meet him outside the home where he lives with his wife and child – the child is ailing, in plain English, he is on the point of death – and the doctor says to him, 'For God's sake, man, get the child down into the valley by the sea where the air is warmer, otherwise he will surely perish,' and Brand says, not these words, but in Ibsen's words to the effect, 'It is God's will, if he is to live he will live, if he is to die, he will die,' and the child dies. And then – I'm sketching about here, which is naughty of me – but in effect the same thing happens to his wife, and in a sense he brings about the death of his wife, it being God's will. In the last scene of the play he confronts God himself, on the mountain. He is standing there with the shepherd girl, played by Olive McFarland, and he sees an avalanche coming and he makes no attempt to get out of its way, it is God's will.

It was Richard Negri's avalanche, and Richard Pilbrow's lighting, and the sound effects that brought about the end of *Brand* at the Lyric Theatre Hammersmith, and on the first night they stood and cheered, and Patrick's career and his life were transformed. I heard later that Michael Elliott, the director, had gone into his dressing room on the first night and said, 'I know what you're going to do, Patrick, you're going to start at the top,' meaning at the top of his performance, 'you're going to sustain it throughout the whole play, and then the audience will tell you when to go into overdrive, and you'll go into overdrive and you will wring their withers.' And so he did, night after night, although the first night had, of course, something very special about it.

I couldn't help thinking, even though he was a mate of mine, this is a real privilege. I am working with somebody now who is actually giving as near to a great performance as you can possibly get. The critic James Agate was always going on about how there were no great actors; he said we call them great, but they're not great. I would have loved Agate to have seen that performance. His eyes – you couldn't take your eyes off him, and they really did drill right through you. Very, very moving, and very, very satisfying as an actor to be in that sort of presence. I don't think it happens very often.

I do know that he was offered James Bond; before Sean Connery did it they offered it to Patrick, and Patrick turned it down. The reason that he turned it down is very interesting. Bond, as everybody knows, is a womaniser, and Patrick is a Catholic happily married to Joan, and they have three daughters. Patrick did not want to play a man who was hopping in and out of bed every other reel, so he turned down Bond.

What he did do, of course, was *Danger Man* for ITV. Lew Grade persuaded him to do *Danger Man*, then Patrick followed that up with his own conception, *The Prisoner*, which he also produced, and that became a famous cult series. But the interesting thing about the character in *Danger Man* and the character in *The Prisoner* is that neither of them is a womaniser. If you can remember a scene in either of those two shows where he actually goes to bed with somebody, a woman, of course, answers on a postcard, please. I don't think you'll find one.

SEVEN

'What a Perfectly Bloody Play'

Those of you who have followed the story so far may remember that in 1939 I was in Barclays Bank, Bloomsbury, Southampton Row. I used to go to a restaurant called Guy Pearce's practically every day for my lunch. I became acquainted, I think that's the right word to use, with a young lady there, and I asked her if she would like to accompany me to the cinema and she said she would, so we went to the Empire, Leicester Square, to see Vivien Leigh in *Gone with the Wind*. I hadn't really taken into account the fact that the film lasted for four hours. We were sitting somewhere in the middle of the stalls, and because I felt that some form of affection was required, if either of us was to get anywhere, I put my arm round her and she made no attempt to dissuade me.

Then the film began, and the first half lasted for two hours. I had no idea it was going to go on as long as that, and by then my arm had lost all feeling, it was like the proverbial withered shrub, and yet I felt if I took my arm away, she would think I had gone off her. We came to the interval at last, I did take my arm away, and surreptitiously I hit it with my left fist as hard as I could and it was dead, dead. By the second half it had recovered itself, and by then I had learnt my lesson and I didn't put it back.

While all this romantic drama was going on, another

romantic drama was being portrayed on the screen in front of us, which was Vivien Leigh and Clark Gable having a good time, well, most of the time they were having a good time. If you had told me that in twenty years from then I would be playing Vivien Leigh's father, I wouldn't have believed it, but that's how it turned out.

In 1959, Noël Coward had done an adaptation of *Look After Lulu*, written by a Frenchman, Georges Feydeau, and Vivien Leigh was going to play the leading lady. We were to do it at the Royal Court Theatre and then it was to transfer to what was at that time the New Theatre, then the Albery and now, believe it or not, the Noël Coward Theatre. It was three years since I had made my unsuccessful attempt to be in *Nude with Violin*, Noël Coward's comedy, when I was dismissed from the play because the author had felt that I was unsuitable. While we were rehearsing *Look After Lulu* at the Royal Court, he turned up on a couple of occasions and both times he asked to see me, and both times I just didn't happen to have been called that day. But I thought it was typical of the man that he wanted to see how I was getting on, and we could have shaken hands. So I was rather sad to miss him, but I was thrilled to be doing *Look After Lulu* with Vivien Leigh, playing her father, and great fun it was.

I have nothing special to tell you about the production except that George Devine had been playing a part in it. George ran the Royal Court Theatre and was playing a German called Herr von Putzeboum, and it had been arranged before we started work that if we transferred Mr Devine would not be going on playing the part that he had been, but that it was to be taken over by me. We did transfer, and the play took off and we were doing pretty well. Then one day the director of the play, Tony Richardson, came to see it and he assembled the whole cast the following day.

I can't remember all that he said, but I do know that he referred to the fact that the play was getting out of hand. The cast were just not doing what we had originally rehearsed, and here was a direct connection with Noël Coward, although I didn't think about it just at the time. But Tony Richardson said, 'I'm sorry to pick out one individual in particular, but Peter Sallis is a good example of what I mean. Peter, you've let von Putzeboum get completely out of hand. You are just – how can I put it? – you're just playing for laughs instead of playing the character.'

I wondered if that was what I was doing with Sir John when Noël Coward fired me. I think it probably was, although I had only had a few days with Sir John to get out of hand, nevertheless that same spark, that same bit of devilment in me, was doing the same thing in *Look After Lulu* as it had done in *Nude with Violin*. Later on, when I was back at the Royal Court, I did meet Mr Coward again under rather different circumstances, which we will come to in due course.

After *Lulu* had closed in 1959 I was offered a job at the Arts Theatre again, a play by Edward Albee called *The Zoo Story*. I was to partner Kenneth Haigh. There were quite a few flashes of theatrical history in this production. To begin with it was the very first play that Albee had written. It had been done in America as a double bill with a short play of Tennessee Williams' called *Forty Wagon Loads of Cotton*, and it was now to be presented as a double bill at the Arts Theatre.

The plays had been brought across the Atlantic by two men. One was in fact what you might call 'the management', and the other was the producer and the owner of the play by Edward Albee. When I say 'owner' he had first call on it, I suppose. None of this was at all clear when Kenneth and I started to rehearse, but it became clear shortly. The producer was also the director, a young man who began by talking about the setting of the play, which was fair enough. It took place in Central Park in New York.

Central Park Zoo was the zoo of the story, a nine-page story about a dog, which was told by Kenneth Haigh's character. Fabia Drake would have admired Kenneth enormously. He had made his name in the original production of *Look Back in Anger*, in which he starred as Jimmy Porter. I had not worked with him before, and he had the book in his hand. I learnt the play as quickly as I could and put the book down. This story that he had to tell, which he told beautifully, I should add, covered nine pages of this particular script that we were working from. I suppose in theatrical terms it must have lasted more than ten minutes, that's for sure, and Kenneth never put the book down until either the first dress rehearsal or the rehearsal before that, but he knew it and it was fascinating to watch him. Fascinating to see how the book just disappeared.

He never really consciously went thump, and put it down, it just went out of his hand and he knew that speech perfectly. It was an example of what Fabia Drake was seeking all the time, she would have been so proud of him, and I was proud of him, but in a different sort of way, because I never would have attempted that. I would have learnt that story as soon as I could, before we even started rehearsing, if I could manage it.

That is not why I am telling you all this, really, because the problem was the director, the young man who was partly in management with the production of the show. He had no idea how to direct. I was sitting on a bench and Kenneth had to come from backstage down to me, where I was reading the paper or smoking a pipe or something, and he spent quite a long time explaining to me what I would see from my bench in the park. In other words. I was looking down Fifth Avenue, running down the east side of the park, from the zoo.

He described various houses and buildings, and after a while I stopped him and said, 'Excuse me, but you know, if a curtain goes up and an audience sees me looking from right to left like this, following these different buildings that you are describing to me, they won't really know what I'm looking at. I know what I'm supposed to be looking at. It will look, for all the world, as though I'm counting the houses.'

Now that was just one little example of what set Kenneth and me on the trail, because day after day Kenneth hardly got on, and when he did get on we didn't move the play very much at all. The director would just talk to us and after a bit Kenneth said, 'I've had enough of this.'

Now backstage of the Arts Theatre was this man's partner, the man who jointly had brought the two plays over, and Kenneth used that immortal expression 'This play is too good to be mucked about like that', so we asked for an appointment to see him and we went in. Kenneth took the lead and I was at what you might call first slip, just behind his right elbow. Kenneth said, 'I'm sorry but this play is too good for this man to be directing. We're not getting any direction at all; in fact, we've barely got past the first page, and we've been at it for several days, I'm sorry, but we want him changed.'

Well, this chap was obviously a bit staggered, I mean the two of them had come all the way from America, and here he was being told to get rid of his partner. But I think he saw the sense. I can't remember how the interview ended, but I think he said that we would be allowed to change. He asked Kenneth whom he had in mind, did he have *anybody* in mind to take over? In fact, Kenneth had, and I could back him up, because this was someone I'd worked for too, a very bright Canadian called Henry Caplin, known as Hank. He was a character in himself and we both said, 'Yes, if you can get Henry Caplin we'll be home and dry.' All this time Edward Albee was around.

Probably we told him what was going on, but certainly he was made aware of the problem.

Fortunately Hank Caplin was free, he *was* able to take over, he read the play and loved it, and said, 'Yeah, let's get going,' so we did.

The man that we had dismissed, I don't know how he took it. I don't think we ever saw him again, but certainly, if he had any sense, stepping out of the picture was the wisest thing he could do. It was a fascinating play, and the story of the dog, this nine-page story that builds as the centrepiece of the play, was a marvellous piece of writing and we both knew that Edward Albee had not written his last play.

I can remember sitting in the Buckstone with him and looking at him. His eyes ... perhaps they weren't black, but they looked black, and there was something deep going on there. He talked about a rather unhappy childhood, and I mustn't go on about that because it's pretty private, but he was a fascinating man and he had written a fascinating first play.

The press were not quite so kind. One or two people likened it to Harold Pinter. Well, they hadn't listened very carefully, because Harold Pinter is in a world of his own, and Edward Albee is in a world of *his* own, and the only similarity is that they were both, when they began, fine modern writers. They were not going backwards, they were bringing the theatre forward. That was the only thing, really, that they had in common.

I had worked with Henry Caplin before and I liked him enormously. He was the right chap for this job, there was no doubt about that. You have to remember this was the Arts Theatre, it wasn't loaded. We didn't have all that much rehearsal time, which is why we were naturally so anxious that the original director should not take up so much of our time by just not doing anything. Hank got cracking immediately. It took him a day or two just to set the piece, so that we knew where we were going, the basic pattern of the moves and that sort of thing.

He also kept a beady eye on me and it was interesting, going back again to *Look After Lulu* and *Nude with Violin*, that he insisted I was fidgeting too much. Not fidgeting in the sense that I was twitching, but that I was not keeping the whole thing tight, and he had a cure for it. 'Keep it simple,' he said, 'keep it simple.' On the first night he wrote on my mirror, with some of my make-up, the letters SIMPUL, and he said, 'That's what you do, OK?' and I did.

The people who usually employed him were Granada Television and something more came out of it for all of us, because they made a television version with Kenneth and me in it, which Hank directed. It was later used at Granada as an example, for newly arrived directors, who perhaps hadn't had much experience, of camerawork and how actually to film, not necessarily a two-hander, but any television play, how to choose your shots and all that sort of thing. It was quite flattering to hear that, I mean flattering from Hank's point of view.

In 1960 my next play was *Rhinoceros* by Ionesco, the avant-garde French writer, with Laurence Olivier playing the lead, Berenger, and Orson Welles directing. We were to do it at the Royal Court, and if all went well we would transfer it to somewhere in the West End. So the cast was assembled and we started work. Orson told me later that the management had approached him and said that Larry Olivier would play this leading part as long as Orson Welles directed it, and then they were supposed to have said that Orson would only direct it if Larry Olivier played the leading part. This is a ploy that has been used many times in the past and will probably continue to be used in the future, no real harm in it, just a bit of chicanery. But they were going to do it together and Orson's approach to it was that he was not only going to direct it, but also design the sets.

It was a pretty good cast. I can't remember all of them, but I know my old mate Michael Bates was there, as well as some older members of the profession: Alan Webb, Duncan Macrae, Miles Malleson. I had always been an out-and-out fan of Miles Malleson, who produced the funniest Polonius in *Hamlet* that I have ever seen. Twice in rep I asked if I could play Polonius. and I played it as though I were Miles Malleson. Joan Plowright was also in it, so it was a good strong cast and we set to.

What Orson did almost immediately was to make it clear that he was going to introduce his overlapping dialogue technique. I don't know whether this had ever been attempted in the English theatre before, certainly I had never come across it. It had appeared with dramatic effect in *Citizen Kane, The Magnificent Ambersons* and in the ferris wheel scene in *The Third Man*. Very simply, when you're watching the film, you truly think that these people are improvising, you really get the feeling that they are overlapping each other, that two or three people are talking at once. If this production was anything to go by, that overlapping dialogue was scrupulously worked out, and this is what Orson had done here. The scripts were not actually marked, it was left to the actors to mark them, having had certain suggestions made to them by Orson. It was based, very simply, on a musical canon, and if you think of it as a musical canon you will get some idea of what we had to do.

Let us just suppose, for instance, that you have got three sentences and three actors on the stage. The first one says, 'Every time it rains, it rains pennies from heaven,' and when it gets to the second 'it rains', the second actor says, 'I keep thinking today's Thursday,' and when he gets to 'today's Thursday', the third actor says, 'It never rains but it pours.' Not all the scenes were treated in this way and not all the scenes had the same number of people. I know that I had scenes with Olivier and with Joan, and then there were other scenes with what I would call the more elderly members of the cast, whom I've already mentioned. We marked our scripts as carefully as we could, and we tried to follow Orson's directions, and in the main we weren't doing too badly. In fact, it was going quite well. But after a week had gone by, Orson started to change it around, so in fact we had learnt one series of cues, and now we were starting to shift them and this led to tension.

In fact, it led to trouble and eventually, although I wasn't aware that this was happening, it was pretty obvious it needed sorting out. Olivier took Orson on one side, and he must have said something along the lines of, 'Look, Orson, you've got your plan, you've worked it out, we find this overlapping dialogue not easy to do, but if you start mucking about with it, if you start shifting where the cues are going to be, then we're going to be in real trouble. In fact we *are* in real trouble. Now be a good lad, go away and let us sort it out on our own. We will stay with the original markings that you gave us and I think we'll be able to do it.'

So Orson went away. He went away for a week or something like that. When he came back we were pretty well set in what we were going to do the first time round. Now all the actors were happy about this and though there was no ill discipline in the ranks, nevertheless you got the feeling that we were getting close to a situation rather akin to that of the *Bounty* when it was running out of food.

Let me make another diversion here to talk about Olivier. I had never worked with him before, and it was very interesting to see his approach to Berenger. Day after day went by and he held the script and he didn't mumble it, but he was just Larry Olivier holding a book and reading from it, and then, all of a sudden, it really did happen overnight, he put the book down and he *was* Berenger, the shoulders slackened, the mouth began to drop and he was a different man. You were looking at Olivier, but you were listening to and watching Berenger, and he never changed back again. He stayed like that all the way through the remainder of the rehearsals and the performance. I just found it interesting that he did it literally overnight.

We opened the play and I was sharing a dressing room with Miles Malleson, Alan Webb and Duncan Macrae, and on the first night, at the interval, Orson Welles came round. He stormed into the dressing room and said, 'There are only three people, Laurence Olivier, Joan Plowright and Peter Sallis, who are doing what we rehearsed!' He slammed the door and left, and that was the last time that we four chaps saw Orson on that first night. Well, the atmosphere in our dressing room was pretty tense. Nobody, of course, took it out on me, but you got the feeling that I was slightly pushed to one side and no wonder.

At the end of the play, the door burst open again and this time it was Noël Coward who said, again at the top of his voice, 'What a perfectly bloody play. This is the author!' He turned round and there was Ionesco, all five feet of him, ears sticking out, smiling broadly and nodding and Noël Coward said, 'He can't speak a word of English.' That is all I remember about the first night.

I know that Orson didn't come round again and we went our separate ways. The play, because it had Olivier in it and was directed by Orson Welles, attracted a lot of attention and we did finally transfer. We went to the Strand Theatre and we had quite a good run out of it, still doing the overlapping dialogue – I'm tempted to say, those of us who could.

I had one scene in particular with Olivier where we had a row. The two characters were both angry in their own separate ways about some aspect of what was going on in the play, and on one particular night, a few days into the run, Olivier got angry plus. He got angry squared, even. I have never seen such anger come from anybody, and I swear that his face turned a shade of green. It is quite possible that he might have had a word with the lighting man and said, 'Look. I'd like you to try a bit of green on me tonight, see what you think,' I don't know, but that is the impression I had at the time, and I remember it still. It frightened the life out of me. He didn't actually advance on me physically, but his looks could kill and the pallor of his face was this dark green.

It never happened again, but I've never forgotten it. If it was acting it was frightening acting, and if it wasn't acting then it may have come from something that had happened to him that day. Do you know, it has only just occurred to me while I have been going through these pages that maybe it was Vivien, because not long after we had been doing the play she announced from America, where she was playing in *Tovarich*, that she was divorcing Olivier because of his adultery with Joan Plowright. So it is just possible that she may have spoken to Olivier on the phone the day that this green effect took place, and that he used it, as any good Stanislavsky actor will tell you, to heighten the effect of his anger on the stage with me. All this is guesswork, but it has some relationship to what was actually going on and it may well be true.

The day that Vivien did announce this divorce, Joan Plowright didn't turn up; indeed, she left the play literally overnight and her place was taken by her understudy. I was understudying Olivier, and when the news got out and we were contacted by telephone to stand by, I thought it was very possible that I was going to take over from him, not permanently, but at least for a night or two. But it didn't happen. Olivier was never off and I never played the part. From a purely personal point of view I have to admit that I was a bit disappointed. Goodness knows what sort of a mess I would have made of it, but the chance of actually understudying Olivier and *playing* for him, now that would have been fun.

I did have one intriguing last encounter with him much later. In 1976 he and Joan Plowright were doing a series of plays for Derek Granger at Granada Television. He had a hand in producing all of them, and appeared in *Cat on a Hot Tin Roof* and Pinter's *The Collection*. I was also working at Granada then, doing some comedy plays for them, and he and I met the day after he had opened the Olivier Theatre at the National. I had watched this on TV, so when we just happened to meet I said how lovely it was to see him do it, and how awful it was that he wasn't going to be there.

A day or so later his secretary came up to me in the bar, and said that he was going to be having dinner in the hotel restaurant and would I like to join him. She said, 'He's done this with other actors that he's bumped into, he asks that if you'd kindly pay for the meal he'd be glad to have your company, and he would buy the drinks.'

I thought that was lovely, so I said, 'Yes, please, thank you.' We sat down to dinner that night, and there were five of us. I was invited to bring a lady, whose name I can't now remember, Joan was there, and Alan Bridges, who was directing their play.

We were sitting at one table, and at the next table there were about thirty people from his company. At the end of the meal I said, 'I understand the rules, but I'd love to buy you a glass of port, may I do that?' He said, 'Yes, of course, that would be lovely.'

The others had gone by then and I said to the waiter, 'I would like a very nice glass of port for Sir Laurence, and I'll have a glass of wine. And I'd like to sign the bill, please.'

When he came back with the two glasses, Olivier said to him, 'What is this?' When he told him, Olivier said, 'Ah,' dived into his pocket and pulled out his diary. I have had diaries like that, but never paid much attention. This one listed all the leading clarets, burgundies, ports etc., it was a Wine-drinker's Diary. He looked it up and said, 'You've bought me the best port that you can have. This is great, baby.' We had our drinks, but by then all he really wanted to do was to get over to the other table where all the gang were. He invited me to go with him and I got a touch of the Angelos.

Angelo used to be the head waiter at the George Hotel in Huddersfield, where I stayed when I was doing *Last of the Summer Wine*. A touch of the Angelos in my case meant raising your hand and snapping your finger and thumb together, 'Angelo, drinks for the table.' I ordered wine for the whole table. Later on, I said to Olivier, 'Why don't you do Lear?'

'Oh, I couldn't do Lear.'

'But you're with Derek Granger now, he's producing here for Granada, do it on television. You could practically do it a line at a time. It's daft that with all the stuff you've done, there isn't a record of your Lear, and it's perfectly possible on tape, you can do a video of it.' The following day I wrote him a letter to his room at the Midland Hotel, putting it in writing, just in case he had forgotten all about it.

When I woke up the next morning I was still wearing my socks, pants and vest, and I realised it had been one of those nights. When I left my room we met by the lift and he greeted me, 'Hello, baby.' The lift doors opened and a chap in a wheel-chair was trying to get out. I went forward to help him, and he just brushed me aside and pushed himself out. Sir Laurence said something in Anglo-Saxon to me, which I had translated later, he said, 'He nearly had your balls.'

We staggered down to Reception and handed in our keys, and said goodbye to each other. I said to the desk, 'I had a meal with Sir Laurence last night and I did buy some wine, and I think I may have used the expression "I will sign the bill". This was only meant to include two rounds of drinks. I would be glad if you could tell me how much I owe you.' It doesn't seem much now, but it was around seventy pounds thirty years ago, so I said, 'I think I've paid not only for two rounds of drinks, but also the food.'

'Yes, you did.'

I thought of home, and disgrace coming to the family when I am probably imprisoned. So I said, 'Well, look, I will pay this. The only thing I ask of you is that you don't ask Sir Laurence to pay it as well. Don't charge us twice.'

'Oh no, there will be no danger of that.'

'Oh good.'

But he did play Lear, and it was quite nice to have had a jolly good drunken evening with Laurence Olivier and to have bought his dinner.

In 1962 I did two plays in the theatre, and also made a television appearance, which had a note of history about it. I cannot now think how the idea was originally conceived, who conceived it or what, in television history, it was supposed to represent. But it was agreed among all the television-producing companies in Europe that each one would do an individual production of a play by Terence Rattigan. The play was called *Heart to Heart*, and it had a solid background in television in the sense that it was one of these cross-examination programmes, a little bit like *Face to Face*, where a well-known figure is brought before the cameras to be cross-examined by the interviewer.

So, at a given hour, on a given day, all these countries would be presenting their own language version of this play by Terence Rattigan, which could be watched simultaneously throughout Europe. You might well say where does all that get us? I'll tell you where it got somebody, it got Terence Rattigan quite a lot of money, didn't it? Imagine, you don't get paid just once, but you get paid maybe six, seven or eight times for the same play on the same night – not bad. But Terence Rattigan was a good man and I wished him the best of luck.

Our production was going to be directed by Alvin Rakoff. Kenneth More was chosen to play the interviewer, Sir Ralph Richardson what you might call the victim, and Jack Gwillim the producer of the programme. I was playing the director, in other words the chap who calls the shots. Also in the cast were Wendy Craig and Jean Marsh. In the play Sir Ralph has a dark secret, which is finally brought to light by the probing of Kenneth More; he has been warned by the Jack Gwillim character that he must not disclose this information, but Kenny is made of stronger stuff and he decides that he is going to disclose it.

I remember two or three things about the production. First of all the actual pleasure of working with Kenny More and also with Sir Ralph again after our time in *Three Sisters*, when I played Fedotik and he was Vershinin. It was fun to be with those two great gentlemen. I was also a drinker in those days, and I remember that Kenny More's character was that of a drinker, which was one of the problems that he had with his producer. There was a shot where you saw Kenny More and Wendy Craig walking along a passageway together when she said to him, 'Why do you drink so much?'

And he turned to her and patted her hand and said, 'Because I can afford it, darling.' I thought that was a good line.

The play went out and I don't think it was ever repeated. Whether the citizens of each country appreciated the fact that it was being shown in a different language next door at the same time I don't know. The effect it had on the history of television I would think was probably very slight, but it didn't do Terence Rattigan any harm.

★

'Ted's coming down!' This was the cry that used to go up at Teddington Studios when Ted Kotcheff, probably the most successful of the band of directors that they had there at the time, started coming down the stairs from the control room to berate the cast and technicians. He never came down with a smile on his face; it was always in order to growl or shout at somebody. But I don't think there was anybody who worked for him in any shape or form who didn't love him. He was a Canadian, he was big physically, and he was one of the protégés of Sydney Newman. Sydney was also a Canadian, and had imported a number of Canadians to work for him in British television. Alvin Rakoff was one, and another was my old friend Hank Caplin.

Ted would bellow, and the more he bellowed the more excited he grew, and somehow this excitement was infectious; so that instead of making you nervous and shivery and wondering how best to please him, you joined in the joke. He just had a way with him, and it never altered in all the years that I worked with him. I've lost count of how many plays we did together. In the movie *Someone Is Killing the Best Chefs in Europe* he did have a go at Jacqueline Bisset, who was playing the leading lady, and Jacqueline was not the sort you shouted at. I'm afraid she was far too sensitive and too modest to take it as all in a day's work, and I think he did rather upset her, but apart from her I never knew it to upset anybody.

What I learnt from Ted Kotcheff was my emotional capabilities. He called me into his office when I was doing my first part for him in an Angus Wilson story; I was playing the leading part, where I had to become emotionally involved. Ted said, 'Look, you've got depths in you that you don't know about and I don't think you've ever explored them as an actor. This part calls on you to develop this emotional talent. I want you to think about it, and I want you to work on it, because you'll find it very valuable as you go through life, and at the moment you just don't know what you've got.' That was in essence what he said and it succeeded in loosening me up.

Another man who did that was Ronald Wilson, who directed me in one of the C. P. Snow series, *Strangers and Brothers*, where I played a Jewish gentleman who had a couple of scenes with his son who he believes is letting the family down. In rehearsal Ronnie said to me, 'No, Peter, no, you're not being Jewish enough, I want some real hot air from you here. Let your hair down, whether it's hot or not, and let's have a bit of real Jewish heat in this.'

I have always admired the Jews enormously, and often used to wish that I were Jewish in the course of my acting career. Well, I wasn't, but he tried to persuade me that I could be, so I did as he asked, and looking at the finished product I think he did get his way up to a point. Ronnie employed me over and over again. He was a fine director, and *The Pallisers* was a marvellous serial. I haven't seen one that compares nowadays with the amount of talent that went into those earlier series from *The Forsyte Saga* onwards.

When Patrick Troughton was playing Doctor Who I was cast in an episode called *Doctor Who and the Ice Warriors*. I played an Ice Warrior which, to put it simply, was casting me rather dangerously, especially as Peter Barkworth was appearing with me. So you had two professional gigglers who would lay down their lives to get a giggle if they could manage it. We tried to take it as seriously as we possibly could, but it was very difficult. At one point we were confronted by a grizzly bear, which emerged from behind a huge rock of polystyrene and bore down on us. There were no stunt doubles, so instead of having the huge grizzly called for in the script, the BBC chose a small baby grizzly. It was a charmer. It was about three or four feet long, with a sweet nose and temperament, but the director thought that if they shot it in close-up it would fill the screen and therefore produce a moment of high tension. I'm sure the BBC meant well, and I hesitate to draw their attention to it, but if you can imagine this baby bear, that everybody in the studio wanted to give a squeeze to, even filling the screen with it wasn't going to turn it into a monster. It stayed just a cuddly baby bear.

Of the two plays that I did in 1962, one was at a theatre which, when it was built, was named in honour of Sir Oswald Stoll, the theatrical impresario. The Stoll Theatre was in a side turning off Kingsway, you couldn't go past it without turning off Kingsway, so it was rather hidden away. Nowadays it is known as the Peacock Theatre. This play was notable, as far as I was concerned, mainly for the fact that the leading man was a famous European actor who had starred in films, both English and foreign, Anton Walbrook, and my old chum Maggie Johnson was there to play his wife.

The play was called *Masterpiece* and it was about the trial of a forger, with Anton Walbrook playing the painter. It was directed by Hank Caplin and was not a success. It was written by two Americans, and I don't mean to blame them for this, but given this marvellous subject of a man who was copying Vermeer's pictures and trading them on the market, I thought something more could have been made of it. As it was we didn't last very long in *Masterpiece*.

The second play was by John Mortimer, and it starred another great man of the theatre and the cinema, Trevor Howard. As its name rather implies, *Two Stars for Comfort* took place in a public house-cum-hotel and Trevor played the lead in it. A good play, and we had quite a successful run out of it.

★

Some time in 1962 I received a telegram from Orson Welles, saying something along the lines of: 'Peter, dear, can you come to Paris and dub a character for me in a film I'm making. Be here on Saturday', or thereabouts. It was around Thursday by then. I went to Kenneth Carten and said, 'Orson Welles wants me to go to Paris and dub for a film he's making.'

Kenneth said, 'You won't be paid.'

I said, 'You seriously think that I care about being paid for going to Paris and doing something with Orson Welles?' and we both grinned at each other, and Kenneth did the best he could over the money.

I didn't even know what the film was, I didn't know what the part was. I didn't know anything about it, but I packed my little bag and went off to Paris, and the recording studio where he had told me to meet him. We were not to start work immediately, I think this was just to get me there. I walked into the studio and there he was with three or four English actors. One I knew, Patience Collier, the others were strangers to me, but I could tell that they were English actors all right. I thought, well, I think we could try this one, this won't do any harm so I went up to Orson and said, 'Hello, Orson, thank you very much for having me, but I'm afraid I don't like the part.' In view of the fact, of course, that I hadn't even been sent the part, everybody could guess that I was having a bit of fun and we all had a good laugh, at least I hoped it was a good laugh.

The following day we started work. The film was called *The Trial* and was based upon the work of Kafka. Anthony Perkins had filmed the leading part, the entire film had been shot and it was all assembled. But because it was Orson, and because it had been shot in Europe somewhere, not all of it in Paris, it was going to have multilingual artists playing the different parts. Romy Schneider was in it somewhere, and the part that he wanted me to do was that of an Hungarian actor. A perfectly good actor, except that he couldn't speak English and so his part was in Hungarian, he was the uncle of K, the part that Tony Perkins was playing. So he spoke Hungarian, and I had to follow the lines across the screen which were in English, while this guy was talking in Hungarian. I had to put them back into English, or in this particular case, as Orson wanted it, in my American accent version of English.

Orson had shot the interiors of *The Trial* at the Gare d'Orsay. This railway station had previously been used by Jean-Louis Barrault as a theatre to stage plays in, so what better person to take it over for a bit than another son of the theatre. He showed me around before we did much work, he showed me the cutting room, he showed me clips from the film and he was, what he had always been I suppose, just a little bit of a child. He had a childlike delight in what he was doing and he wanted to share it with somebody, so he shared it with me, and I was flattered and pleased that he did. I couldn't make much of it, of course, just watching the odd scenes that he had put together, but never mind. It brought us together, and when I saw the film I realised that the interior apartments seemed to have a lot of drapes hanging down, with which Orson disguised the iron girders of the railway station. A lot of swagging went on, and protective clothing was hung about on odd places to cover up the nuts and bolts.

We made our way to the recording studio. In the middle of the room was the console, just a small desk, and at it sat a rather small French operator. The screen was in front of just the three of us. There was the operator, then Orson and then me; the microphones were hung appropriately and we started work. You have to bear in mind that the operator was French, and he was listening to a voice that was very much a background voice, on a guide track, speaking in Hungarian. Then he was going to have superimposed on that my voice speaking, projecting a bit, in English, or rather American, so he had to be pretty well on his toes, and I did feel a smidgen of sympathy when Orson began to get cross with him.

I could see that the guy had got his hands full, and how he had managed with the other characters I don't know, maybe they had all been giving him trouble. This went on for quite a while, as we were working away, and Orson eventually turned to me and said, 'This man is a four-letter word!' and I got the message. We worked away, and worked away, and eventually Orson said, 'Let's eat.'

So we went outside and stood on the pavement, and I thought that we were waiting for a taxi, but no, we were waiting for Orson's van and it rolled up, with two sliding doors that opened like a cattle truck. Orson got in and I followed him. There were two benches facing each other, like an old-fashioned stagecoach, and he sat on one and I sat on the second, facing each other, and Orson explained, 'I can't get into a taxi.' It hadn't really dawned on me that he was that big.

The van took us to the restaurant where Orson had booked a table in advance, and we got out and made our way in. We had only gone a couple of paces when he froze and said, 'Jesus, it's the management,' which I took to mean that they were the executives of the film that we were making, seated at a round table. There were about five or six of them, and the one who was clearly the top man, the producer, immediately engaged in a conversation with Orson in French, of which I understood very little.

So I stood back and he didn't introduce me, and eventually I saw that the producer man was looking at Orson, and looking at me and looking back again, and to-ing and fro-ing, and eventually he interrupted and put his hand halfway out and said, '*Excusez moi.*'

'Yeah,' said Orson.

He pointed at me and pointed at Orson and said, '*Votre fils?*' Well, I don't know which of us was the more embarrassed. Neither of us said a word. Orson almost darted away from the table, not that it was possible for Orson to dart anywhere, but he did his best, and we sat down at the table that had been reserved for us.

Neither of us said a word about the incident and we began eating and, in Orson's case, drinking straight away. I think I can say that it's the only time I have ever seen Orson nonplussed. But there was a reason for it. I mean, I was round of face. I had a sort of semi-crewcut in those days and it would never have occurred to me in a thousand years, but I suppose you could say that there was a slight resemblance.

We had our meal. Orson had the table piled with dishes: salami and beef and ham and prawns and lettuce, and goodness knows what, and a huge carafe of red wine. I didn't drink, I stuck to water, and he did his best to finish all this off. In the meantime, with his mouth full, he chattered away. I wish to goodness I could remember what he talked about. He talked about a lot while we were together those few days, but I can't remember any of it, except reminiscing, from time to time, about *Moby Dick*, the play that we had done, and in particular about Gordon Jackson. He obviously had an affection, as who didn't, for Gordon. He was less, shall I say, accommodating about McGoohan, but I suspect that this was because McGoohan had his measure, and McGoohan could have taken him the whole eighteen holes, if you know what I mean. Gordon was made of less strong material.

We finished our meal and the van took us back to the recording studio. Work began again and nothing really had occurred to make the operator any more efficient. I still felt a bit sorry for him because of the circumstances in which he was working, but Orson, encouraged by the claret he had drunk, and the food he had eaten, wasn't going to put up with it much longer, I could tell that. Eventually he turned on the man, and I have never seen anything like it except in cartoon films. He stretched out his hand, he got hold of him by the scruff of his collar, lifted him out of his seat and carried him, with his feet just off the floor, all the way to the door and threw him out. Then he came back, sat down at the console, pulled his microphone down over him and began to work the thing himself, giving me my instructions. I fed him my lines and we worked like that until the job was done. At the end of it, when we had finished and were on our way back to the hotel, I took the liberty of saying to him, 'Orson, I always thought you were a great director, but now I know you are.'

Of course, hundreds of people, thousands of people, had worked with Orson more than I had and knew him better than I did, but in the short time that I was with him I became very fond of him. There was something intensely likeable about him, and although he hadn't forgotten all the sadnesses and the bitternesses of films like *The Magnificent Ambersons*, they disappeared into the past. As far as Orson was concerned, I am sure he was one of those people who couldn't be left alone, and shouldn't be left alone. He wanted a companion and I was very happy to fill the breach for a short time.

I watched the film of *The Trial* again not all that long ago. It is not a great film, but there are things in it that only Orson could possibly have provided. I mean who, in 1961 when the film was made, could have known Albinoni's G Minor Adagio? Something that clutters all the record shelves these days. And the opening title sequences. Who but Orson would have discovered two people called Alexander Alexia and Claire Parker with their pinscreens?

Let me try to describe what a pinscreen is. Imagine a huge breadboard, many feet long and many feet square, made of thick, thick wood and into that board you hammer literally thousands of needles, and then you project a light horizontally on to the needles, but you don't photograph the needles, you photograph the shadow that they cast. If you were to see *The Trial*, you would know immediately what I mean. It produces a really spooky effect, and when you see that figure of the man, who has been waiting outside the gates of the law all his life, waiting to be let in, when you see that done with pin or needle shadows, you get some idea of the nature of the film that you are going to see. It is Kafkaesque, to coin a phrase.

Orson must have spent at least an hour or two with me explaining this needle screen, and showing me the finished results on his machinery in the railway station. Fascinating stuff, fascinating, and absolutely spot-on right for this particularly depressing movie, although, of course, he and Tony Perkins wanted to make it into a comedy. Well, in a kind of way you can see what they mean. If you watch the film with the idea of it being comedic, if you think of it that way, it does come over, but you have to be told that it is funny before you laugh at it. He told me that he and Tony Perkins had gone to see a press showing in Paris, and they were sitting at the back of the cinema roaring with laughter and nobody else in the audience was.

EIGHT

Wait Until Dark

A Shot in the Dark was to be done at the Lyric Theatre, Shaftesbury Avenue, in 1963, with Judi Dench and George Baker. It was, as you've probably already guessed, the beginnings of what you might call the *Pink Panther* films. The play (an adaptation by Harry Kurnitz from the French) had been done on Broadway and the management was headed by Richard Rodgers, of 'Rodgers and Hart' and 'Rodgers and Hammerstein' fame. I formed the opinion, quite early on when I knew that I was going to be in it, that if Mr Rodgers came over to England at any time to see this play I was going to have a word with him, just to say hello and thank you, thank you, thank you.

It had happened a couple of times before where I was in the presence of great people and froze. One of them was at the Mermaid Theatre, when it was in St John's Wood, and we were using the house as a rest centre when we were not on the stage. I was in a room somewhere in the house, and who should come through in his wheelchair, propelled by his wife, but T. S. Eliot. They nodded and acknowledged the fact that I was there, and I acknowledged the fact that they were there, but what fun it would have been to have stopped, just for a moment, and said, 'Excuse me, Mr Eliot, but I just wanted to say hello, Tom, and get a rhyme from Nova Scotia.' Something jolly like that, that might have sent him paddling away even faster. Then there was Burgess Meredith going to produce a play in London, which was actually an evening with James Thurber, a sort of Thurber Carnival Evening, and he was holding auditions for it.

I was one of the participants in the auditions, and I remember being in the stalls with Burgess Meredith talking about the production, and sitting just a few seats away from me was James Thurber, and I actually found myself at one point sitting next to him. It would have been so easy to have said, 'Hello, Mr Thurber, you can't see me, but I can see you and I just wanted to say thank you for the hours of pleasure that you have given me.' I expect he probably would have given a bit of a grunt and a sniff, and gone on with his private thoughts. Never mind, there was the idea. That's what I wanted to do.

But then we did do *A Shot in the Dark* and Mr Rodgers did cross the Atlantic to see it. We were doing it at Brighton, and I knew that he had been coming backstage to see Judi and George, so I spoke to the company manager and said, 'Look, if I am just standing in the corridor here when you bring him along to see Judi and George, perhaps he wouldn't mind if I just said a few words to him.' He said, 'No, I'm sure that'll be all right,' and indeed it was all right.

Mr Rodgers came along, a smallish, dapper figure. I said, 'Excuse me, Mr Rodgers, but I can't let you be here and not say to you thank you so much for all your music. It has meant an enormous amount to me over the years.'

'Oh,' he said, 'thank you, thank you,' and he nodded his head and went on. Well, I had done it, at least I had spoken to him, and I felt better for it. I don't suppose he felt any better, but maybe he did, you never know with these quiet geniuses.

I think that the American director of *A Shot in the Dark* must have been given directions from above to produce on the stage in London exactly what he had done in New York. Fortunately, in a way, I can't remember the name of the actress who played the leading part, the Judi Dench part on Broadway. In fact, I don't know the names of any of the cast, now that I'm writing about it, but this director wanted Judi to do everything that this other lady had done and in exactly the same manner, even to wearing the same clothes.

'No, Judi, excuse me . . .' he would say, 'Miss X would always rise at this point and she'd move towards the settee, almost as though she was . . . no, no, no, I've got that wrong. Yeah, I'm getting it, Judi, I'm getting it, almost as though she'd forgotten something, and then she carries on. You understand me, Judi?' Stuff like that was going on all the time.

I had a long section in one part of the play where I was reading out a transcript of what some prisoner or somebody in the witness box had been saying – I can't remember any of the details now – but whatever it was, this man who was directing us managed to crush any attempt that I made to make it sound spontaneous and a little bit interesting. It's not fair on him to go on too long about it, but I just know that on the first night, Peter Bridge, our producer, came round and said, 'That bit where you were reading that stuff out, why on earth did you do it like that?'

'Because I was told to,' I said.

'Dear me, dear me,' said Peter, tut-tutting away.

So it came to none of us as a surprise that the show closed but, to my surprise and delight, I was back at the Lyric almost immediately. This time I was doing a musical and it was a Hal Prince musical. Now that was something else again!

It was called *She Loves Me*. The score was written by Jerry Bock and Sheldon Harnick, and I think they hadn't yet opened *Fiddler on the Roof* on Broadway, which was of course their biggest hit. The score that they presented us with for this musical was an absolute delight, but more to the point, it was a Hal Prince musical. Hal was not only in management with Richard Pilbrow, presenting it in London, but he was also directing it, and it was then that I learnt something of the magic and mystery of Broadway.

The show itself was a delightful tale taken from an Hungarian story which, in turn, had been made into a movie called *The Shop Around the Corner* starring James Stewart and Margaret Sullavan. As a story the film was charming, and we were shown it by Richard Pilbrow before we started rehearsals. It seemed to me, as far as I could judge these things, that the score by Bock and Harnick had exactly captured the atmosphere. The shop in question, where the whole setting of the story was laid, was a perfumery, and the leading man and the leading lady engaged in a private correspondence, they were writing to each other under the nom de plume of 'friend'. Dear 'friend', that was how they wrote to each other, but they didn't know who the other person was. Eventually they do discover each other, and all ends happily.

Somewhere in the cast there was the lecherous villain, played by Gary Miller. I had never met Gary Miller before, and he came into my life like a treasure. He was such a nice guy. He had a family, three boys and a charming wife, Joy, and he just took me under his wing. He knew it was my first musical and he had been a song and dance man. He had worked the clubs and done just a couple of musicals, but in this show he was great. Harold Hobson said in his first night notice, 'When Mr Miller was on the stage, I could not take my eyes off him,' and I agreed with Mr Hobson.

Alan Ainsworth was the musical director, and I had a number in the show called 'Perspectives', and the bottom line was singing to the hero, 'George, George, keep your perspective and whatever happens, do not lose your job.' I had to audition for this, and Hal Prince heard me do it and gave me the job. A word about Hal at this stage. Of course I knew the man by reputation for his work on Broadway, especially as one of the producers of *West Side Story*, and I liked him immediately. He is still an intensely likeable man.

You didn't get any ruffled feathers with Hal Prince. He knew what he wanted, he asked you to do it, and if you had any sense you just did it. Once I stepped out of line, I'm not even going to waste your time with that, I just draw your attention to it to show that we're all human, but I had the greatest respect for him, and I finished up by doing three Hal Prince musicals in reasonably rapid succession. This was the first, and when we opened we got what can be described as mixed notices. For some reason or other the public didn't really take to it. I couldn't fathom why, unless it was the fact that the show for that time in 1963 was too sentimental, perhaps the people in it were almost too nice.

I thought it was a shame and, to be fair to everybody concerned, a few years later a management came along and repeated *She Loves Me* in London, and they ran for a year and jolly good luck to them. I know that as far as Jerry and Sheldon were concerned, they had a special love of the show and were very disappointed when we didn't succeed, and very pleased when the second company who came along years later actually did succeed.

Naomi Capon was still going great guns at the BBC around this time, and I did two television programmes for her in the mid-1960s. One was *Colombe*, the Anouilh play, and she brought Françoise Rosay over from Paris to play the grande dame in that. Dorothy Tutin played the title part, and the rest of the cast included Sean Connery, Patrick Wymark, Richard Pasco, Freda Jackson, William Mervyn and me, not a bad line-up.

She followed that by doing the other great Anouilh play,

Ring Round the Moon, in which Keith Michell played the twins, Sarah Miles was the girl, and Martita Hunt was also in it. I would have loved to have taken Martita Hunt on tour, just so that I could sit in her dressing room and listen to her stories. She was the best female raconteur I ever came across, and I wish I had written down all her stories of the theatre, I wish I could tell them to you now. She was a lovely lady, a great wit and a fount of stories.

In 1964 I had a call from Hal Prince in America, asking if I would go there and do another musical for him. This one was called *Baker Street*, from which you might deduce that the leading man was Sherlock Holmes, and you would be right. I was to play Dr Watson. I thought, my goodness, this is getting better and better, now I am not only doing a Hal Prince musical, but I am doing a brand-new one on Broadway! I had never been to America before, so of course I said, yes please. He sent me the script and told me a little bit about the song that I had, which was called 'A Married Man'. I got in touch with him and said, 'Do you think you could send me a tape of the musical accompaniment?'

He said, 'No, Peter, no, I want you to start from fresh with me and I don't want you to get bored.'

This was a reference to a point in the musical *She Loves Me*, when George and I went into a nightclub to meet this person who might be the secret correspondent, and he asked me if I could see her. I looked around the room and said, 'Yes, there she is,' and instead of pointing with my hand, I pointed with my foot. Now I don't want you to think for a moment that this sums up Hal Prince's abilities as a director, but he loved it. After a little while I cut it out and I just nodded or pointed with my hand, and I remember him saying to me, 'Why did you do that, Peter, why did you stop pointing with your foot?'

I said, 'Well, I just got a bit bored doing it.'

And he said, 'No, no, no. I love it. Don't leave that out.' So clearly he didn't want me to get bored with my number 'A Married Man' before I had even got to America, not that there was much danger of that.

I am not going to take up your time telling you about living in New York; there was nothing very special about it as far as I was concerned. I was a bit nervous at first. I was warned not to walk in Central Park after dark, and one or two other precautionary notes were given me by my colleagues, but it was those colleagues who I thought were absolutely marvellous. It was pretty obvious that Sherlock Holmes should be played by somebody who was totally convincing as an Englishman, even if he was being played by an American, and Fritz Weaver, who played Holmes, was about as near perfection as you could get.

He had the right figure, the right angular approach to the part, and even if his accent had just a touch of New York in it, or wherever it was he came from, really from an American you couldn't have asked for a better vocal delivery, and he knew how to sing. The rest of the cast welcomed me, and were so kind to me from the start to the finish of the run, and it was nice to be taken aboard like that. The thing that I did miss was just not being in England or, to put it better than that, the fact that England was such a long way away. You never felt, when you were going on tour in England, that you couldn't get home if the necessity arose in well under twenty-four hours, wherever you were. But in New York, 3000 miles away, that feeling never really left me.

However, I wasn't going to let it get me down at this stage, even if the play wasn't a great success. It ran for about six months, it could not be written off as a failure, but there was something about it. I never discussed it with anybody at the time, not even with Hal, but my feeling then was that that 'something in the show' was that Sherlock Holmes had what you might call a fleeting affair. Not in the sense that they went to bed, but let us say, a friendly affair, if there is such a thing, with Irene Adler, a visiting American singer and performer who is appearing in London, and the audience was rather led up the garden a bit into thinking that they are going to go off together, arm in arm.

But since Holmes was a totally confirmed misogynist there was no way in which he was going to go off arm in arm with Irene Adler at the end of the show, so the whole romantic build-up all came to nothing at the end. Maybe you were left to think the two might just meet up again, but nobody, I believe, was really taken in by that.

But I had my little number in it, which I enjoyed, even though one first night critic wrote that the audience went out singing the sets, which were by Oliver Smith. Hal wasn't too happy with the original score, and he got Jerry Bock and Sheldon Harnick in to ghost two or three numbers. Now this is what you go out of town for. We went to Boston and to Toronto as a try-out, but usually the try-out numbers are re-scored, or new numbers are written by the original team. In this case Hal had left the original team on the sidelines and gone back to Bock and Harnick.

So these were signs of weakness which, to a trained Broadway observer, could only have led to one thing, and that was that this show was not going to run and run, and I'm afraid it didn't. But there were rustlings in the Broadway undergrowth, and just before the show finally closed I was offered another chance to work on Broadway. Anthony Page was to direct it, John Osborne had written it and the play was called *Inadmissible Evidence*. It had opened in London with the leading man played by Nicol Williamson, who scored an immediate hit.

It was, in my opinion, probably Osborne's second-best play after *Look Back in Anger* and the part was probably written for Nicol, because it was difficult to imagine anybody else playing it. It had been brought to America by the impresario David Merrick, and I had a very short gap before finishing *Baker Street* and starting to rehearse *Inadmissible Evidence*. I was going to play the part that Arthur Lowe had played in England with Nicol, his clerk, Wally. I hadn't met Nicol before, but did he make an impression on me! I thought, this is the chap for me. I mustn't say that I fell in love with him, but you know what I mean.

Everything he did I just thought was sheer gold dust, even when he was being at his most irritating. We hit it off and he seemed to quite like me – I suppose he wanted a bit of companionship – and we went off on tour with it. In fact, we only went to one theatre and that was in Philadelphia. We were rehearsing in Philadelphia and had yet to open, and I was a bit surprised when I walked by the theatre one day and there were no notices up at all. There was no indication that next week you were going to see *Inadmissible Evidence* starring Nicol Williamson, presented by David Merrick. I thought that was a bit odd. We opened and the first night went very well, as far as one can judge these things, and it was to be followed that night by a photocall; the cast were asked to stay behind after they had done the show to have their photos taken for the front of house, which up until now had been rather bare.

So we sat in our dressing rooms chewing our lips and just waiting to get out of the place, and after a bit I thought, this is absurd. Twenty minutes, half an hour had gone by and nobody had called us, or started taking the photographs, and I thought I'm going to have a word with Nick. So I walked down the passageway, and as I went towards his dressing room a man came out of it whom I half recognised as one of David Merrick's management team, and as he went past me he was almost in tears. He was shaking his head and saying, 'He didn't oughta have done it, he didn't oughta have done it.' I thought, oh, didn't oughta have done what?

I got to the dressing room and knocked on the door, and Peter Murphy, a friend of Nicol's helping to dress him and generally look after him, opened the door and said, 'You can't come in.'

I said, 'But what's going on?'

'I can't tell you, I can't tell you. Just wait in your dressing room. Somebody will come along in a minute.' So I went back to the dressing room and there was another pause, and then we were told that we were to be dismissed. In other words there was not going to be a photocall. I thought, oh well, so I went back to Nicol's dressing room, and to my surprise it was practically empty.

I said to Peter Murphy, 'Where's Nicol?'

'He's gone, he's gone, he's left for London.'

'What do you mean, he's left for London?'

He said, 'There's been a row. There's been a row and he walked out and now he says he's going back to London.'

I said, 'Well, not without *me*, he isn't!' I chased out of the building and I saw him going down the street. He was hatless and coatless and just striding off. I ran after him and I caught up with him, and I said, 'What are you doing? What are you doing?'

He said, 'That man, that man, I've just hit him!'

'Who have you just hit?'

'That Merrick!'

I said, 'Why?'

'He wants to cut the show.'

'Do you mean take it off?'

'No, no, no, he just wants to cut it, and Tony Page won't have it and I'm backing up Tony, so I hit him!'

I went back to my hotel. I didn't like the idea of leaving for England with Nicol without my passport or even any clothes, and I thought at least I had better get back to the hotel. By then it was something like one or two o'clock in the morning, and after a few minutes the phone went and it was my old chum Peter Bull phoning from London.

He said, 'Is it true? Is it true?'

'Is *what* true?'

'Well, it's on the grapevine over here in London that Nicol Williamson has punched David Merrick in the jaw.'

I thought to myself, don't get too far into this, sunshine, keep as much on the fringe as you can. So I said, 'Yes, it might be true.'

And he said, 'Don't you know?'

I said, 'I don't know. I don't know, and I don't really know what's happened.' Well, of course Peter Bull was right, and I was also right not to give anything more away than I did.

The following day I caught up with Nicol and it turned out that the play, in David Merrick's opinion, having watched just that one performance, was too long and needed cutting. Now I have to say that I was in agreement with David Merrick, but it was none of my business. I thought it was overlong. It didn't need much, but it just needed something. Apparently that evening David Merrick had made his announcement in Nicol's dressing room in front of Anthony Page and John Osborne. John Osborne was a bit inclined to side with Merrick, not wholeheartedly, but you could tell, Nicol said, how his feelings were.

But Anthony Page absolutely refused. He said, 'No, we've got to run this thing in, it's only the first night, for goodness sake, give it a chance. I think this is a great play and I don't want to cut any of it.'

It was at that point that David Merrick said, 'Mr Page, I want to cut it, the author is prepared to cut it, you don't want to cut it, you'll have to go, I'll get another director.'

And Nicol said, 'Oh no you won't,' and he threw half a glass of Budweiser in David Merrick's face and hit him, not very hard, but on the other hand Nicol was a big man, so he didn't have to hit very hard, and David Merrick collapsed.

Somehow or other, and I imagine it was probably John Osborne who did the hard work, everyone was calmed down, and during the following day it was decided that there would be some cuts and that the show would go on. But it made an exciting little moment in our lives and I thought it was fairly typical. It summed up the characteristics of all the contenders. The show opened at the Belasco Theater, and I think it was a matter of convenience, more than anything, but we did transfer to the Shubert Theater. Maybe the Shubert Theater held more. It was not a roaring success, but it was a success, and Nicol made a personal triumph out of it, as he had done in London.

So in one sense, it was *the* play to see, and in another sense it wasn't to everybody's taste, and it wasn't in any sense of the word an American play. We were very, very English, if you know what I mean. One day there was a company call and we were told to expect this tough guy from David Merrick's office. He was the man that David Merrick would send to fire you. If he hadn't been in Nicol Williamson's dressing room at the time, he would have sent somebody else to tell Anthony Page that he was fired in Philadelphia. This man was known as 'the hatchet man' and he arrived in the room where we were all waiting for him.

He took off his coat, put it down, and without bothering to say who he was or anything he said, 'Everybody's to take a thirty per cent cut.'

I said, 'Excuse me?'

'Yeah?'

'Why? Why?'

'Yeah?'

Nicol wasn't there. He had already agreed to take a cut, but we didn't know that. Faces were turned towards me and I said, 'Well, for a start, let's consider Philadelphia. I went past the theatre before we opened in Philadelphia and there wasn't any sign that the play was going to be done the following week, and I think that a little advance publicity there would have brought in a few more seats. I'm not suggesting that it might not have ended in our having to take a cut, but it seemed to me to be an indication of the management attitude towards the play, that they couldn't even be bothered to announce it in Philadelphia the week before.'

This was brushed aside and we did take a thirty per cent cut, and one of the American ladies in the cast came up to me afterwards and said, 'Peter, it's all right for you, I mean you don't live here, you don't work here, but we have to, well, to put it very simply, we have to toe the line.'

I said, 'Well, I'm very sorry. As it happens no harm has been done, but yes, of course, I see what you mean, I'll keep my mouth shut in future.' We continued to do the play. I can't remember how long it lasted, but probably about six months.

I was into the jazz scene when I arrived in New York to do *Baker Street*. I made enquiries, got the necessary trade papers, and had a few weeks in Greenwich Village, actually living there, before we went off on tour. When we came back from our tour and opened in *Baker Street*, I moved to the east side of New York, to a flat, I may add, which was actually owned by Noël Coward.

But before that, when I was in Greenwich Village, there was one place in particular I remember called the Five Spot, and I went there several times. I recall one occasion in particular. They would have selected artists come along to do the odd week, and this particular week they had got Coleman Hawkins. It was probably a Sunday, when we were not playing, but I arrived as soon as the doors opened and I was the first person there. I got myself a drink, and the tables were arranged rather like forms in a school. They were long tables, which stretched across the room and then the platform – you could hardly call it a stage – was there and the players would come up on to it.

I saw Coleman Hawkins and I was not going to make a fool of myself. I wasn't going to go up and touch his sleeve or anything like that, but I thought, this is one of the people whose records I have collected. He sat down and he had a piano and a double bass to accompany him. I had a glass of wine in front of me and he played his opening note. It was a blast, it was one prolonged honk. It didn't shatter the glass, but it shattered me, and then he went into the number, which I think was 'Liza', and I sat there enraptured for a couple of hours.

Later on, when I was in New York doing the play, I discovered Jimmy Ryan's. There were two nightspots that I knew about, one was Jimmy Ryan's and the other was Eddie Condon's. Jimmy Ryan's was quite nearby. It was more or less on the way to the apartment block where I was staying, Noël Coward's apartment, on the way from the theatre, and I used to drop in there practically every night. There was a group of five who usually played there, led by a man with an Italian name. I'm going to make this up – Tony Porenco – something Italian-sounding like that, and then there was a trombonist, a pianist and a drummer, and probably a double bass.

Of that group, the one that I sought out immediately was the drummer, because he was Zuty Singleton and I used to go in there after the show. I never stayed very long, but long enough to buy them all a drink and have one myself, and then maybe another drink, and that was how I spent the later part of the evening. One day I went up to Zuty Singleton – I knew them all by now – and said, 'I've got something to tell you.'

And he said, 'What's that?'

'Well, you remember doing some broadcasts a year or so back that were arranged by Alistair Cooke, they were transmitted from America to England, and they went out live and I think it was called *The Alistair Cooke Hour* or something like that?'

He said, 'Yeah, I remember.'

I said, 'Well, you were the drummer, not all the time, but you were there more often than not, one of the pick-up groups.'

He said, 'Yeah, I do remember.'

'Well, see if you can believe this. I have an exercise book back in England, which I got when I was a schoolboy, and on a blank page you will see a whole lot of lead pencil dots, and underneath is written "St Louis Blues", Zuty Singleton, the tango section.' And by now his mouth was open. So I had to come to Zuty's rescue. I said, 'Those dots, Zuty, were made by me with a lead pencil as you were drumming, and when you switched to the tango rhythm I just kept on going, and so these dots are totally meaningless, but they're a record of your drum beat in that particular broadcast.' First of all I think he thought that I must be crazy, and secondly I think he thought crazy in a nice way. That cemented what was needed, if anything was needed, to seal our friendship, and I loved going there.

One day when I was buying a round of drinks the manager said to me, 'Tony' – referring to the clarinet player – 'Tony's cracked alcohol.'

I said, 'What do you mean, he's cracked alcohol?'

'Well, he starts pretty early in the evening, somewhere round about six or seven, and by the time you get here he's been through the alcohol barrier and come out the other side. He's got drunk and now he's sobering up, and you're still buying him drinks but it's all right, it's all right, he won't fluff a note.' He didn't, and I think that the manager was probably actually pulling my leg, but Tony certainly was able to put it away and he never showed the slightest sign of missing a semiquaver.

When we were doing *Inadmissible Evidence* I took Nicol to Jimmy Ryan's, and Nicol thought it was just great. He also liked to sing, and once or twice they let Nicol sing. He had a pretty good voice; in fact, he made an LP and very good it is too.

Nicol has different ways of working. He has ways of working when he is into that part of the play where he knows that he's got to turn it on, and then in other parts of the play he will relax. In the case of *Inadmissible Evidence* the relaxation came in the first half of the play and several passages of it were with me. I played his clerk, and I also played the judge who opens the play in a prologue section where he sends Maitland down. But in the opening scenes of the play, after the judge prologue, there were scenes between me and Nicol, and my name was Wally but he persisted in calling me Wall-I, much to the audience's confusion, I would have thought, but oh boy, it was great working with him.

He could do the play with the apparent utmost facility and his depth of character and his depth of feeling were quite astonishing. Sometimes I would go down in the second half when I wasn't on and had left the play, just to watch him. I have never known anybody whose mind worked at such a rate. Osborne had written one passage where he was talking to his daughter, and he was talking about a woman. He had a passage which went, 'she is . . . she is . . . she is . . .' and then in between the 'she is'es Osborne had written a descriptive passage of this particular woman. Just short sentences, but I could watch Nicol do it over and over again.

His mind was ahead of you, he was thinking out what the woman was and saying it in the next millisecond; he was thinking out each phrase, yet he spoke with a rapidity and a poise that you knew was absolutely genuine. In other words he hadn't just learnt it and was gabbling it off. He knew exactly what he was saying at any particular point. This is nothing much, but it was an indication of the volatility of his mind. And as for emotions, he could create more atmosphere with a flick of his wrist than most actors can in a month of *Hamlets*.

He had a fine mind, there is no doubt about that, and he was entirely self-taught. Or, to put it another way, you couldn't tell Nicol how to do anything. You wouldn't have wanted to, but if the thought had crossed your mind, he wouldn't have taken any notice of you. He should have developed into a West End star of first proportions, but his star blazed and then rather died away, and I don't feel happy saying this, but in some ways I think he was his own worst enemy. He did have this thing about audiences which was understandable: coughing, children in the audience talking while they're watching the play. Yes, he did walk off the stage, and he did talk to the audience and say, 'If I have any more of this, I'm going off', and all those kinds of remarks that he made.

It is difficult really to describe on paper, and if you hadn't witnessed it or heard about it you wouldn't know, but it was there. While we were in New York no such problems existed, but he did not play the matinées. He had his understudy do the matinées. I know that I found his understudy a real charmer and a good actor, but he was an under-actor. He did not, in my opinion, really project. I sometimes wondered how the audience could follow what he was actually saying, and I'm not going to disclose his name, because I saw him in a film a year or two later, where he played a very, very important part, and he was absolutely marvellous, so there's no doubt that he could do it, but he wasn't really a theatre actor. He was a film actor who hadn't got the knack of projecting.

After a few matinées of this I went into Nicol's dressing room one evening and said, 'Nicol, you've got to do the part, I'm not going on with this guy any more. Even I can't hear him. Look, I'd rather act with my mother than with this guy.' It brought no response at all from Mr Williamson, of course.

After the first night, I was going to Sardi's, the famous theatrical restaurant in New York, which I enjoyed enormously, and I'd brought my tuxedo, as they called it, or dinner jacket, to wear there. I can't remember now who I took with me, but I'd brought my dinner jacket and of course Nicol, the swine, pinched it on the first night. He had got Peter Murphy to go into my room and snaffle it off the hook and hide it.

My agent arrived, Milton Goldman, a lovely man, an enormous help to me in many ways while I was in America, and Milton came in with Joan Fontaine. She was his guest for the evening, and they were going off to dine somewhere, and I was standing there in my pants and vest. I said to Miss Fontaine and to Milton Goldman, and anybody else who would hear, 'That bastard has pinched my dinner jacket!' Miss Fontaine, being brought up in a theatrical family, of course, could handle it and so could Milton Goldman, but I thought, oh, I had a chance there of having a chat with Joan Fontaine and I've ruined it. But those days with Nicol were still very good days.

When we got back to England Tony Page had arranged that we would film *Inadmissible Evidence*, so we did. It was shot in the City and on location almost entirely, and it was also in black and white, which I don't think affected the film at all. It was a black-and-white movie, why spend the money on lots of colours that you're not going to see, really, on the set. But the film disappeared. I did manage to catch it in the West End before it vanished. As far as I know it has had only one late-night showing on television. I really don't know why. It wasn't, of course, to everybody's taste, the play as a whole was a pretty heavy drama, but my goodness when you think of Nicol's performance alone, it was worth preserving. All those films are shown over and over and over again on television, yet this one, for some reason or other, isn't. So if you're listening out there – how about it?

When I was in New York, during this last time with Nicol, I got a letter from Peter Bridge. Peter Bridge, you may remember, is the man who produced me in my first play ever, the Noël Coward *Hay Fever* at Cranwell. In his letter Peter told me to go and see Lee Remick in *Wait Until Dark*, and he added a few more touches, and that was really the end of the message. I didn't go and see Lee Remick in *Wait Until Dark* and when I got back to England, probably about the time when we'd finished making *Inadmissible Evidence*, Peter sent for me and said, 'Did you see Lee Remick?'

I said, 'No, no, sorry.'

'Oh God! Well, here's, the script. It's called *Wait Until Dark* and I want you to play Roat. Thank you and good afternoon.'

I went away and I read it and I thought, wow! It was by Frederick Knott, who had written *Dial M for Murder*, which was an enormous success in the theatre and on film, then another mystery thriller play which was not, and then came *Wait Until Dark*. It is a difficult play to read and a difficult play in a way to put over, but he had assembled a good cast. It was headed by Honor Blackman, and when I was in discussion with him about doing it, not that I really needed to discuss it and nor did he, I said, 'Who is playing the girl?'

He said, 'Honor Blackman.'

I said, 'Oh, well, thank God for that!'

The play has three nasties, three villains, and they have killed a girl, but for some reason or other they've killed her for the drugs that she is carrying, and they put her in the basement of the block of flats where the action takes place, in other words Honor Blackman's flat. It was written by Freddie Knott to take place in New York somewhere, but for the London production the venue shifted to somewhere such as South Hampstead.

At the beginning you do wonder why the three villains had made such a hash of it, so that the body and the drugs all finish up in this basement. It is vaguely explained, but it makes for a rather difficult opening to the play. Once it gets under way and you know what the problems are – can the nasties get the drugs? Can the girl stop them? – once you get over that, I don't mean you're home and dry, but it then settles down to be a straightforward thriller, with the head of the nasties, Mr Roat, battling it out theatrically with Honor Blackman, who was playing the blind girl.

When I agreed to play Roat I was particularly thrilled that it was Honor who did me the honour, if I may put it that way, of saying to me, when we met to start work, 'I'm so glad it's you.' We had worked together before. I had been in one of her *Avengers* films, when she was tossing men about like cabers. This time she wasn't going to toss anybody about because she was blind.

It is an out and out thriller. As the play progresses, two of the three nasties drop out, until the last big scene is a confrontation between the girl, Susy, and Roat. Susy has brought in a sixteen-year-old girl who is living in the same block of flats. They know that something terrible is going to happen, but they don't know what and they don't know why, they don't know anything about drugs, they just know that this man Roat is a nasty piece of work. They do various things, take certain precautions; for instance, they remove all the fuses out of the box so that the lights can't work in the kitchen, which is where the action takes place. There are various highlights in the last scene. For example, at one point you really think she's got the better of him, because she hits him and he goes down with a great thud behind the sofa, and you think she's done him in or at least knocked him unconscious and then a few seconds or even half a minute later, he leaps up from behind the sofa and comes for her again.

At this point, on the tour, the audience would scream, and Peter Bridge used to phone from time to time and say to one or other of us, 'Did you get the scream?' and if we said 'Yes, we got the scream last night' he was happy, he just put the phone down. It was a kind of signpost. If we got the scream, we knew we'd got the audience, and on the first night in London we did get the scream, and we did get the audience, and we got the notices and we were a hit.

It was the nature of the piece, the thriller atmosphere that was conjured up by Freddie Knott and maintained by Anthony Sharp, our director. You couldn't have found a better director to run the play. He was like a captain on the bridge of a destroyer in the middle of a minefield. He knew exactly how to get us to go. The very first thing he said to me – we weren't friends, but we knew each other – was, 'Peter, do you think you could do a fall?'

I said, 'Well, it depends where and how far.'

'It's not very far, but you've really got to make it convincing.'

So I said, 'Well, we'd better rehearse it until I convince you, and if I can convince you then we should be all right.'

So we left it like that, and I did do the fall. It was the fall that preceded my coming up from behind the sofa and getting the scream. There was also another part where the whole theatre was blacked out as much as we could get it. We weren't allowed to turn off the exit lights over the doors altogether, but we were allowed to turn them down so that there was the absolute minimum amount of light, and when Roat was chasing Honor at the end of the play, there was a point when he suddenly had a brainwave. The whole place was in blackness, but he opened the fridge door and the light from the fridge, which Susy had completely forgotten, blazed out like the head-lamp of a car and it lit up the whole stage and part of the auditorium as well.

This didn't get a scream, but it certainly kept the audience on their toes, and thanks to Anthony Sharp, this whole last scene was so well choreographed that the excitement was intense and we ran and we ran and we ran. I had never been in a play that ran as long. I think it did three years altogether. I did a year and three months, Honor left at the end of a six-month contract, her place being taken by Barbara Murray, and then Barbara Murray and I left together, and our parts were taken by Alana Morris and my understudy, a man who had faithfully stood by me for the year and three months that I was doing it. He was rewarded by being given the part to play full time.

Such was the success of the play that Peter smothered the Strand Theatre, which is where we were doing it, with huge blown-up pictures of me doing nasty things to Honor with a chiffon scarf. Our names were in lights over the front-of-house marquee, the first and only time it had happened to me. It said, 'Honor Blackman in *Wait Until Dark* with Peter Sallis.'

One bright sunny day I was walking towards the stage door of the Strand Theatre when coming down the pavement on the same side towards me I saw Sir John Gielgud. 'Hello,' he said.

'Hello,' I said, and it was important we find out how we both were, and it turned out that we were both fine.

And he said, 'What are you doing at the moment?'

So I looked at him, and then I looked up at all these posters and bills and everything, and said, 'Well, I'm in this.'

'Ahhh,' he said, 'ahhh. I hear the girl's very good.'

NINE

'The Scenery has Stuck'

In 1968 Hal Prince asked me to do another musical. I could hardly believe it. The show was *Cabaret*, which had run on Broadway for quite a while, starring Joel Gray as the Master of Ceremonies, probably the most important part in the show apart from Sally Bowles. He had asked Judi Dench to play Sally Bowles in London, and Barry Dennen, an unknown, was to play the Master of Ceremonies.

Hal took me out to lunch with his assistant producer, Ruth Mitchell, who had been with him through the other two shows that I had done, and he said as follows: 'You're not Jewish, are you?'

I said, 'No.'

He said, 'You're playing a Jew, though?'

'Yes, I realise that.'

'Well, the point is this, I've cast you in this part because I don't want the audience to realise straight away that you *are* Jewish. It's the way the play unfolds, and if you come on and they just accept you as a perfectly ordinary greengrocer, which is your job, then fine. Later on, as the play develops, let them realise, let them find out that you are Jewish. OK?'

'Yes.'

'Right, let's go.'

The show was developed from Christopher Isherwood's

stories set in Berlin before the war, and it was a matter of the Jews versus the Nazis. As we began work at the Palace Theatre, I realised why I had always thought of Hal as a great stage manager, that is to say somebody who manages the stage. He had got Boris Aronson to do the sets, and I remember standing at the back of the theatre when we were dress rehearsing, and looking at it thinking this is a masterpiece of stage engineering. One set was living inside another and we went from the cabaret scenes with Barry Dennen, the Master of Ceremonies – 'Wilkommen, Welcome' and all that – to the other sets, which were built around it. It was just marvellous the way he and Boris Aronson created this setting.

We had previews before we opened. I have to explain about previews. In those days, and I suspect it is probably pretty much the same now, if you were doing a big show like this you couldn't take it on the road first, at least not in England. Having done it on Broadway, Hal knew the layout, he knew how to shape it and direct it, so we were to have something like a week's run of previews.

Jewish charities would buy up a huge number of seats and, if you haven't already discovered it for yourself, let me tell you that the Jews, both in London and New York, certainly at this time, held up the theatre. They were enormously generous providers and they loved going to the theatre. They didn't go there just for charity's sake, the theatre was part of their life. You have only to look back over the songwriters, the Gershwins, Irving Berlin and the others, to realise what strength they have in the actual operation of the theatre, as well as from an audience point of view.

I am saying all this because when we did these previews they were not very well attended. You could see that from the stage, you could just see the empty seats, and I wondered why. I didn't say anything to anybody. I didn't discuss it with anybody in the cast. I never mentioned it, of course, to Hal; it was just a fact that we were not doing very well and one or two of the charity shows that we did hardly sold any seats at all. I thought, this is word of mouth. This has come, possibly, from America. I really am guessing at this. Don't think for one moment that I knew the real reason, but I thought, they don't like this show in advance. It was the Nazi versus the Jewish element.

We opened and we got pretty good notices. They weren't bad at all, and Barry Dennen, in particular, and Judi Dench received special praise. Barry was terrific. It was interesting that he broke through into the part about two dress rehearsals before we were due to open. I remember Hal saying to him, 'You haven't got it yet, Barry.' What they talked about I have no idea, but there was some keynote that was obviously missing. By the time we actually opened, Barry Dennen had found it and he was an enormous success.

Judi has a slight catch in her voice, which was ideal for Sally Bowles. She and I had no scenes together, but I watched her a lot. I never thought about her becoming a great star at the time we were doing *Cabaret*, although she was already doing pretty well, and for one reason only: her size. I don't mean you have to be physically large like Edith Evans to be a big female star, but Judi is a relatively diminutive figure. I hope she won't be insulted by me saying that, but nobody could say she was tall and willowy, like Evelyn Laye, for example. Evelyn carried stardom with her and Judi has had to work for it.

But she has produced a range of parts that are quite extraordinary and the public can't get enough of her. She is the number one star in England at the moment, and has been for a few years; I mean above the men, there is no man working in the West End at present whom you would put ahead of Judi in terms of box office. She has earned it the hard way, by doing things she probably shouldn't do and still convincing the audience.

But nevertheless, despite the rave notices for Judi and Barry, the show never really got going, although it was doing well enough for Judi, who had only a six-month contract, to be on the brink of leaving the show, and Elizabeth Seal was asked to take her place. Elizabeth had actually started rehearsing when we came to the point of Judi leaving, and Emile Littler, who owned the theatre, took it off. So that was the end of the rather chequered history of *Cabaret* in London.

This is very naughty of me, but I can't leave *Cabaret* without telling you of two matinée days when Peter Sallis came on and did a turn. It was to do with the scenery. This scenery that Hal and Boris had arranged between them was power-driven, at least the motors to operate the scenery were power-driven, and they were up in the flies, so at a given point somebody pressed a button and all the machinery got into motion, and the set glided from one scene to another. But there was one matinée, not all that long into the run, when the scenery started to move and then it stuck. And it stuck.

There was nothing that anybody could really do about it except the stagehands and the stage manager who, to his great credit, actually performed miracles, facing some danger up there in the flies, scrambling about trying to undo whatever it was that had frozen stiff. But the pause between the scenes mounted and mounted, and after about ten minutes I thought this was absurd. So without asking permission of anybody, because there was nobody to ask as they were all up in the flies trying to get it to work, I went in front of the audience with the curtain still up and said, 'I'm sorry, ladies and gentlemen, but we've had a breakdown here,' and I turned to the conductor Gareth Davies and said, 'Let's give them "Mieskeit".'

Now 'Mieskeit' was my solo number and Gareth looked a

bit doubtful, so I said, 'Come on, look, they can't sit here like this.' And to the audience, 'I'm terribly sorry, but the scenery has stuck, it's obvious, and I'd like to do something to entertain you.' Eventually the band found their parts and I said to the boys and girls of the chorus, who were going to be there with me on the stage when I came to do the number later, 'Come on, come and join me.' So they came on and we did 'Mieskeit', and when it was all over there was a ripple of applause, as if to say well done. I said, 'When we get to it in the show pretend you haven't heard this.'

There was a phone call almost immediately. A friend of mine, who was out front, had seen what had happened and had phoned the *Evening Standard*, and the *Evening Standard* phoned me. I said, 'No, I'm terribly sorry, I'm not going to tell you what happened. Something did go wrong, but I'm not going to talk about it to the press because it may damage the run of the play if something like this gets out. Thank you very much,' and I put the phone down. About a week later it happened again, but this time I was ready for them and by then I had got some props in my dressing room – my portable radio, a camp stool and a book and some letters.

The scenery was jammed up again, there was no question about that, and I wasn't going to just dash on and do this, but I didn't wait ten minutes this time. I went on, put my camp stool down, put my radio down, which was playing gently, and said, 'I'm sorry, but there is a fault with the scenery, as you can tell, and this is a matinée. If we aren't careful the evening audience will come in while you're still here, so I thought at least I'd entertain you a bit. I'd like to read you some of my fan mail.' I opened this letter and I read out, 'Dear Mr Sallis, take your hands off my daugh . . . Oh,' I said. I also managed to slip in the old gag of 'I expect you're all wondering why I sent for you' and one or two other things like that.

Fortunately, I don't think Hal ever found out because he was back in America, and I don't think Richard Pilbrow was exactly carried away, but it was a fact that the audience sat there for something like fifteen to twenty minutes in both cases, before anything happened. That's my story of the run of *Cabaret* and at this late stage I don't really mind who knows it.

In 1980 my old friend Peter Bridge got in touch again, but this time in a completely different way. He sent me the script of a play by Dion Boucicault called *Old Heads and Young Hearts*. Boucicault was a late nineteenth-century writer who was pretty prolific. He wrote plays mainly for himself, the most famous being the one that Donald Sinden revived with enormous success, *London Assurance*. It was far and away Boucicault's most successful play and an interesting sidelight is that his daughter Nina played the first Peter Pan.

Old Heads and Young Hearts was not an easy play to read, and I could understand why nobody had done it since Boucicault himself. It is very difficult to describe it. I can make fun of it by saying you have three people who leave the house, let's say at eight o'clock in the morning, and the next scene it's seven o'clock in the morning, in other words they've gone back an hour, and they're somewhere quite different from where they said they were going.

The play was shot through with those kinds of funny errors but I started to think, as I read it and as I began to work on it, that in fact it had got some fine stuff in it, and I did work very hard on it. I rewrote complete scenes, and two things occurred to me. One was that it was probably an ideal play for Chichester, the festival theatre. I had never been there and had never seen anything on its thrust stage, but I knew that Olivier had started the National Theatre there, and that John Clements had taken over from him and made an enormous success of it. The audience surround the stage in a semicircle. Thinking of the different entrances and exits that the cast had to make, and using these tunnels that came up from below and let you on to the stage, I thought this might be just the right sort of play for Chichester.

I was over-optimistic in the sense that I had never *been* to the theatre, but nevertheless the thoughts that I had were in the right direction. So I adapted it and finally I sent it to Chichester and they accepted it. Peter Dews, whom I knew but had never actually worked for, was running the theatre at the time and decided do the play in tandem with *Much Ado About Nothing*. He offered me the part of Verges in *Much Ado About Nothing*, and the part of an elderly cleric who is the principal maker of the story in *Old Heads and Young Hearts*. He was the chap who got things going, mostly in the wrong direction, so that things became worse under his guidance rather than better, but every-thing worked out in the end.

The other thing that spurred me on was that there was a marvellous part for Lally Bowers. It was not the lead, but it was the leading character actress, and I found myself writing lines for Lally, one in particular where she came on in the last scene of the play. Looking around her, she put her lorgnettes up to her eyes and said, 'So this is Middlesex?' I can't explain why, but it got the biggest laugh of the evening.

Michael Simpson directed the play. He had previously dir-ected me in the television version of the musical *She Loves Me* and had become a good friend. He was married to Jane Freeman, who played Ivy at the café in *Last of the Summer Wine*, which we will come to later on. *Old Heads and Young Hearts* had some success at Chichester. In fact, we took more money at the box office than any of the other plays that season.

In 1985, I did a six-month season at the Criterion Theatre, in one of Ray Cooney's farces, *Run for Your Wife*. Ray actually

Last of the Summer Wine
The original trio, with Bill Owen as Compo and Michael Bates as Blamire.

The second trio, with Brian Wilde as Foggy Dewhurst.

Riding to the rescue?

A cheerful moment in the café with the full cast.

The third trio, with Michael Aldridge as Seymour
'The pleasure it gives me to go back there and climb up those hills.'

Guess who plays the squaw?

The present trio with Tom Owen and Frank Thornton.

Recording the voices for Wallace and Gromit with Nick Park.

Wallace and Gromit: the Curse of the Were-Rabbit wins the Oscar in 2006.

My favourite picture as Clegg in *Last of the Summer Wine*.

directed the takeovers. In other words he had originally directed the play and he was in charge of anybody who was
coming along to take over, so he was in charge of me and, my
goodness, did I enjoy that. He was precision exemplified, he
knew exactly where you should be at any point of the play on
the stage; he knew exactly how to place you and how to arrange
the business for you. There was a military precision about it,
and when you threw the text aside and you knew it well, and
just let yourself go, his instructions saw you through the play.
I can't describe it any better than that.

He was really from what I call the old school. The theatre
was littered with those people at one time, and it was a great
treat to come across one of them working now in the West
End and being able to work for them. We didn't get through
the six months that I was there without me collapsing almost
completely on the stage, and taking Jack Smethurst with me.
The Medical Association, or some such body, approached the
theatre and asked if the cast would be prepared to have instru-
ments attached to them, to measure their blood pressure and
heartbeats and so on during the run of the play.

Where this was going to get anybody I don't know, except I
suppose you could put it this way, that if we were dropping
down dead at regular intervals it might be due to the play.
Fortunately, we weren't dropping down dead in *Run for Your
Wife*, but the cast agreed to have it done, to have these things
strapped to their chests and to their arms, and also to have their
blood taken. I turned it down. I didn't like the sound of it at all
and I didn't have to do it, but I think everybody else in the cast
did, including Jack Smethurst. He was just as reluctant as I was
but he didn't actually turn it down. He said, 'Yes, all right, you
can do it if you like.'

So we had these medics, two or three of them, in the wings
with their measuring devices and all that sort of stuff. They

took blood from those who had volunteered, and I saw Jack Smethurst's blood being placed on the table in the wings in a flask and he went on to do a scene. I was just about to go on after him when somebody bumped into a table, and I watched as Jack Smethurst's flask of blood rolled gently off the table, fell to the floor and broke, and his blood ran on to the floor. I was immediately on, and I came on and I'm afraid that I was just in tears.

If Jack hadn't been quite so against it, perhaps I wouldn't have found it quite so funny, but because he hated the idea and had still gone through with it, I couldn't control myself. When I got on to the stage I never said a word, I was just laughing and the audience, of course, wondered what was going on, so I said, 'Well, excuse me, ladies and gentlemen, but something's just happened in the wings that I have to tell you, because at the moment I just can't continue with the play. We're having blood tests and heart tests while we're doing the play.'

I turned to Jack and said, 'I'm terribly sorry, Jack, but your flask of blood has just rolled off the table and the flask has broken, so you'll have to give some more.' Well, the audience then joined in. Yes, they thought, that wasn't quite up to Ray Cooney's usual standard, but it would do to be going on with. Jack, to his great credit, didn't punch me on the nose, nor did he run into the wings to see how badly his blood had been spilt. No, we managed to pick it up and to continue through to the end of the play, but it made a beautiful incident while it lasted. I never told Ray!

In 1986 I became involved in what turned out to be a lovely production of *Pride and Prejudice*, mounted originally by the Cambridge Theatre Company. The producer-director was Bill Pryde, for whom I had done a couple of shows at the Birmingham Rep, so we knew each other's work. He offered me Mr Bennet. The way it had been adapted by David Pownall, Mr Bennet, I have to admit, really ran the show and it was a lovely part. It was very difficult to learn and there was a great deal of Jane Austen's prose, beautiful stuff to speak, but a lot of it, and we did more than one production. We did it at the Cambridge Arts Theatre and tried it out in the provinces, and nobody bought it.

But then we did it again, and this time we were more successful. We did it at the Leicester Haymarket Theatre when David Aukin was running it, and he got it to the Old Vic. The Old Vic had just been renovated by the Mirvish family from Canada, great benefactors of the theatre, and it was done beautifully. I had been there years before, when I was playing a small part in *Timon of Athens* for Tyrone Guthrie, but now I was playing the leading part and I had the number one dressing room.

Just close your eyes for a minute and imagine that you are an actor. You are not a star, you are me, and you find yourself playing at the Old Vic, not perhaps the oldest theatre in London but the most prestigious old theatre in London, the home of Lilian Baylis, and you have the *star* dressing room. I didn't let it go to my head too much, but the play was a success. It was a limited run, but we did do extremely well and I thoroughly enjoyed it, and Bill Pryde did a lovely production. The adaptor, David Pownall, had the audaciously brilliant idea of dropping two of the daughters, so there were only three daughters in our version, instead of Jane Austen's five, and I think this single cut in itself helped to tighten the play and make it more concentrated.

It was a beautiful thing to do and I was very lucky, and those evenings at the Old Vic – what a way to come near the end of your theatre career, because I was getting near. In the following year, 1987, I was phoned by my friend Michael Aldridge, who was with us doing *Last of the Summer Wine*, playing Seymour, the former headmaster, and Michael explained he was poorly.

I don't know what it was he had wrong with him, but he was due to play the doctor in the Greenwich Theatre's production of *Three Sisters*. The doctor's name is Chebutykin and it is a lovely part. When we did it at the Aldwych for Tennent with Sir Ralph, Chebutykin was played by Harcourt 'Billy' Williams, and I was now to play his part.

I should say that what happened was that Michael had phoned me to ask me if I would like to play the part if he got both Alan Strachan, who was running the theatre at the time, and the director of the play, Elijah Moshinsky, to agree. Both did. It was great to be in Chekhov again. I have said elsewhere that I wished I had played Uncle Vanya. There were two or three other parts in Chekhov that I would have loved. But I did play the doctor in *Three Sisters* at the Greenwich Theatre and we were a success. It was going to transfer to London and I was offered the opportunity of doing it, but I had already agreed to do *Last of the Summer Wine*, so I had reluctantly to turn it down. Nevertheless, I had played it at Greenwich and oh, did I enjoy it.

I think that I can tell you this, showing off a bit, but never mind, I got a first night postcard from Elijah Moshinsky, our director, saying, 'You showed us the way.' Well, you can't explain that on paper. I'm not even going to attempt it, but it was a most complimentary remark to make and I was happy enough with that.

Then in 1989 Moshinsky asked me to do two plays for the Duncan Weldon management at the Strand Theatre. They were *Ivanov*, a little-done play of Chekhov's, and *Much Ado About Nothing*. We ran them, or were supposed to run them, in tandem for a season, but in fact *Ivanov* didn't do terribly well. It is not a very good Chekhov, if there is such a thing as a not very good Chekhov, and it starred Alan Bates and Felicity Kendal, who were both perfectly fine. I had a good part in it and so did Frank Thornton.

It was the first time that Frank and I had worked together, and he was great to work with; in fact, it emerged in the course of doing *Ivanov* that really we were a kind of Russian Morecambe and Wise, a cross-talk act, that was how we thought of ourselves, and we enjoyed working together enormously. In *Much Ado About Nothing* Elijah had cast me as Dogberry and I said to him, 'Elijah, please let me play Verges. I've done it before. I did it at Chichester. I was *born* to play Verges. Please don't ask me to do Dogberry, because I haven't the faintest idea how to go about it. I knew what he should be, but I know what I am and the two aren't really similar.'

He said, 'We can't afford to pay your salary and have you just play Verges. No, you've jolly well got to play Dogberry. I want you to play it anyway, like that old lady in *Last of the Summer Wine*.'

I said, 'What old lady? Do you mean Thora Hird?'

'Yes.'

I said, 'You want me to base my performance of Dogberry on it being played as though it were played by Thora Hird?'

'Yes, yes, something like that.'

'Oh boy,' I said, 'no. If I'm going to do it at all, I'll do it my way.'

My way turned out to get the laughs, using the old-fashioned trick, if you can't get any laughs with the dialogue you bump into furniture. So I bumped into the furniture quite a lot, and finally I developed a technique of bumping into the scenery, and my final exit in the theatre, in the West End, was me bumping into the scenery as I played my final line, which always got a round, and so I managed to get a round on my last exit in the West End. Nothing to be proud of, I'm afraid, no, sir, but at least I enjoyed it and it wasn't a bit like Thora Hird.

Orson Welles said that in order to succeed in films the camera has to love you or, perhaps more specifically, to love your face. I think it could be said that my film career is best summed up by saying that the camera in my case was not even infatuated. I like to put it this way: I did about twenty films and I did about twenty days' filming in order to achieve that number of films.

I think it is best summed up by referring to the film *The Millionairess*, which starred Peter Sellers and Sophia Loren. It was shot in MGM's Borehamwood studios and I was invited to take part in it. I was going to play a scene, I don't know what character I was, I might have been a servant or something like that, and it was actually with Peter Sellers, so of course I was agreeably excited and pleased at the idea. A bit abashed, because of the similarity of our names and the fact that people often thought I was starring in his pictures when in fact, of course, I was not.

So I got into my car and I drove to Borehamwood, plenty of time to start filming, and I was told when I went to the reception that they hadn't got a dressing room for me. I said that I would be in my car in the parking lot, and I went and sat there. Fortunately, I had had the foresight to bring with me a book. It was *Act One* by Moss Hart. It is the story of Moss Hart and George Kaufman working together in the theatre and in films. To say that I couldn't put it down is absolutely true because there was no need for me to put it down. I just sat there reading *Act One* and I was absolutely enthralled by it.

Every now and then I looked at my watch, and after a few hours had gone by I thought probably it was time I had some lunch, so I went back to the reception and reported in, and said I was just going to have some lunch and I would be in my car.

'Right,' they said, and I went back to the parking lot and continued reading. Eventually I actually finished *Act One* and a few minutes later I was told that they were ready for me. So I made my way back. I went to my dressing room, which I'd got by now. I suppose the actor who had occupied it before had gone off, so they had a spare room. I got changed. I went on to the set and the director, Anthony 'Puffin' Asquith, and Peter Sellers were there.

By now I had got so absorbed by *Act One* and, I'm tempted to say, indifferent to the film that I was supposed to be taking part in that when I came to rehearse the scene with Peter Sellers – nothing to do with him, I don't mean any reflection on him – I know I didn't do it very well. We had just one run-through, then he took the director to one side, there was a little bit of a conversation, and the first assistant came over to me and said that they were sorry, but they wouldn't have time to do my scene that day and they'd be in touch.

So I went back to the car and I drove home and they were not in touch. I don't know what happened to *The Millionairess*, or the part that I was supposed to be playing but it never affected me. That was the last I heard of it, but years and years later I had the charming experience of meeting Kitty Carlisle-Hart, the widow of Moss Hart. Well, I will tell you this much, that I was in the audience, and she came on and made an appearance on the stage, and I thought, what a good-looking woman.

Now she must have been approaching ninety. The legs, the legs alone, and the rest of her. I have no doubt that she was sheltering under a lot of make-up, but wow! Did she look good. Later that evening I met up with her again and I took the opportunity of telling her this little story. She did think it was rather sweet, but particularly, of course, she was so thrilled to meet somebody who had read *Act One*. Thousands of people must have read it, but it was published a long time before this conversation took place between Kitty Carlisle and me. I think it brought back memories, so that was a lovely evening as far as I was concerned, to have actually spent five minutes in her company and to think that I had read her husband's book while I was waiting not to be in *The Millionairess*.

Radio is quite a different story. Goodness, I've been lucky in radio. I have done scores of broadcasts, by which I mean mainly, of course, plays. So many that I daren't try to categorise them or say anything about them, except to pick out one or two particular favourites. First of all, John Tydeman. He asked me to do a play with Brenda Bruce, written by Raymond Briggs, who is most famous, I would imagine, for *The Snowman*, but this was a radio broadcast called *When the Wind Blows*.

It was Raymond Briggs's satirical version of the effect of an atomic explosion on a middle-aged to elderly married couple. I cannot remember much about it, but it was beautifully acted by Brenda and, I suppose, it was acted all right by me. John Tydeman made a marvellous job of the production and Raymond Briggs had done a great script and we won the British Press Award for Best Programme (not just Best Drama Programme) of the year. I have worked again for John down the years, but that was the first one that we did together and in every way it was the high spot, I think.

Somebody else that I worked for and had got very fond of was Enid Williams. I first heard from her when she invited me to play Hercule Poirot in a Christmas edition called, believe it or not, *Hercule Poirot's Christmas*. I knew enough about the man, having read Agatha Christie's stories, to know that he was in fact a Belgian, and I had a gramophone record that gave lots of accents and dialects right across Europe, and also some local English accents, but not Belgian. The nearest that it contained was in fact French.

I thought, well, I've got to make a start somewhere, so I went to the library and just got *any* Hercule Poirot off the shelf and took it home and studied it, got out my little tape recorder and practised it. Now, admittedly, I knew that I was not doing a Belgian accent, but I thought, I've got to work up something that will convince me, if not Enid Williams, that this is OK for me to do. I worked on it quite hard, and I phoned her and said, 'Enid, may I come and audition for you?'

This sounds as though it took for ever, but in fact it was only two or three days before I made this call and she said, 'Well, yes, of course, if you want to, but I mean there's no question that I want you to play the part.'

'Well, thank you,' I said, 'but yes, I'd like your confirmation that I'm going to be all right.' So armed with this in my head, I took the book along and said, 'Look, I'm going to read to you from one of these Agatha Christie books, just so that you'll get a feel of what you think about my accent.'

I read it and at the end of it she said, 'Oh Peter, that's a marvellous Belgian accent!' So I let it go at that. I thought, don't push your luck, son! OK, we'll do it. Now we did it and it was great fun to do. This was the first time I had worked with her, but I didn't realise how enjoyable she could make the whole thing, as well as professionally sound, and I remember that we came near to overrunning in the studio.

It was quite a long play and she said, 'I've never overrun, so I'm going to ask you all to concentrate hard and we may have to speed it up a bit.'

We did finish in time, and said goodbye to each other, and I went home, and that Christmas I listened to it on the radio. It went out on Christmas Day and the phone went actually in the middle of it. I said, 'Yes, who is it?' and it was Michael Aldridge phoning from Greenwich. He and I were working on *Last of the Summer Wine* then. Michael said, 'I just had to tell you that I'm trying to stuff the goose and I simply can't, because I'm in tears. I don't know whether I'm going to be able to listen to this to the very end, because I'm almost rolling about on the floor.'

I said, 'Well, thank you very much indeed, Michael, how kind of you to even *bother* to listen to it, but I can assure you that Enid Williams thinks it's all right,' and I put the phone down. But I must admit I had to agree with Michael, not entirely, but a bit. I didn't think it was very good. I hadn't got that lovely facility that John Moffatt has. John took over from me because when Enid asked me to do another one I said, 'I'm sorry, Enid, you may be happy about me, but I'm afraid I'm not. I'm not convincing myself that I am a Belgian. It just sounds like me doing an accent.' Well, bless her, she was disappointed I know, but I did feel that I was right, and Johnny Moffatt is still doing Poirot.

The other broadcast that I would like to mention is because it brought Leslie Sands and me together again, side by side, actually acting together professionally. Leslie was doing a radio series about an Alan Bennett character called Lord Raingo, and I had a part in one of the episodes. All I can remember about it is the two of us standing shoulder to shoulder at the microphone, and both getting paid for it, but I do remember the experience with great affection.

Then there was *Death at Broadcasting House*. Val Gielgud, the brother of John, was Head of Radio Drama for many years and he had written this play before the war. Enid had got hold of the play and adapted it, and we were going to do it again. I was going to play the detective who finally solves the mystery, and I had another mate in it whom I worked with several times, Nicky Henson.

Nicky and I enjoyed each other's company and we loved working together. He was playing my sergeant but it didn't really matter what we played, we just enjoyed it, and there was a tendency, even in the most serious of situations, for us to get the giggles. You put us with Enid Williams and there was no question that we were going to get the giggles. Val Gielgud had done quite a good job on it and at the time when he wrote this there was no television, so it must have brought people inside Broadcasting House, when they were listening to it, in a very clever way.

Of course there came a point when Nicky Henson, Bill Nighy, his wife Diana Quick and I – there were quite a bunch of us – actually got the giggles. I don't know quite why, but it was a chase scene around the studio, 'Look out, he's going to shoot!' 'Bang!' one of those sorts of scenes, and it was too much for Henson and me. We had to sit down and have a quiet sob for a few minutes. I tell you, really, you must be gathering a terrible impression of me and it's absolutely true. But it made quite a good broadcast; I remember listening to that one too. Whether Michael Aldridge listened to it I'm not at all sure.

TEN

Last of the Summer Wine

In 1972 a script arrived from the BBC. There was a letter accompanying it written by a director-producer called James Gilbert. Jimmy and I had been at RADA at the same time, although we didn't really know each other there, but I knew his reputation as a director of television comedy for the BBC. I looked at the title page and the script read *Last of the Summer Wine* by Roy Clarke.

I knew Roy Clarke and had done a couple of his scripts. The first one, *Spyder's Web*, was part of a series, and the second was also part of a series, a mystery type of playlet called *The Millicent Sisters: Whatever Happened to Them?*. In this playlet I partnered Jeanette Jenkins. We played a brother and sister who ran a theatrical boarding house, and a married couple arrived, the wife being played by Sheila Hancock.

The first shot in this playlet established that I was a transvestite. When you first saw me, you saw this not unattractive woman in a rather smart suit walking up the path of the front garden. She let herself in, came into the house and took her hat off, and talked like I do. Obviously the viewers think it is a woman, but it isn't, it's a sort of man, me.

That was one of the little surprises that Roy had up his sleeve, but as the play went on it began to develop that Mapes was a complete transvestite, always changing from being one character to another. We were under-running at one point and Roy wrote a five-minute scene for me. The married couple were having breakfast and Mapes was serving them, and I came down for breakfast dressed as a priest. I made a few perfunctory blessing signs and launched into a sermon.

That sermon introduced me to Roy Clarke's slightly imaginative and rather quirky approach to religion. He used this more than once when we were doing *Last of the Summer Wine*. After we had completed filming *The Millicent Sisters* I had a long chat with Roy. He had done so many things in his life, although he didn't tell it all to me then; among other things he had been a policeman, I think in South Africa.

He had taken up a career as a writer and it seemed to me that he wasn't doing too badly. Now he had written this script. I read it and I thought, oh yes, oh yes, oh yes, this is all right. This is all right. The BBC's idea at that time was that they would launch maybe six different comedy programmes in one year as a try-out. They would do an episode of each *Comedy Playhouse* that they had in mind, and that was what they were going to do with us. We were coupled with five other *Comedy Playhouses* and, in a sense, we would be competing. At the end of the season the BBC would decide which ones were going to be made into a series.

Jimmy called the three of us together, Michael Bates, Bill Owen and me, and we went to the Television Centre to meet him and talk about the script and our general feelings about it. We were not actually going to read it, but just talk about it. It turned out that Bill thought it was gold dust. Michael Bates, who was playing Blamire, thought that it was a very good part for him, and I, of course, had already had some experience of the writer.

Before we had our meeting, I thought about what I was going to wear as Clegg, the character that I was going to play, and I took into account the fact that I knew Yorkshire, where we were going to film. I knew it a bit because I had been in the Sheffield Rep. I also knew that where we were going was close to the Pennines, and the Pennines are rather upsetting at times, they can pour with rain when everywhere else has bright sunshine. I thought, I'm going to protect myself against this, so I got out some clothing and chose a pair of trousers and a waistcoat from an old suit of mine that I'd had made for me in the 1950s when I was at Sheffield Rep.

It was the only article of clothing that I had ever had made for me, and I thought if I wear this dark pair of trousers and a dark waistcoat, but with a fawn sports jacket over it, it will give it an imbalance that might be rather quirky and rather nice for Clegg. I thought about the weather, and I thought, what I am also going to do is to wear a long-sleeved cardigan underneath the waistcoat, so that I am as protected as I can be against the vagaries of the weather. I turned up for the meeting wearing these clothes in order that I could show them off to Jimmy Gilbert and we settled down to talk about the script.

While we were talking I could see that Jimmy Gilbert was eyeing me a bit oddly, and so was Bill Owen. He was not quite sure about me, I thought. I already knew Michael Bates, because we had worked together on *Look After Lulu* and shared a dressing room. I knew his wife, Maggie Chisholm, as we had also worked together. I had never worked with Bill, but of course I knew his reputation in films, playing leading and very good supporting parts. I remembered him in *The Way to the Stars* playing an air force sergeant. I knew he was a good character actor and so, indeed, for that matter was Michael.

We were chatting away and after we had said pretty well all that was going to be said, a date was arranged when we were to go up to Yorkshire and start filming the first pages of the script. I got ready to go and, as I stood there with my hand on the doorknob, I said to Jimmy, 'Oh, by the way, Jimmy, these clothes I'm wearing, I thought they might be rather good for Clegg.' A look of what I realised later was relief went over his face and Bill cheered up too. Obviously they had thought that I was pretty near the dole queue and was only scraping clear as a result of having to do *Last of the Summer Wine*.

We said our goodbyes and we next met one day in June at the Television Centre. The three of us with the director Jimmy Gilbert, the designer Andy Diamond, the lighting cameraman, the sound man, the continuity girl, a group of about a dozen of us, and we were going up in a minibus. The minibus took off with us in it and made for the M1, and started to move north. Without wishing to sound overdramatic, none of us had the faintest idea that we would still be doing this programme, those of us, I hasten to add, who are still alive, thirty-four years later.

When you drive up the M1 you have to turn left to go to Holmfirth. I have always thought of it as a village, although I suspect it is actually a town – it has cobbled streets, but not really any quaint Georgian cottages; it has a worn, work-manlike look about it. Holmfirth was built in a valley. If you get above it and look down there it is, nestling in a valley of the hills. An attractive place, in fact, if you forgive the slightly grimy, used look that some of it has.

So we turned left off the M1 to go to Holmfirth, and it had been, up until then, a fairly bright and sunny day, but as we moved westwards, the clouds began to gather and it was not very long before it was pouring with rain, and it was still thundering down when we got to Holmfirth. We were booked in for lunch at a pub called the Elephant and Castle. We got there pretty well on time. But when we arrived we realised quite quickly, because the landlady told us, that she hadn't actually cooked our lunch yet, and she was going to give us pork. Well, you can't cook pork in a minute and a half, so it was about two hours after our arrival at the pub before we actually left to start filming.

We were going to shoot some scenes that afternoon, that was part of the plan. While we were waiting for the pork to be cooked I did something a bit naughty, which I don't usually do, but I felt that this was an occasion for a little bit of a celebration, so I had a couple of vodkas, and the others were also not shy about joining me in a glass or two. The scenes that we had to do that afternoon, when eventually we started them, were of us walking across a field, walking along a road and along a lane, most of them in medium or long shot and the dialogue was going to be dubbed in later. It would not actually be recorded live at the time, or maybe if it was, it would only be as a soundtrack.

I mention this just as a defence against the fact that I had had a couple of vodkas. I knew in advance that I was not going to have to do any real acting with dialogue. We got to one of the scenes walking across a field and Bill said, 'Who's going to tread in the cowpat?'

Michael said, 'Oh, well, I thought I'd do that.' I didn't say anything. I hadn't thought about a cowpat at all, but I mention it because it is quite an important little point. It is only a little point, but actors would understand – well, you will all understand – that Bill had made a suggestion, Michael had picked it up and that was what we were going to do. One of us was going to tread in a cowpat.

Now Bill might have taken offence – I mean, he had made the suggestion so why couldn't he do it? But he kept quiet and Michael did the business, and that attitude towards our work permeated all the time that we were together, until Michael tragically had to leave the programme and shortly afterwards died. We worked as a team, we kept each other going all the time in that first episode and, as it happily turned out, in subsequent episodes. We would exchange ideas, somebody would come up with a thought for the other person and that sort of thing.

The teamwork was helped enormously, of course, by the dialogue, which was just delightful. I won't put it any higher than that. It was unusual. It was quirky. At one point we went into a little chapel. Bill was bouncing about in his wellies and Michael said, 'You're on consecrated ground.'

And Bill said, 'Well, yeah, but I'm wearing my wellies!'

The whole flavour of the thing was quite different from anything else I had done, except possibly those previous two scripts of Roys. That afternoon we finished what filming we had to do and we were booked into a lodge, I suppose you would call it a rather large public house, on the edge of Marsden Moor called the Coach and Horses. We were going to spend our week up in Holmfirth, but actually stay in this pub on the edge of the moor.

We had not been there very long, we were just chatting, and Michael said, 'I'm going out for a walk. I'm going to explore the moor.' He left Jimmy and Bill and me and went off, and the landlord, who was keeping a friendly eye on us, said after a few minutes, 'Where's your friend?'

One of us said, 'Well, he's gone for a walk on the moor.'

'He's what?' and the man was out of the door before you could say night. He came back ten minutes later with Michael, and he said to all of us, 'I've just been speaking to this gentleman. It's getting dusk now, and the night is closing in, and if you go for a walk on those moors, as sure as anything you will get lost. You think the path is behind you and then you turn round and you can't see it, and all around you is moorland and it all looks the same. It's a bit like the desert, only with grass. I just suggest to you gentlemen that you don't go off walking across the moors, because people do get lost, and quite often.'

So we took all that to heart and sat down to have our meal. I should explain that Michael Bates was slightly to the right of Margaret Thatcher – except that, of course, she hadn't been invented then – and Bill was slightly to the left of Lenin. I hadn't yet realised this, but by the time we had got to the end of the soup course the two of them were at it, hammer and tongs. They were raising their voices and both of them were getting really quite angry. It was all politics. Now I've hardly ever had a political thought in my mind in my life. My father voted Conservative, so I have always voted Conservative, but I have never understood politics, not in the way that these two were rowing about it.

They were getting really hot and bothered, and Jimmy Gilbert stood up and said, 'You two, come with me.' He took them out of the dining room and they were away for quite a while. Eventually they came back and sat down, all three of them, and Bill and Michael were fairly subdued; in fact, they were very subdued. The talk was desultory and we finished our meal. I didn't ask any questions and I wasn't told anything, but it wasn't long after that that Jimmy explained.

He said, 'I took them outside and I said, look, you two, we've got a great script on our hands, there's every likelihood that this is going to be turned into a series, and if you two are going to take this attitude towards each other and you are going to behave like that, then I'm taking the whole lot back to London and I'm going to recast it.' Well, his remarks obviously went home. They never mentioned politics again in all the five years that Michael was with us. Jimmy had made his point.

I wondered, in those early days, just how Roy had got around to approaching the trio as he did. He had written a series for television called *The Misfits*, and it was seen by Duncan Wood, the BBC's Head of Comedy, in 1972. Duncan liked the slightly quirky nature of the dialogue, and he asked Roy to go and see him. The two of them talked and quite how it happened of course I don't know, but as a result of their conversation Roy was commissioned to write this pilot episode with the idea that it might be turned into a series, and he went away to think about it. Now I must admit that when one thinks about how you describe a series about three old men in a Yorkshire village passing the time of day, if you suggested that as an idea to anybody nowadays they would show you the lift, but Duncan was different, and Roy went away to think about it and he was looking for a clue.

He was looking for some way of actually making it a bit different from just three retired old chaps, and he came up with the idea that they all behaved like children. This has been the cornerstone of the way that the series has been written. Probably Clegg, out of all the different characters in the series, has been the only one who seems to have both feet on the ground and has a fairly normal, commonsensical attitude towards life, although even Clegg has been known to slide down a hill on a tin tray.

Let us go back to the filming of that first episode. The next day the political rumpus was not mentioned, everybody was in high spirits, it was not a bad day, the sun was trying to shine, and Michael and Bill had the first scene together. I sat on the kerb or perched on a wall to watch them. There were no artists' chairs in those days, you either sat on the kerbstone or you perched on a wall, and I was perching.

It was a joy to watch them doing their scene together, two experts at it. The dialogue was crisp and unusually funny in places, and Michael was supposed to be taking his landlady's dog for a walk, except it was quite a small dog and he spent most of his time carrying it. Bill was there and they had this half-teasing, half-antagonistic attitude towards each other, but

Bill as Compo persisted, and Michael as Blamire had difficulty in shaking him off. At the end of the scene, Bill ran after Michael saying, 'Lend us a fag, Cyril, and I'll give you a sniff of me socks!'

It was my turn next, and in my scene you saw me in close-up, riding a bicycle and carrying a little posy of flowers, and the camera pulled back to show that I was actually hanging on to the back of a hearse, which is engaged, of course, in a funeral and it drove up to this little chapel, a chapel that, I'm sorry to say, no longer exists. It was at the top of one of those hills that look down on the town, a charming little building with a small graveyard, and my purpose in going there was to lay a small posy of flowers on the gravestone of my wife. I was a widower. Then I went and sat on a bench at the front of the chapel overlooking the town. The vicar came and joined me and after a bit I offered him a cigarette, and he took one, saying, 'In my position I should be seen, I suppose, trying to live for ever.'

Then we were joined by Compo and Blamire, and the scene continued. We went into the chapel and we had the little bit about the wellies and the consecrated ground. Then we went to the library. This was obviously where, in Roy's imagination, we were going to go probably every day. In fact, at one point in the early discussions I suggested he call the series *The Library Mob*. Fortunately he took no notice of me. We were in the library having a read of the newspapers for nothing, and we were thrown out for some reason. So we went down to a little stream with a jam jar between us and collected this tadpole in the jam jar, put a bit of string round it, and went back to the library, where again we were thrown out because, of course, we'd got a tadpole in a jam jar, and that brought us to the end of the episode. It sounds a bit foreshortened, the way I have just explained it, but it took half an hour.

We left the library to go home. Blamire and Compo went

their way, and I went round to collect my bicycle. As I got on it the last line of that particular programme was me saying to myself, 'I think I'll go and get a bit of sausage for me tea.' I don't know why, but I've never forgotten that line and in an odd sort of way it seemed to me to sum up *Last of the Summer Wine*.

I would like to tell you the story of how Bill Owen saved my life. One or two of you may not know what happened and for that lucky couple here it is. We were doing the second series. Jimmy Gilbert had been promoted to Head of Comedy, so we had a new producer-director, Bernard Thompson, and one of the episodes centred around the River Wharfe in Wharfedale. We went there one glorious August Bank Holiday and we were going to do a canoeing scene. Michael, Bill and I were going to get into a canoe, and we were going to paddle it towards this arched bridge, go under the bridge and out the other side, and the camera was going to be on top of the bridge.

It was, as I say, an August Bank Holiday. The pub nearby was milling with people and when they saw a camera, saw it perched on top of a bridge, they thought, oh, a bit of filming going on, just the job for a Bank Holiday, so they gathered around. There were dozens of them. I'm tempted to say hundreds, but anyway there was certainly quite a big crowd. They had no idea who we were or what we were going to do, but there was a camera and they wanted to see what was going to happen.

We had decided that we would wear bathing costumes. Michael wore short trunks and Bill did the same, but I, cautious as ever, decided that I would wear a one-piece bathing costume, the sort with shoulder straps, but underneath it I was going to wear my thermals, in case I got a bit chilly. So you saw me in my bathing costume, and underneath it you saw these long johns and a long-sleeved vest and, to cap it all, I was wearing a cap, just in case my head got a bit draughty. We were going to paddle the canoe towards the bridge and under it. I looked at the water and saw that it was pretty choppy, and was moving quite swiftly, and sometimes you couldn't see the bottom of the river bed.

I approached the director, Bernard Thompson, and explained to him, 'Look, I can't swim, I've never been able to swim, and I just want you to know that if I fall in, I want the entire unit to come to my rescue. Never mind about those two, just concentrate on me, otherwise I shall drown.' I didn't really finish the sentence because he had walked away; however, I like Bernard Thompson, there's nothing really wrong with him.

We got into the canoe. Michael was taking charge and he said that he knew about these things, he was going to be in the back, or the stern as he called it, and he was going to be able to steer the canoe as we went along. I was going to be in the middle, and Bill was going to be up the front or, as Michael called it, the bow. We got in, the camera rolled, and off we went. We made quite good progress and were heading straight for the archway to, as they say in nautical terms, shoot the bridge. We *did* shoot the bridge, and we came out the other side, and then I felt the shakes. I don't know why, but all of a sudden the canoe started to shudder from front to back. I said, at the top of my voice, 'We're going over!'

And Michael said, 'No, no, no, it's all right, I've got it,' but of course he hadn't got it and the canoe, like an accommodating harlot, turned on its side and we shot into the water.

I went down, bubble, bubble, bubble. I kicked out and struck out with everything I've got. I was absolutely terrified, and after a bit of thrashing about, fortunately my left foot hit something hard. I got a purchase and gave a good push, and I came out of the water like a cork out of a bottle, and I could feel gravel beneath me. I was partly on land and I scrambled up, crawled up, staggered up the bank of the river on to dry land. The audience, not knowing whether we were supposed to do that or not, nevertheless realised that I had had a bit of a job getting out of the water, and one or two of them actually applauded.

I took no notice of them. I didn't look back to see how Bill and Michael were, I just looked straight ahead, I got through the crowd and I got into a field, and I was just standing there, thinking, thank God, thank God, I'm safe, I'm safe, when I felt a tug on my sleeve. I turned round, and there was a man beside me and he said, 'I hope you don't mind me mentioning it, but weren't you Samuel Pepys?'

Oh, I nearly forgot, how did Bill Owen save my life? Well, when I fell into the water and I was thrashing about, and my left foot hit something hard and I got the purchase and I shot out of the water, what my left foot was resting on was Bill Owen's head!

When Bill died, and Compo died, we lost, in my opinion, the best comedy performance that has ever been seen on television. Bill Owen and Compo had absolutely nothing in common, except that they both weighed the same and they were the same height. He created, with Roy's help, this character who should have been given some sort of an award, a BAFTA or something, for this extraordinary performance. I have been watching television since 1938, and I have never seen a more complete and utter transformation of someone's character as Bill created. Wilfred Brambell was marvellous in *Steptoe and Son*, but while he was doing it you could still see Wilfred through the gauze.

For a start, Bill was a cockney, he had never been anywhere near Yorkshire in his life. The second thing was that he was very smart, Bill dressed very well. He liked to put on a bit of a show, he never let his trousers drop or anything like that, and his whole creation of Compo was something that was alive. I envied his way with children; I have never been very good with children, but they used to flock around Bill when we were filming. He used to go through the contents of his pockets, which in a Stanislavskyan way were always stuffed with bits of childlike things, like an old pencil stub or a bit of string or a conker, things like that, and he would show them to the children and hand them round.

Bill was lovely, he really was, and when Compo died, Truly (Frank Thornton) said to Clegg. 'Do you think he was heavenly material?'

And Clegg said, 'Oh yes. Oh yes, to be of little children, that was him, never lost it, did he?'

When Bill died, I think we all thought that would be the end of the series, but Roy was on his mettle. Not that he was ever off it, but he wrote three episodes which he called *Elegy for Fallen Wellies*, and when we heard that he was going to be writing them I took the liberty of phoning him and asking, 'How are you getting on, Roy?'

He said, 'Well, I'm all right. Of course the trouble is, it's a comedy programme, it's supposed to be funny.'

Well, it was funny, some of the scenes in those three *Elegy* episodes were some of the funniest he had ever written. Frank Thornton got some marvellous one-liners, which of course he delivered with his usual aplomb, and altogether the pathos was mingled with great fun and larks. An extraordinary bit of writing. The best writing, in my opinion, that Roy has ever done, and Alan Bell, the director, and he conceived the idea that Bill should go for a last tour around the countryside. We had just had the funeral service and he was in his coffin in the hearse, and I said, 'We thought you'd like a last look round, old chap.'

You saw the cortège move off, Ronnie Hazelhurst's lovely waltz that introduces every programme was playing, and a choir sang these words to the music, written by Roy, and it went like this:

> Now all of your summer's gone
> Those urgent days when he was young
> Those girls he loved
> That soon moved on
> To drink his summer wine.
> Now perfumes of earth and vine of meadows
> When the rain has gone
> These friends with their black armbands on
> Salute his summer wine.
> The memories he'd left to me
> Here in my cup of sweet short days
> Bitter days
> Now all drunk up.
> The fullness of the life that slipped
> The other day all mortal pain
> Free now to roam fresh hills and lanes
> And taste eternal wine.

This is not intended to be an obituary column, but I think it is as good a place for me now to pay my respects and tributes to those who have been in the programme. Michael Bates was the first of us to go, a very clever and amusing comedy actor, but also in films making a great mark for himself as Montgomery in *Patton* with George C. Scott. Then we lost Blake Butler who played the original librarian, the social climber, climbing up, I may say, the adorable body of Rosemary Martin, who played the other librarian and who has also died.

John Comer – I had such admiration for John Comer, I used

to watch him in those café scenes leaning over the counter, doing his little crossword puzzle, and without even turning his body, giving dear Jane Freeman back for the remarks that she was making to him. He was a master of doing very, very little.

Joe Gladwin. It is not, I think, generally known that Joe was a Papal Knight of the Roman Catholic Church, an honour he shared with Matt Busby of Manchester United. They were both Papal Knights, and I remember when Joe told me, and the pride on his face when he told me. He was very, very proud of that, and why not?

Brian Wilde, thank goodness, is still with us at the time of writing, but Foggy Dewhurst I suppose really dominated the screen while we were doing it with him, and he had some marvellous things written for him by Roy. I remember the wonderful one when he envisages the fact that he is going to be in charge of the Queen's corgis, a brilliant bit of writing, and a lovely bit of playing by Brian. As I say, fortunately he is still around, but not with us on the screen, and his place was taken by Frank Thornton who is, thank God, still with us as I write.

In between we had Michael Aldridge as Seymour, the former headmaster, inventor extraordinary and headmaster not so extraordinary, would be my guess. A lovely performance. Michael had to retire from the programme because his wife was taken seriously ill and Michael is dead now.

Dame Thora Hird and Gordon Wharmby, Mr and Mrs Wally Pegden, those newspapers on the floor, a great trick of Roy's. A lovely bit of business for Thora and for Gordon. Gordon's job was mainly to provide transport for the three of us, an old beaten-up Land Rover, which he used to drive around the countryside and pick up the trio to bring us back to town. Of course, there was more to his part than that, but that was really his essential role. Sadly, both he and Thora died within a short time of each other, and Roy Clarke had to find another provider of transport.

Who but Roy would have thought of casting Burt Kwouk? (I'm tempted to say Burt Quirk!) Burt made his name with Peter Sellers in the *Pink Panther* films, where he used to appear out of the fridge and wrestle with his master on his return home. Invariably, because Peter Sellers was playing the lead, Burt would come off worse. When Gordon Wharmby died Roy brought in Burt as a Yorkshire Chinaman, who has been with us for four years now. His name was Entwhistle, he was about as Chinese as you get, and he was also about as Yorkshire as you get.

But I would like to finish like this. The cast list over the years has grown and grown, in every sense of the word. We started off with, I suppose, about six of us, playing what you might call principal parts, and now it is over sixteen. And who knows where Roy will take us next? But I cannot describe to you the pleasure that it gives *me*, certainly – I mustn't speak for the others – just to go back there, and climb up those hills, or be driven up those hills, more particularly, to look across that landscape; it is magical. You can stand there filming and you have a break from your scene, and I find myself standing or squatting, sitting and just looking at it and thinking, you lucky sod to be here doing this with a great writer behind you, a fine director, and let's call it a ripping cast, very, very lucky indeed.

Early in the 1980s Roy had written a script for the theatre, a play, and he offered it to the three of us. Brian didn't want to do it, but Bill and I did, and we were lucky to get the services of Jan Butlin, a lady who had written scripts for television. I knew her work there, but she had also worked in the theatre, and she took on the direction. We opened at the Bob Hope Theatre in Hanwell in Middlesex, and on the first night there was a scene between me and Bill and another man, when we were sitting at a table downstage right. As we did this scene we were putting our elbows on the table, and generally not just sitting quietly still, and the table began to rock. It actually gave way, and Bill and I picked it up and threw it off into the wings, and got on with the scene.

This attracted a round of applause from the audience, and a certain element of that continued through both the years I was in it with Bill. He did a third year. We moved on from that original theatre, we went to the Devonshire Park Theatre in Eastbourne and did a season there, and the following year, 1984, to Bournemouth and a season on the Pier. The dressing rooms, I must say, at the Bournemouth Theatre were the hottest dressing rooms I have ever been in. I think that was largely due to the fact that we had a heatwave that summer.

The idea of something going wrong haunted us, really. I remember in one scene, on the stage there was a huge put-u-up sofa, and when you unwound it and straightened it up, you could actually get a human being into the sofa, and close it and put the lid back on. On one occasion I just couldn't get the thing open, and there was nothing else for it but to ask the stage management to come on and help me with it, and that, too, attracted a great deal of attention.

It may not have been the greatest play ever written, but we certainly got a lot of fun out of it. In one magical moment at the Devonshire Park Theatre, quite early on in the run, we were standing in a line to take our curtain call when a butterfly, not a cabbage white but a real butterfly, like a red admiral or whatever those things are called, fluttered down from the flies and settled on Bill's head. He was wearing his Compo cap at the time, so actually it settled on his cap, and we all thought that was pretty marvellous, and the audience gave that an extra round of applause. But even more remarkable, on the last night at the Devonshire Park Theatre some three or four weeks later, a butterfly, and I'll swear it was the same butterfly, came down and landed at the curtain call on Bill Owen's head, and that, I thought, was theatrical history. It had come to say goodbye to us. But how did the butterfly *know* that this was our last night?

ELEVEN

Where are the Tunes?

Constant Lambert was a wise man who said, in effect, that music is occupying too much of our lives. You get it in the lifts, you get it out in the streets, you get music wherever you go, and he is certainly right. He has become more and more right as time has gone by. The radio, for instance, is the biggest distributor of musical sounds, I suppose, in the whole world. But I have never really minded it, only because I have been living with music all my life. It has been in the wings all the time. I am a hummer, for instance. Everywhere I go, whether it is at home or out in the street, or even when I am working, if I am not interfering with the sound man, I am humming or singing. I used to be able to whistle, but I can't whistle any more. My taste in music is a mixture of what you might call Beethoven and Rodgers and Hart, and I am delighted for myself that I have this taste and ability to reproduce a little bit of the sound that I would like to be hearing.

My mother, as I mentioned at the beginning, introduced me to music; we would go to musical shows and listen to the wireless. And then, as I got older and went to work I could afford to buy gramophone records and learn from them. But although my mother enjoyed classical music, as did my father, I was virtually self-taught. Not, of course, to play an instrument. I have never been able to play any musical instrument, but self-taught in the sense that when I was earning enough at the bank to buy gramophone records I was lucky enough to read a book by a Frenchman, Romain Rolland, entitled *Beethoven the Romantic*, and I devoured it.

The interesting part to me, looking back on it now, is that what I learnt from him was more to do with chamber music than with the symphonies or concertos. EMG, Hand Made Gramophones, was a shop in Soho Square where you could ask them what they thought was the best recording of, say, Beethoven's *Pastoral Symphony* and they might say, 'The Vienna Philharmonic, sir, conducted by Bruno Walter,' so that was what I bought as one of my first records, and I think they were right.

The other advantage in those days, and maybe it is still worth it today, although you don't get multiple disc collections in the same way that you did then, was that a symphony, for instance, would cover five twelve-inch records more often than not. They would allow you to buy them a record at a time. So taking my guide from Romain Rolland, and reading what he had to say about the late quartets of Beethoven – just reading it off the page brought it to life for me – I went to EMG and bought what he considered to be the deepest part of the work, the Cavatina. I think it is the fifth movement. Maybe he did mention the Grosse Fugue, which is how Beethoven first ended that quartet, and his publisher said, 'No, chum, no, this is not going to sell any copies, you've got to come up with something a bit more easy for the public to understand.' We are talking about Opus 130, to finish the quartet, which I have only once heard played live, and that was at the Wigmore Hall a few years ago when they played the Grosse Fugue as the proper ending, which is what it should be.

Enough of that highbrow stuff. What I am trying to get at is the fact that I found the quartet, gradually I built up all five or six records, or however many there were in the set, I loved it, and even now I can listen to it with the greatest pleasure. Of course I know that the whole point about that kind of writing by Beethoven, and others of his ilk, was that the more you hear them the more they endear themselves to you. So I became a collector of gramophone records in a very modest way, but it has continued ever since. Now there are CDs, and I love my collection and in that sense you can say that I am musical.

I was so lucky to have been born exactly when I was, in 1921, because as my ear became attuned to the music I was growing up with it, and what was it providing me with? It was providing me with that great sound of what we call 'popular music' composers. I am not going to give you a long list, but even though they are obvious, I want you to hear them: Irving Berlin, Jerome Kern, Richard Rodgers, Harold Arlen, Harry Warren, Jimmy Van Heusen.

These men were writing great melodies. Great tunes, if you think melody is too high-toned a word for what they wrote. And with them, hand in hand, were their partners. Of course in the case of Irving Berlin and Cole Porter, the most obvious examples, they wrote their own lyrics. But Rodgers and Hart, Rodgers and Hammerstein, Harold Arlen with Johnny Mercer, formed teams. They swapped around, of course. Hoagy Carmichael, probably the most gifted of them all or the one who was always a little bit ahead of the field, had one great collaborator who really launched their careers together when he wrote the words for 'Stardust' – Mitchell Parish. He went on to write another lovely song with Hoagy Carmichael, 'One Morning in May', which has always been my favourite. They were writing glorious tunes, and they were writing wonderful words and you could hear them. Now what I mean is what I'm going to come to shortly, so please hang on to it.

When you hear Sinatra, Crosby or Ella Fitzgerald, any of

those great singers, when you are listening to their songs you are hearing every word that is sung, because the notes that the composers have given the lyric writer are within the range of the human ear actually to understand. A lot of the trouble with what I would call 'classical' music, 'vocal' music, is that the words are not written to be understood very clearly.

Now I am going to take you to the opera house. I saw the original production of *Peter Grimes* at Sadler's Wells and I thought Britten's opera was marvellous. In fact, I came away thinking I don't believe he will ever write anything better than that; a lot of people would think he has, but for me he hasn't. I just think the whole idea is marvellous: a great dramatic story of this fisherman and the two boys. But when I went to hear it the other day I couldn't follow it. They didn't have subtitles, because of course it is in English, so you are supposed to be able to understand it, but I couldn't. Indeed, the only bit that I could hear clearly was something that I remembered from the first production. I got the general sense of the plot, mainly because I had seen it before and I had loved the libretto when I had first seen it. But if I had been relying entirely upon the sound the singers were making I would not have understood it at all.

Something has been happening over hundreds of years to the human voice, which was meant, when nature provided it, simply to meet the need to be able to convey information, like 'shut that door' or 'stand up when I speak to you'. It can cope with that in any language without any difficulty at all, but then you discover that that same voice can rise – I am not musical, so I won't go raving mad – but it can rise by octaves, or lower itself by octaves, and still make a sound that is in pitch and in key, and all those other things that the voice can do. People have been using it, but it does not mean that the notes that they are putting down on paper, and that are being sung by the singers, can be understood by the audience. It is a physical musical impossibility.

I know a man who has been a chorister for many years and has sung with a number of big choirs. Choristers have a terrible job. They think that you can understand them because the notes are there, and the words are there in front of them. As he said to me the other day, 'Our coach is very happy with what we are doing, and I'll tell you why exactly, it's because he's got the words in front of him, or if he hasn't got them in front of him, they're in his head. He knows that the noises they are making fit those words like mauve, yellow, brown, whatever. What he doesn't take into account is the fact that the audience, if they don't know the words, can't necessarily follow them.'

Let us go back to Britten. Last Christmas I listened to a ceremony of carols, sung by one of the Cambridge choirs. There is nothing wrong with that choir at all, they sang most beautifully. The noise that they were making was glorious, but I could not understand one word of any carol that they were actually singing. I admit that one or two of the carols I didn't know, I had not heard before, or could not remember, but that is my point. You should be able to, but you see the conductor knows the words, he has got them in front of him. The choristers know the words, they have got them in front of them, and the coach knows the words, everybody knows the words except the audience. It could be 'Good King Wenceslas Looked Out', but if it is something that they have not heard before they don't stand a chance.

The spoken word doesn't escape either. I have been to theatres and watched people doing plays, and very frequently I cannot understand what they are saying. The actors can understand what they are saying. The director, if he happens to be out front, has got the book in front of him, he knows what they are saying, but the audience have not got the book and they don't know, and that is just speech.

But it can be done, and in order to show how it can be done you need to go back to the twenties, thirties, forties, fifties. You need to go back to Cole Porter and people like him because, you see, what was happening in those years was not that they were writing the songs, but *who* they were writing them for. Hanging over the whole lot in a little place – it was little when it started – in America in Los Angeles: Hollywood.

Hollywood was big business, and it helped to increase the sales of records and sheet music, and the radio was climbing just as fast as Hollywood. Hollywood in turn was echoed by Broadway and London was not very far behind, with shows like Noël Coward's *Bitter Sweet*, a group of excellent writers, really great writers, not just the Americans. These people were writing to have their songs and their tunes understood. If people can't understand them, they won't buy them, they won't sing them. Imagine Gene Kelly doing 'Singing in the Rain' if you couldn't understand a word he was singing. The answer is, of course, that Hollywood would have scrapped it and made somebody else's.

I have been very lucky. I have lived through that golden age when the songwriters were producing the songs, and the singers could sing them, and fifty per cent, at least, of their effort was put in to make sure that you could hear those words.

Here is a little thought that has just struck me, and that is that when Beethoven wrote the 'Ode to Joy', the words were, of course, written by somebody else, but when he wrote the notes for the 'Ode to Joy' in the choral symphony at the end he was stone deaf, and I wonder if that is why he chose to have just short notes. I hum that tune in my head and there are not many what I would call extended notes. They are all short notes. I wonder if some instinct told him to keep them short:

keep them short and the audience will understand them. I wonder.

Here is another helpful suggestion, which I don't think will be taken up by anybody. Let's say it's a choir, and you have somebody sitting out front who doesn't know the work at all and who cannot actually read music. In other words, me. I am sitting there and the choir is singing whatever it happens to be, the conductor can understand what they are singing, the choristers can understand, the coach can understand, and then I put up my hand, and say, 'I'm sorry but I can't understand a word of it.'

I think their instinctive reaction would be, 'Can you find your own way out, Mr Sallis?' It is just possible that they might say, 'Stick around, Peter, for a bit, and let's see if we can improve things. Let us know when you can understand the words.' It would be quite an interesting experiment to see whether it can be made to happen. I really don't know. I think the answer is no. It is just in the nature of the beast.

It is a characteristic of singing that the higher, the lower, the longer the notes are, the more difficult they are to understand. If you finish something, say, that ends in the word 'moon' and it is right up there, an octave above whatever, 'moon' is an almost impossible word to make clear. It is bound to come out as 'moo'. You cannot get the consonant, the 'n', at the end of it. Not unless you put another note on and sing moo-n, which of course you wouldn't.

I am going to have one more grumble, and that is at people who are writing music in what I would call the classical idiom, in other words 'serious music'. I wonder just how much of this is going to last these days, because from what I hear of it it does not seem to me to have any melody in it at all. Melody seems to have gone out the window. You get lots of scraping sounds and noises, but where are the tunes? Beethoven wrote great tunes. Nowadays they don't seem to be able to do it and I am sorry to pick on him, but it is only because I happen to have watched a television programme about Sir Michael Tippett after he had died.

The BBC replayed an interview that he had once given, and he was sitting in his drawing room and talking to the interviewer, just chatting away about his music, *all* music, and there was a man sitting at the piano in the corner who was playing Gershwin's 'Summertime'. Sir Michael stopped in the middle of what he was saying and said, with such astonishing frankness that I just loved him for it, 'You hear that. I've never been able to do that. I've never been able to write a melody.' I think he was probably right.

I remember going to hear his *A Child of our Time*. I went to the first performance. It didn't strike me then that you don't have to fill your ears with tunes, but my goodness I think it does help. I have been to a few of these modern musicals, and very rarely have I stopped short and thought, now *there's* a good tune. People don't seem to be able to write them any more. The other day I was in a popular London store, and they were playing tracks over our heads of something or other, which sounded to me like a duet for whips and carpet beaters. It didn't have a note of recognisable music in it. It was just um-ching, um-ching, um-ching, noise. I thought, I can't imagine any barrow boy whistling that, but they all play it so somebody must like it. No, I don't think much of that; as far as I'm concerned I was born at the right time and I shall go out at the right time. So I think I should stop grousing and consider myself very lucky. Very lucky indeed. Constant Lambert, here I come.

TWELVE

Wallace and Gromit

In 1983 my agent phoned me to say that there was a young man at Beaconsfield Film School who would like me to record a voice for him on an animated cartoon film that he was making, and would I like to talk to him. I said, 'Yes, fine, give me his number,' and I phoned.

His name was Nick Park and he said, 'Hello.'

And I said, 'Hello.'

Look, I've got this script. It's a cartoon film that I'm making. It's just one character who actually speaks in the cartoon. Would you come and do it for me at Beaconsfield Film School?'

'Well, yes, but supposing you don't like me?'

'No, no, there'll be no difficulty there, I'm sure.'

'Well, let's play it safe. Have you got a script?'

'Yes, I've got a script of what this character says.'

'Send it to me and I'll do my best. I'll record what I think is an appropriate voice and see how we go from there.'

'Oh, all right then,' he said. The script arrived. The film was called *A Grand Day Out*, and I read it, and it was about a man and his dog. The man was called Wallace and the dog was called Gromit. I didn't realise straight away, but in fact what I had been told was true. I was the only voice, the dog didn't speak, and there was another character who was known as the 'moon man'.

I recorded perhaps not the whole script, but chunks of it, and sent it back to him. He listened to it and said, 'Yes, please.' So I went out to Beaconsfield. I liked Nick immediately. He was young. I learnt later that he was twenty-three, he came from Preston and he had a lot of charm. You felt that he couldn't do harm to anybody and that he was just a very nice chap. His father was good to him, and good for him because they had a garage, which he allowed his son to use as a workshop. I got to Beaconsfield and he explained straight away 'I'm sorry, but I haven't got the models. Well, I've got them, but I'm not ready to show them to you yet because I'm not happy with them. They need more work.' These were the models for the man and his dog, Wallace and Gromit.

We sat down beside each other in the studio at Beaconsfield. The microphone was pointing towards me and we started to record. I was doing what I had said I would do in my tape to him, and what interested me was that he never once commented on the actual noise that I was making. He said, could I be more this, more that, or the other. Where he did tell me what to do was more in the way in which the words were said. 'From a purely acting point of view, Peter, could you take that line a bit faster?' or could I do this with the line, or that with the line. But he never once said, 'Peter, this voice is not right.' It seemed as though I had got it, in a sense, in one. We came to the end of our session together, and we shook hands and I went home and that was in 1983.

Then, in 1989, the telephone rang and a voice said, 'Hello, it's me, it's Nick Park. Remember me?'

'Yes, of course I remember you.'

He said, 'Well, I've finished it!' and I thought, six years, wow! But I said, 'Oh, that's great.'

He said, 'But I'd like you to come to a studio,' and then he named a real studio, not the school studio, but one in Soho.

He said, 'I'd like you to do some more what we call oohs and ahs.'

'Yes, I know what you mean,' I said. So we met up in Soho and there was me as Wallace, going 'ooh, ah, oh', or whatever it might be. Not just words of the script, but noises of the script, and now I could see it joined up. I could see the figures, and I must admit straight away that I was struck by both of them.

I wasn't so struck by the moon man. I thought he looked too much like a petrol pump, but in fact I have even grown to love him over the years, as I have watched the programme from time to time. There is something fascinating about him, especially when he ends up skiing over the moon slopes, using the twisted and buckled bits of the moon machine that Wallace and Gromit have constructed between them – the spaceship that they used to get to the moon and to get back – the moon man used bits that had fallen off in order to ski over the moon's slopes.

It has all been great fun, and I am just surprised that it took six years, but Nick explained: 'Well,' he said, 'you see, I have gone to these people called Aardman, they specialise in Plasticine,' and he told me that both these characters and the moon man were all made of Plasticine. That was the material with which he worked and in which Aardman worked. So he had joined their studio in Bristol to work together, they had helped him to finish off *A Grand Day Out* and also with their help he made this film called *Creature Comforts*.

When we were doing the second Wallace and Gromit, *The Wrong Trousers*, I said, 'You know, Nick, *Creature Comforts* was your *Citizen Kane*.' In fact, what happened was that he had completed *A Grand Day Out*, the Wallace and Gromit film, and he had also completed *Creature Comforts*, and both were in the Oscars for the Best Animated Cartoon Film. *Creature Comforts* had won it. I don't know where *A Grand Day Out* came in the voting, but it had been nominated and it competed with *Creature Comforts*. So there he was. He had got off to what might be called a flying start by having two cartoon films nominated in the same year and winning the Oscar.

In 1990, almost immediately after the Oscar ceremony, we started work on the second film, which was called *The Wrong Trousers*, and again it was I who had to provide the voice first. People have asked me over the years, do I do the voice first or do they do the animation first and then I post-sync to the animation? But it is my voice that they need first, and I will tell you a little story about that in just a second.

The Wrong Trousers attracted me more than *A Grand Day Out* almost immediately, because not only were Wallace and Gromit still there, and they were my favourites, but there was also this penguin – a villainous penguin. The penguin doesn't speak either, but he is the villain, so he has to have a disguise, which he achieves by getting a red rubber glove and sticking it on the top of his head. This transforms him immediately into a cockerel, so he can go about disguised as a chicken. What a villainous penguin.

It is a jewel robbery film, based very loosely on *Topkapi*, and it has always been my favourite because it was the one that was the greatest fun to do. It certainly was fun when I went back once more to Soho, having recorded it all in a day or two initially, to do all the oohs and ahs again. This time there were even more oohs and ahs than there were in *A Grand Day Out*.

I was watching this particular section of the film, which Nick had already planned and shot. It was the end of the film where you saw the penguin running away from Wallace and Gromit in their own house. They were chasing it in this toy train that they have, and Gromit was lying across the front of the train, laying the track before him as the train goes along, so that it was clip-clip, clip-clip. He was putting the tracks down as the train approached the penguin, and I stopped Nick in the middle of all this and said, 'Nick.'

'Yes, Peter.'

'Nick, I'm sorry to have to say so, but you know, this isn't going to work. This is absurd, that they can lay the track in front of the train like this and finally catch up with the penguin.'

And Nick's voice came back, 'Trust me, Peter.'

'Oh sure, oh yes, of course, Nick, of course.'

At the preview in Leicester Square the cinema had an invited audience, mainly of all the people who had worked on the film, because now, of course, it was attracting more actual workers to do the animation than he ever had with *A Grand Day Out*. I was sitting in the same row as Nick. There were two or three people sitting between us, and I was chatting away before the curtain went up, when a guy turned round and looked at me and said, 'Peter Sallis?'

'Yes, hello, hello.'

He said, 'If I hear that voice of yours once more, I'll break your bloody neck!'

It turned out to be one of the animators; in fact, he was the principal animator for Wallace. What had happened was that this man had spent hours, for days on end, in a studio putting me through my motions as they followed me with a camera. They had taken goodness knows how many shots just to cover twenty seconds of film, and I think we have all got the message now, even me, that this was where the real work was, in doing the actual animation. So for this chap to hear me saying 'What, no cheese, Gromit?' or whatever it might be, over and over again, while he adjusted my face and arms and legs, well, I could see his point. Fortunately for me he didn't break my bloody neck and I suppose, to some extent, fortunately for him.

This film, *The Wrong Trousers*, was then shown in the 1993

Oscars and it won. But going back to this preview at the Odeon Leicester Square, when it got to the bit where Wallace and Gromit were chasing the penguin through the house, and Gromit was lying at the front of the train laying down the track as the train raced along towards the penguin, as he lies down and puts the track in place, clip-clip, clip-clip, clip-clip, the audience erupted. They screamed and they clapped and they cheered, and Nick leant forward from his seat and turned to me, and I leant forward in my seat and turned to him, and we waved to each other. 'Trust me, Peter.' Boy, have I done so ever since!

Now with two Oscars under their belts, Aardman and Nick Park were going into what you might call overdrive. The next Wallace and Gromit was planned, and I went along to do the voice. I don't think I am in overdrive, but at least I am Wallace. This time the film was called *A Close Shave* and it introduced a love interest. Yes. Wendolene, who comes close to being what you might call the heroine. In fact, I suppose she is the heroine, and the villain is her dog, whose name is Preston. Nick Park comes from Preston, so what are we to deduce from that?

He is certainly a villainous dog and there is a nearly helpless victim, and this time it is in the form of Shaun the Sheep. By now I am getting the picture. I am realising that Nick, and his friends around him, are being really inventive, they are coming up with astonishing characters. In her own way, Wendolene is a fairly astonishing character, in the sense that she and Wallace actually touch hands over a skein of wool when he upsets some things in her shop where she sells wool. There is a tingle of excitement as their hands touch. Where is this going to lead them? Well, where it's going to lead them is that Wendolene is captured by the nasty Preston, by the villain; it takes a lot of ingenuity and bravery on everybody's part to rescue her and at the end of the film she comes to visit Wallace.

He comes to the door and there they are, looking at each other, their eyes are locked. Do you lock eyes? I don't know. He says, 'Won't you come in?'

And she says, 'Thank you' and is making a move.

And he says, 'We've got Wensleydale today.'

'Oh, oh, I'm sorry, but I'm afraid I don't like cheese.' Wow! Wallace is crestfallen and he has to say goodbye to her. She says goodbye to him and she goes out of his life. Oh dear, oh dear. Wendolene was played by a lovely actress, Ann Reid. I never saw her film, *Mother*, a year or so ago, in which she made such a big success, but that was a feature film and she had the most marvellous notices. Clearly a lovely actress. Dear Ann Reid.

Nick Park, in the meantime, had had *A Close Shave* nominated for an Oscar and in the 1996 Oscars it won him his third. When I say him, of course, I mean him and Aardman. One mustn't forget all the real hard work that was being done in the background by Aardman, while Nick was supplying the ingenious twists and turns in the plot. But between 1990 and 1996 this young man had won three Oscars. Where was he going to go next?

Well, where he went next was to Hollywood. Or perhaps I should say Hollywood came to him, as Dreamworks, a branch of the Spielberg organisation, approached him. I had nothing to do with the making of *Chicken Run*, as Wallace and Gromit were not involved. Mel Gibson played the voice of the hero in this case. I saw the film and I thought it was jolly good. Again it showed their ingenuity. Aardman and Nick were able to change tack completely and present the world with another animated film, only this time it was full length, about an hour and a half. It was fine.

I loved the sequence near the end, when they escaped from the chicken run by driving this multi-bladed airship-cum-galleon-cum-warship over the fence where all the chickens were penned in. This film, as it happens, didn't win an Oscar. But it goes to show that we are only human. So Aardman and Dreamworks had what you might call metaphorically a good night's rest, and what were they going to do next? Well, much scheming and plotting and thinking went on, and I think it was in about two years, or something like that, I think it must have been in 2001, when they decided on the path they were going to take.

The title had been chosen, probably before the story was really properly mapped out. It was to be called *Wallace and Gromit: The Curse of the Were-Rabbit*. I had lunch with Nick and Steve Box, and they were talking about the story so far. They gave me a script, which I took home and read. I have still got it, but I wouldn't like to *have* to tell you what resemblance it bears to the final product. Sufficient to say that the biggest problem, I think, was the ending, roughly the last half-hour of an hour-and-twenty-minute film.

Jeffrey Katzenberg came over from Dreamworks. He had been a constant help to them during the making of *Chicken Run*, and now he was at it again over *The Were-Rabbit*. His advice was invaluable, giving the American point of view and helping where he could with the storyline. I don't know how many times Jeffrey must have crossed America and the Atlantic, but I would say it averaged out at something like once or twice every month. He was on the go all the time, helping and advising. Eventually it was finished and it too was nominated for an Oscar. That is almost another little chapter on its own, because Wallace put in an appearance at the Oscars, and I would like to tell you a little bit about it.

On a year-to-year basis I love the Oscars. I used to watch them on television, and sometimes I would sit up and watch them live. I loved it when those young ladies suddenly won an

Oscar for a supporting part, and they would come on in tears and say how they loved everybody, and their mummy and daddy, and so on. It all seemed corny, but I loved it. Then there were the big men, the Clint Eastwoods, the Gene Hackmans, popping up every now and then and winning an Oscar. I found the whole atmosphere, the whole Hollywood pizzazz, just won me over completely, so the thought that if the film was nominated I might possibly go to Hollywood, well, it hardly bore thinking about.

But the film was nominated. The opposition, in a strange sort of way, was not all that strong, not in numbers. I think there were only two other nominations for Best Animated Film, and Nick Park and Stephen Box represented Aardman and Dreamworks. So they would go to the Oscars and be present in case it won, and they would accept the award on behalf of the team.

But Nick did something for me that I shall never forget, and which I found very touching. He invited me to go with him as his guest. Although really this was a producer's and director's award, not an actor's award, I was going to be allowed to go into the hall when the actual Oscar ceremony took place. I am just going to say it again, I was so grateful just to *be* there, never mind whether we won or not, although of course everybody thinks about winning, but it was just the idea of being there.

We flew over on 2 March and the actual Oscar ceremony was on 5 March, then we returned on the 7th. They put me up in the same hotel as them, so I was part of the team and very well looked after. I have to emphasise the fact that of course I can't see very well now. I am sprightly, but I am eighty-five, so every little helped me. We came to the day of the Oscars, the interviews were being given, and it was now being held, not in the Dorothy Chandler Pavilion, which I remembered seeing

to go to. But not me, no, I'm ready for beddy-byes by then. I said goodnight to them and blessed them. They were very sweet to me and the limo took me back, on my own, to the hotel. And that was the Oscars. Well, well, well.

But there is a postscript. When the film was shown at the première I realised when they ran the credits that they just went on and on and on. I think they took about six or seven minutes to get to the end of them, the credits of all the people who had had anything to do with the making of *The Curse of the Were-Rabbit*, and I was determined to find out how many there really were. Somebody was kind enough to do the adding up for me and it turned out that there were 614 names in those credits. So when we all got back to England and they had their get-together for the crew, what I'll call the engine room staff in Bristol, I went down there to be with them. Nick asked me to say a few words, so I said the magic number, 'Six hundred and fourteen. That's the number of you who worked on this film and who are in the credits, and I would just like to add my congratulations to that number. Well done, everybody! It's you, really, who won the Oscar.'

THIRTEEN

By Way of a Goodbye

This is by way of a goodbye. I would like to go back to those ladies and gentlemen, all of them stars, with whom I have had the privilege of working, where we have had duologues, either on the stage or occasionally on film, and not for any reason other than to say goodbye.

I would like to begin at the beginning, in 1948, with Lally Bowers. Dear, dear Lally and *The Way of the World* at Guildford. Sitting on the stage in her chair, fanning herself very gently and wiping the floor with me. Not that I minded, good gracious, quite the reverse. I just wish that I could have done better. But she was a mistress of her art, the art of the spoken word; I was aware of it and I didn't let it get me down. I just did the best I could in my own particular way, but it was Lally you were watching and she was marvellous. I wish she were here now to read this, because I never really said it to her face. Dear, dear Lally.

Then *The Way of the World* again, in 1953, with Sir John's company at the Lyric Hammersmith, playing Waitwell this time, to Margaret Rutherford's Lady Wishfort. Ah, Margaret Rutherford, a charmer off stage and a charming killer on stage. I don't know how conscious Margaret was of how good she was. Possibly it was one of those cases where the less it's talked about the better, but all of us who watched her, and there must have been millions over the years, on film as well as in the theatre, grew to love her, and she was a genuinely funny person. Funny in the way that she delivered the lines, and it was my pleasure to go on to the stage with her and feed her the lines that she needed. Great stuff, great stuff. She was very friendly off stage, and I just loved her enormously. Dear Margaret.

Googie Withers, that first night in particular, at the Aldwych Theatre, when it dawned on me as the seconds ticked by that this lady was as aware as I was that the audience were not finding this as good a play in London as they had in the provinces. But it made absolutely no difference to her, she just moved through the part with great ease and enormous skill, and I finished that first act, as I have told you, wringing wet. She was so much more experienced an actor than I was and yet, at the same time, it didn't come over very consciously, it was just there and it was great to work with her, it really was. I learnt an enormous amount from her.

In Honor Blackman's case it was our mutual regard for each other and our discipline that I think created the excitement, helped enormously, of course, by Freddie Knott, the author, and by Anthony Sharp, the director. We did *Wait Until Dark* together for six months until Honor withdrew. I had always admired her in the *Avengers* films, the way she hurled someone about and so on, but this was a different Honor, this was Honor the actress, and boy, was she good. This was not just hurling somebody about the stage. This was the real thing and it was great to work with her.

Then John Gielgud. We had just that one week of *Nude with Violin* before I was fired, but while it was happening I enjoyed it so much. I suppose the simple truth is that I enjoyed it *too* much. But it was great being on the stage with such a lovely actor and such a lovely man. I enjoyed every minute of it and I was sorry when it came to an end so abruptly, but at least I had done one week. It was a bit like being in weekly rep. He went on to do yearly rep, if you see what I mean. It was a year before he left the play. Dear, dear Sir John. While he lived he was the most loved and most distinguished of us all. Shine, shine, shine, Sir John.

Orson Welles. I think that Orson was lovable. Not to everybody, probably. I would not have liked to have caught him in one of his rages. Well, I did, actually, yes I did, but it was not directed at me and it was short-lived. I was so fond of him and I enjoyed his company so much that I was lucky enough to have it for some time, and he was an extremely gifted man. As you might know, he nearly became a senator, and acting and directing was really only one of his what you might call hobbies. Great company, great man.

Laurence Olivier. That one night in *Rhinoceros*, when he really did frighten the life out of me, and I still don't know whether it was him or the lighting man or what it was. I was glad he was not going to repeat it. I was glad that he only did it once, and I was glad and proud and privileged to have the pleasure of working with him throughout a whole play for a whole season. Thank you, Sir Larry.

Patrick McGoohan, on that first night of *Brand* at the Lyric Theatre Hammersmith, when he became a star overnight. That applause, and standing on the stage with him, and knowing that between us all, including the author, the translator and the director, we had created a moment of theatrical history by bringing *Brand* to life. Patrick was about as near great as you can get, I would say, in the theatre. Take care Patrick, take care.

Nicol Williamson. What a different man he was from Patrick, and yet the two of them when I worked with them were in what I call the young generation, or just emerging from it, and I would have loved to have seen them together. I don't know what they would have done, what play they would have done, but I would have loved to have seen the two of them acting together. That would really have been worth the price of admission. As it was, I just did this one play with Nicol and the movie of the play, and he was wicked towards me, but I didn't resent that at all. In fact, I felt quite chuffed that he thought he could do it. What an actor, what an actor.

Ralph Richardson. In *Witness for the Prosecution* I was Sir Ralph's valet, we had scenes together, short scenes in front of the camera, and he was just lovely. I admired him right from the word go, everybody did. He was the best Falstaff I have ever seen, easily the best. So moving as well as being chuckling funny, and at the end of our film together, when I had completed my last scene, he said to me, 'Very good, you just breathed on it. It was good.' Well, as you can gather, I will never forget that.

I had just one day's filming with Alec Guinness at Borehamwood. He was doing a film called *The Paragon* by Daphne du Maurier and the scene was set at the Channel crossing, at Dover. He was sitting in his car, a little open-roofed tourer, I was the customs man and I was examining his passport. We had arrived that morning, we had never met before, we didn't speak to each other, I mean he said 'Good morning', but I thought no, this is up to him, if he wishes to chat, fine, I will of course join in. If he wishes to be quiet, that is his prerogative, so we didn't say a word to each other. There was a luncheon break, and he went to lunch one way and I went the other way, and then we came back.

The purpose of the scene was for me, as the customs officer, to explain to him that his passport was only valid for three weeks. So he listened and he thanked me, and then he drove away. End of the day, end of the scene. It was about half past five. He was getting ready to leave the set and so was I. He came up to me, shook me by the hand and said goodbye and I did too. He turned away, and then something struck him and he came back. His head was slightly cocked to one side as he said to me, 'Are you working at the moment?' Only Alec Guinness could have thought of a line like that. Lovely man.

And finally, Gromit. Never work with animals or children, but I think the way they created Gromit, the way that Nick created him, and then the animators in the films that came and manipulated him, was brilliant, absolutely brilliant. Watching this latest film, *The Curse of the Were-Rabbit*, I am full of admiration for what they did, but I am going to stick to the fact that this was a dog, and never act with children or animals. This bears it out. The eyes, the ears, no mouth. The eyes and the ears do it all with a bit of help from the nose. I can see Gromit after Wallace has gone to bed. Gromit curls up in front of the television and watches old Lassie films and old Rin Tin Tin films. And probably old Buster Keaton films, growling quietly to himself. Sleep well, Gromit.

Well, goodbye now. Thank you for having me. See ya, Compo.

Index

59 Theatre Company, 126

Aardman, 222, 225–9
actors and acting: and instinct, 40–1;
    learning lines, 41, 85–6; film acting,
    41–2; improvisation, 86, 107;
    auditions, 93; casting, 119; repertory,
    122; great actors, 128; overlapping
    dialogue, 136–7; projecting, 169–70;
    spoken word, 216–17
Adam's Rib, 84
Adkinson, Ella, 59
Adler, Irene, 160
Agate, James, 52, 128
Ainsworth, Alan, 156
Aither, Mary, 9
Albee, Edward, 131, 133–4
Albinoni, Tomaso, 151
Aldridge, Michael, 185–6, 191–3, 208
Aldwych Theatre, 62, 80, 84, 118, 186, 233
Alexandra Palace, 39
Alexia, Alexander, 151
Altaras, Jonathan, 44
Archer, William, 126
Arlen, Harold, 214
Arnaud, Yvonne, 115
Aronson, Boris, 177, 179
Around the World with Orson Welles, 108
Arts Theatre, 38, 131, 133–4
As You Like It, 40
Ashcroft, Peggy, 30
Asherson, Renée, 61

Asquith, Anthony 'Puffin', 189
Assassins, The (Sondheim), 45
Atkins, Robert, 39–40, 120
Attenborough, Richard, 34
audiences, 169, 177, 217; London, 118, 233
auditions, 93
Aukin, David, 185
Austen, Jane, 185
Avengers, 172, 233

Baker, George, 153–4, 158
Baker Street, 158–61, 165
Bank of England, 71–2
Banks, Daphne, 32
Banks, Leslie, 32
Barclays Bank, 7, 13–16, 129
Barkworth, Peter, 56–9, 80, 145
Barnes, Sir Kenneth, 33–6, 39–40, 42–3
Barrault, Jean-Louis, 148
Barry, Michael, 39, 119–20
Bates, Alan, 187
Bates, Michael, 136, 195–6, 198–205
Bateson, Timothy, 66
Bath Festival, 46
Baxter, Jane, 125
Bayldon, Geoffrey, 54, 77
Baylis, Lilian, 185
BBC, 31, 39, 126, 157, 219; and *Pepys's
    Diary*, 120, 122, 124; and grizzly bear,
    145–6; and *Last of the Summer Wine*,
    194–5, 200
Be My Guest, 125

Beaconsfield Film School, 220–1

Beaumont, Hugh 'Binkie', 57, 60–2, 84, 90–2, 110, 115–16

Beecham, Thomas, 29

Beethoven, Ludwig van, 4, 30, 212–14, 217–18

Belasco Theatre, 164

Bell, Alan, 206

Ben-Hur, 82

Bennett, Alan, 124, 192

Berlin, Irving, 11, 177, 214

Bible, The, 83

Birmingham, Repertory Theatre, 184

Bisset, Jacqueline, 144

Bitter Sweet (Coward), 46, 217

Black, Kitty, 74

Blackman, Honor, 171–2, 174, 233

Bloomsbury, 7, 14–15, 33, 129

Bluecoat School, 124

Bock, Jerry, 155–7, 160

Bolton, 22–3

Bonaventure, 57

Borehamwood studios, 188

Born Yesterday, 89

Boston, 160

Boucicault, Dion, 181

Bournemouth, 11; Theatre, 210

Bowers, Lally, 46–7, 51–2, 182, 232

Box, Stephen, 227–30

Boyfriend, The, 57

Brahms, Johannes, 29

Brambell, Wilfred, 205

Brand (Ibsen), 126–8, 234

Brando, Marlon, 112

Bree, James, 90

Bridge, Peter, 5, 24, 40, 155, 181; produces *Wait Until Dark*, 171, 173

Bridges, Alan, 140

Bridgewater, Leslie, 87

Briggs, Raymond, 190

Brighton, 32; Theatre Royal, 68, 91, 154

Bristol, 222, 231

British Actors Equity, 38–9, 109

Britten, Benjamin, 215–16

Broadway, 44, 92, 153, 155–8, 160, 176–7, 217

Brook, Clive, 109

Brook, Peter, 74, 81–2

Brown, Pamela, 49, 52

Bruce, Brenda, 190

Buchanan, Jack, 10

Buckstone Club, 63–4, 103, 134

Bulawayo, 79

Bull, Peter, 163

Busby, Matt, 208

Butler, Blake, 207

Butlin, Jan, 209

Cabaret, 176–81

Cambridge, Arts Theatre, 184–5

Campion, Gerry, 64–5

Canada, 69

Caplin, Henry (Hank), 133–4, 144, 146

Capon, Naomi, 65–6, 157

Carey, Joyce, 113

Carlisle-Hart, Kitty, 189–90

Carmichael, Hoagy, 214

Carten, Kenneth, 44–5, 57–8, 64, 73, 93, 117

Caruso, Enrico, 11

Castle, Ann, 113

Cat on a Hot Tin Roof (Tennessee Williams), 140

Cavallaro, Gaylord, 68

Chaliapin, Feodor, 11

Chalkwell, 13, 15

Chandler, Colin, 38

Changeling, The (Middleton), 73

Chappell, William (Billy), 96, 100, 110

Cheats of Scapin, The, 126

Chekhov, Anton, 186–7

Chester, 109

Chesterfield, Repertory Theatre, 54–5, 82

Chevalier, Maurice, 10–11

Index

Chichester, Festival Theatre, 46, 69, 181–2, 187

Chicken Run, 226–7

Child of Our Time, A (Tippett), 219

Child's Play, 64–5

Chisholm, Maggie, 196

Chitty, Eric, 73

Christie, Agatha, 190–1

Churchill, Diana, 61

Churchill, Donald, 111

Churchill, Winston, 4

cinema, 10–11, 28, 82–3; *see also* films and filming

Citizen Kane, 28, 106–7, 136, 222

Clarke, Roy, 194–5, 199–202, 205–9

Clements, John, 11, 109, 181

Close Shave, A, 225–6

Clunes, Alec, 117

Collection, The (Pinter), 140

Collier, Patience, 147

Collins, Anthony, 97, 100

Colombe (Anouilh), 157

Columbia Pictures, 105, 107

Colville, Alison, 111

Comedy Playhouse, 195

Comer, John, 207

Congreve, William, 48–50, 52, 54, 82

Connery, Sean, 128, 157

Constable, Theo, 37–8

Cooke, Alistair, 167

Cooney, Ray, 182–4

Cooper, Gladys, 10

Count of Clerambard, The, 109

County Wicklow, 114–15

Coward, Nöel, 25, 130–1, 165–6; and *Nude with Violin*, 110, 112–16; and Ionesco, 138

Craig, Wendy, 143

Cranwell, 4, 23–5, 32–3, 35–6, 40, 42, 171; Music Society, 4, 28–31; production of *Hay Fever*, 5, 24, 171

Creature Comforts, 222–3

Creditors (Strindberg), 126

Criterion Theatre, 182

Crosby, Bing, 214

Curzon, George, 46

Dana, Leora, 43–5

Danger Man, 128

Danton's Death, 126

Dark Is Light Enough, The (Fry), 79–80, 84

Davies, Gareth, 179

Daviot, Gordon, 14

Davis, Reg, 9

Davison, Flight-Sergeant David, 28–9

Dean, Basil, 45–6, 116–17

Death at Broadcasting House, 192–3

Delius, Frederick, 45

Dench, Judi, 153–5, 176, 178–9

Dennen, Barry, 176, 178–9

Desk Set, 84

Devine, George, 130

Dews, Peter, 182

Dial M for Murder, 171

Diamond, Andy, 197

Diary of Samuel Pepys, The, 120–5

Dido and Aeneas (Purcell), 72

Doctor Who and the Ice Warriors, 145

Domesday Book, 6

Donald, James, 80

Donat, Robert, 40

Donlan, Yolande, 90

Drake, Fabia, 40–2, 132

Dreamworks, 226–8

du Maurier, Daphne, 235

Dublin, Olympia Theatre, 112–13, 115

Duchess Theatre, 68

Duke of York's Theatre, 93–4, 97

Eastbourne, 56–7; Devonshire Park Theatre, 210

Eastwood, Clint, 228

Eddie Condon's club, 166

Eddington, Paul, 56, 121–2

Edinburgh, 22

Eliot, T. S., 153
Elliott, Denholm, 117, 119
Elliott, Michael, 126–7
Erskine, Chester, 89
Eugene Onegin (Tchaikovsky), 62
Evans, Edith, 46, 80–1, 84–5, 178
Evening Standard, 180

Farjeon, Herbert and Eleanor, 39
Ferrer, Kathleen, 117
Festival of Britain, 59–60
Fiddler on the Roof, 155
films and filming, 188; for television, 135; pinscreen technique, 151–2; *see also* cinema
Firstborn, The (Fry), 82
Fitzgerald, Ella, 214
Five Spot club, 165
Flagstad, Kirsten, 72–3
Flecker, James Elroy, 45
Fontaine, Joan, 170
Forbes-Robertson, Jean, 10
Forsyte Saga, The, 145
Fortune Theatre, 117, 125
Forty Wagon Loads of Cotton (Tennessee Williams), 131
Fox, William, 46
Freeman, Jane, 182, 208
Fry, Christopher, 80–3

Gable, Clark, 130
Garrick Theatre, 109
Gershwin, George and Ira, 11, 177, 219
Gibbs, A. G., 7
Gibson, Chloe, 118–22
Gibson, Mel, 226
Gielgud, John, 14, 32, 36, 61, 174–5; and *The Way of the World*, 48–9, 52–4, 232; and *Richard II*, 53, 73–6, 79; receives knighthood, 76–7; and *Venice Preserv'd*, 77–8; visits Rhodesia, 78–9; and *Nude with Violin*, 110–16, 131, 233–4; *Death at Broadcasting House*, 192–3

Gielgud, Val, 192–3
Gilbert, James, 194–7, 199–200, 203
Gladwin, Joe, 208
Glenville, Peter, 67
Globe Theatre, 74–5, 91, 111
Goldman, Milton, 170
Gone with the Wind, 129–30
Goodwin, Harold, 42–3
Goossens, Leon, 30
Gordon, Ruth, 84–5, 87–90, 92; acting ability, 85–6
Gough, Peter, 31–2
Grade, Lew, 128
Granada Television, 135, 140–1
Grand Day Out, A, 220–4
Granger, Derek, 140–1
Gray, Joel, 176
Greenwich Theatre, 186
Greenwich Village, 165
Griller String Quartet, 29
Guildford, Repertory Theatre, 39, 48–54, 76, 232; Yvonne Arnaud Theatre, 51
Guinness, Alec, 61, 235–6
Guthrie, Tyrone, 55, 68–70, 84, 86–7, 185
Gwillim, Jack, 143

Hackman, Gene, 228
Hackney Empire, 105–6
Hadleigh Castle, 15
Haendel, Ida, 29
Haigh, Kenneth, 131–3, 135
Hale, Lionel, 24
Hamlet, 102, 136
Hammersmith, Lyric Theatre, 48, 73, 126–7, 232, 234
Hammerstein, Oscar, 214
Hammond, Kay, 109–10
Hancock, Sheila, 194
Hanson, Harry, 26
Hanwell, Bob Hope Theatre, 209
Harnick, Sheldon, 155–7, 160
Harringay, 13–14

Index

Hart, Lorenz, 11, 212, 214
Hart, Moss, 14; *Act One*, 188–90
Hassan, 45
Hawkins, Coleman, 166
Hay Fever (Coward), 5, 24, 115, 171
Haye, Helen, 109
Haymarket Theatre, 32, 63, 87
Hazelhurst, Ronnie, 207
Heart to Heart (Rattigan), 142–3
Hecht, Norman, 29
Hedda Gabler (Ibsen), 52
Hello Dolly!, 84
Helpmann, Robert, 116
Henry IV, Part One, 31
Henry V, 32
Henson, Basil, 76, 113
Henson, Nicky, 192–3
Hepburn, Katharine, 84–5
Hercule Poirot's Christmas, 190–2
Hill, Arthur, 87
Hird, Thora, 187–8, 208
Hitler, Adolf, 4
Hobson, Harold, 156
Hollywood, 85, 92, 217, 226, 228–9
Holmes, Sherlock, 158–60
Holmfirth, 197, 199
Horne, David, 113–15
Houston, Donald, 50
Houston, Glyn, 50–1
Howard, Trevor, 146
Huddersfield, 141
Hunt, Martita, 158
Huston, John, 83

I Have Been Here Before, 25, 27
Inadmissible Evidence (Osborne), 160–5, 168; film, 170–1
Into Thin Air, 89–92
Ionesco, Eugene, 138
Isherwood, Christopher, 176
ITV, 128
Ivanov (Chekhov), 186–7

Jackson, Freda, 157
Jackson, Gordon, 97–101, 106, 150
Jameson, Pauline, 52
Janus, 117–18
Jarvis, Martin, 34
jazz, 165–8
Jenkins, Jeanette, 194
Jews, 145, 176–8
JFK, 41–2
Jimmy Ryan's club, 166, 168
Jodrell Bank, 30
John, Elton, 231
Johnson, Celia, 61
Johnson, Margaret, 66, 80, 146

Kafka, Franz, 147
Kanin, Garson, 84–5, 88–93
Katzenberg, Jeffrey, 227
Kaufman, George S., 14, 188
Keaton, Buster, 236
Kelly, Gene, 217
Kendal, Felicity, 187
Kern, Jerome, 214
Kerr, Ronnie, 39
Kirby, Eileen, 87
Knott, Frederick, 171–3, 233
Korda, Sir Alexander, 33, 38
Kotcheff, Ted, 144
Kurnitz, Harry, 153
Kwouk, Burt, 209

Lady's Not for Burning, The (Fry), 52, 80, 82
Lake District, 36
Lambert, Constant, 212, 219
Lascelles, Reg, 30
Lassie, 236
Last of the Summer Wine, 141, 182, 186–7, 192, 194–211; stage play, 20–1, 209–11; filming first episode, 198–9, 201–3; teamwork, 198–9; origin of characters, 200–1; deaths among cast, 205–8

Latham, Robert, 123–4
Laughton, Charles, 33
lawyers, 41
Laye, Evelyn, 46, 178
Legge, Walter, 60–1
Lehmann, Leo, 116
Leicester, Haymarket Theatre, 185
Leicester Square, Odeon, 224–5
Leigh, Vivien, 85, 129, 139
Leigh-on-Sea, 12–16, 18
Leighton, Margaret, 61–2
Leopold Pearls Mystery, The, 9
Levine, Sam, 88
Lime Grove studios, 120
Littler, Emile, 179
Lomas, Herbert 'Tiny', 74–5, 78
London Assurance (Boucicault), 181
Look After Lulu (Feydeau), 130–1, 135, 196
Look Back in Anger (Osborne), 132, 161
Loren, Sophia, 188
Love Parade, The, 10
Lovell, Professor Bernard, 30
Lowe, Arthur, 161
Lucky Day, 125
Lyric Theatre, 153

Macbeth, 26
McCallum, John, 117
McCowen, Alec, 87, 109, 111–12
MacDonald, Jeanette, 10–11
MacDonald, Murray, 109
McFarland, Olive, 127
McGoohan, Patrick, 56, 97, 102–3, 107–8,
150; as *Brand*, 126–8, 234; turns down
James Bond, 128
MacNaughtan, Alan, 56
Macrae, Duncan, 136, 138
Magdalene College, Cambridge, 123
Magnificent Ambersons, The, 136, 151
Malleson, Miles, 136, 138
Manchester, Royal Exchange Theatre,
69; Opera House, 117–18
Marsh, Jean, 143

Martin, Rosemary, 207
Mason, Brewster, 45, 74
Mason, Hal, 65
Masterpiece, 146
Matchmaker, The (Wilder), 84, 86–9
Matriarch, The, 44
Matthews, Denis, 29–31
Maxwell, James, 126
May, Val, 125
Melford, Jill, 90–1
Melville, Herman, 94, 99
Men of Good Nature, 25
Mercer, Johnny, 214
Meredith, Burgess, 154
Mermaid Theatre, 71–3, 153
Merrick, David, 161–4
Mervyn, William, 157
Messel, Oliver, 80
Meyer, Michael, 126
Middleton, Thomas, 73
Midsummer Night's Dream, A, 26, 32, 39,
119
Miles, Bernard, 71–2
Miles, June, 25–7
Miles, Sarah, 158
Miller, Gary, 156
Millicent Sisters, The, 194–5
Millionairess, The, 188–90
Mills, John, 89
Minchenden School, 6, 13
Mirvish family, 185
Misfits, The, 200
Mitchell, Keith, 158
Mitchell, Ruth, 176
Moby Dick Rehearsed, 94–108, 110, 150
Mockingbird, The, 24
Moffatt, John, 192
Moiseiwitsch, Tanya, 69
Montague, Lee, 71, 111
More, Kenneth, 14, 143
Morell, André, 69
Morris, Alana, 174
Mortimer, John, 41, 146

Index

Moshinsky, Elijah, 186–7
Mother, 226
Much Ado About Nothing, 182, 186–7
Murphy, Peter, 162, 170
Murray, Barbara, 174
music, 212–19; *see also* jazz

National Theatre, 14, 24, 181
National Trust, 123
Negri, Richard, 126–7
New Theatre, 130
Newcastle University, 31
Newman, Sydney, 144
Nighy, Bill, 193
Nottingham Playhouse, 125
Nude with Violin (Coward), 110–16, 130–1, 135, 233

Old Heads and Young Hearts (Boucicault), 46, 181–2
Old Vic, 63, 68, 70, 185
Olivier, Laurence, 26, 32, 85, 90, 137–9, 140–2, 234; and *Richard III*, 26, 39, 48; receives knighthood, 76–7; and *Hamlet*, 102; and *Rhinoceros*, 135–40, 234; divorce, 139; starts National Theatre, 181
Olivier Theatre, 140
Once in a Lifetime, 14
Osborn, Andrew, 14
Osborne, John, 163–4, 168–9
Oscars, 92, 222–3, 225–31
Ost, Geoffrey, 55–6
Otway, Thomas, 77–8
Ouspensky, Peter, 25
Owen, Bill, 20, 195–207, 209–11; politics, 200; saves PS's life, 203–5; and Compo character, 205–6; death, 205–7

Padgate, 20–1
Page, Anthony, 160, 162–4, 170
Palace Theatre, 177
Pallisers, The, 145

Palmers Green, 8, 11–12
Paragon, The, 235
Paris, 147, 152; Gare d'Orsay, 148
Parish, Mitchell, 214
Park, Nick, 220–31, 236
Parker, Claire, 151
Parker, Joy, 74–5
Pasco, Richard, 157
Pat and Mike, 84
Patton, 207
Pears, Frank, 29
Peck, Gregory, 96, 105
Perkins, Anthony, 147–8, 152
Perry, John, 74
Peter Grimes (Britten), 215
Peter Pan, 10
Philadelphia, 161, 164–5
Pilbrow, Richard, 126–7, 156, 181
Pink Panther films, 153, 209
Pinner, 18
Pinnock, Trevor, 124
Pinter, Harold, 55, 134
Plowright, Joan, 97, 136–40
Poirot, Hercule, 190–1
Porter, Cole, 11, 214, 217
Porter, Eric, 62
Power, Hartley, 90
Pownall, David, 185
Present Laughter (Coward), 112
Preston, 221, 225
Price, Dennis, 125
Pride and Prejudice, 184–5
Priestley, J. B., 25
Prince, Hal, 56, 155–8, 160, 176–9, 181
Prisoner, The, 128
Private Life of Henry VIII, The, 33
Pryde, Bill, 184–5
Pygmalion (Shaw), 27

Quartermaine, Leon, 46
Queen's Theatre, 61
Quick, Diana, 193
Quitak, Oscar, 63–4

Rachmaninov, Sergei, 30

RADA, 31–40, 42–5, 56, 73, 93, 120, 194; PS auditions, 33–5; homosexuality inquiry, 42–3

radio, 11, 21, 190; growth of, 212, 217

Radio Times, 124

Rakoff, Alvin, 143–4

Ranelow, Freddie, 36

Rattigan, Terence, 142–3

Rawlinson, Colonel A. R., 120

Redcar, 21–2

Reed, David, 29

Regent's Park, Open Air Theatre, 39

Reid, Ann, 226

Remick, Lee, 171

Reynolds, Jimmy, 16

Rhinoceros (Ionesco), 135–40, 234

Rhodesia, 78

Richard II, 53, 73–6

Richard III, 26, 39, 48

Richard of Bordeaux, 14

Richardson, Ralph, 10, 31; in *Three Sisters*, 61–2, 143, 186; in *Witness for the Prosecution*, 62–3, 235; as Falstaff, 63, 235; receives knighthood, 76–7; in *Heart to Heart*, 143

Richardson, Tony, 130–1

Rin Tin Tin, 236

Ring Round the Moon (Anouilh), 158

Rivals, The, 109

Robertson, Alec, 31

Robinson, Mark, 24

Rodgers, Richard, 11, 153–4, 212, 214

Rolland, Romain, 213

Rosay, Françoise, 157

Rose, Guy, 2

Rose and the Ring, The, 39

Rose Marie, 10

Rowe, Alan, 121

Royal Court Theatre, 130, 135

Run for Your Wife (Cooney), 182–4

Rutherford, Margaret, 232–3

Rutland, John, 56

Rye, Daphne, 57–9, 73, 81

St James's Theatre, 44

Sainthill, Loudon, 74

Sallis, Peter: childhood, 8–13; education, 5–7, 13; career in bank, 7–8, 14–16; RAF service, 4–5, 8, 16–24, 28, 35; acting in RAF, 5, 24–7; and music, 28–30, 212–19; decides on acting career, 5, 31–3; voice and accent, 31, 36–7, 43, 190–1; auditions for RADA, 33–5; RADA training, 36–8, 40–5; West End debut, 38–9, 59–62; joins Equity, 38–9; television debut, 39–40, 65–6, 120; acquires agent, 44; first professional role, 46–7; works in repertory theatre, 48–59; works with Gielgud, 48–9, 52–4, 73–9, 110–15, 131, 233–4; joins Tennent, 59–60; works with Richardson, 61–2, 143, 186, 235; film debut, 63–5; appears at Old Vic, 68–70; flies for first time, 71; joins Mermaid Theatre, 71–3; contract artist with Tennent, 73–89, 92; unemployed, 92–3; works with Welles, 93–107, 135–8, 147–52, 234; sacked by Coward, 114–16, 130–1; as Pepys, 120–5; romantic episode, 129; works with Olivier, 135–40, 234; dinner with Olivier, 140–2; emotional capabilities, 144–5; plays opposite grizzly bear, 145–6; reaction to great people, 153–4; first musical, 155–7; in America, 158–70; love of jazz, 165–8; fills in when scenery sticks, 179–80; end of theatre career, 185, 187; film career, 188; radio career, 190; *Last of the Summer Wine*, 194–211; choice of clothing for Clegg, 196–7; politics, 200; Wallace and Gromit, 220–31, 236; and Oscars, 227–31

Sands, Leslie, 24–7, 192

Sardi's restaurant, 170

Index

Scheming Lieutenant, The (Sheridan), 38
Schneider, Romy, 147
School for Scandal, The (Sheridan), 46–7
Scofield, Paul, 73–5, 70, 79
Scott, George C., 207
Seal, Elizabeth, 179
Secret of the Blue Room, The, 10
Sellers, Peter, 188–9, 209
Selznick, Myron, 44
Seyler, Athene, 109
Shakespeare, William, 23, 26–7, 39, 67–8, 75
Shand-Gibbs, Sheila, 67
Sharp, Anthony, 173–4, 233
Shaw, Bernard, 24, 34
Shaw, Maureen, 25–7
She Loves Me, 155–8, 182
Sheffield, Repertory Theatre, 55–9, 82, 196
Shop Around the Corner, The, 156
Shot in the Dark, A, 153–5
Shubert Theatre, 164
Sibelius, Jean, 29
Silence of the Sea, The, 14
Simpson, Michael, 182
Sinatra, Frank, 214
Sinden, Donald, 181
Singleton, Zuty, 166–7
Smethurst, Jack, 183–4
Smith, Oliver, 160
Snow, C. P., 245
Snowman, The (Briggs), 190
Someone Is Killing the Best Chefs in Europe, 144
South Africa, 195
Southgate, 5, 8, 13
Spielberg, Steven, 226–7, 229–30
Spyder's Web, 194
Stanislavsky, Konstantin, 33, 139, 206
Steptoe and Son, 205
Sterland, John, 114–16
Stewart, James, 156
Stoll Theatre, 146

Stone, Christopher, 11
Stone, Oliver, 41
Strachan, Alan, 186
Strand Theatre, 138, 174, 186
Strangers and Brothers, 145
Stratford Ontario Theatre, 69
Streetcar Named Desire, A (Tennessee Williams), 66
Sullavan, Margaret, 156
Summer and Smoke (Tennessee Williams), 66–8
Sunday Times, 52
Sutherland, Donald, 41
Swinstead, Joan, 73
Sylvester, William, 66–7

Taylor, Valerie, 109, 117
Teddington Studios, 144
television, 14, 63, 105, 118–19, 205; PS's debut, 39–40, 65–6, 120; filming technique, 135; history, 142
Tennent, H. M., 52, 57, 66, 110, 186; PS joins, 59–60; PS under contract, 73–89, 92; Tennent Television, 116
Test Match Special, 105–6
Thames estuary, 12
theatres: repertory, 35, 41, 47–59, 122; thrust stage, 69, 181–2; in the round, 69; raising of curtain, 80, 94; West End, 94; Matcham, 105; Jews and, 177; previews, 177
Third Man, The, 136
Thompson, Bernard, 203–4
Thomson, Margaret, 65
Thornton, Frank, 187, 206, 208
Three Sisters (Chekhov), 59–62, 143, 186
Thurber, James, 154
Times, The, 53
Timon of Athens, 69–71, 185
Tippett, Sir Michael, 219
Topkapi, 223
Toronto, 160
Toscanini, Arturo, 29

Tovarich, 139
Towb, Harry, 67
Tracy, Spencer, 84–5
Trial, The, 147–52
Trick to Catch the Old One, A (Middleton), 73
Troughton, Patrick, 145
Turin, 108
Turley, Veronica, 74
Turner, Clifford, 36–7
Tutin, Dorothy, 157
Twelfth Night, 27, 40
Two Stars for Comfort, 146
Tydeman, John, 190
Tynan, Kenneth, 73; on Moby Dick Rehearsed, 94, 101–2, 104

Urquhart, Robert, 36, 42–3
Uxbridge, 16–18

Van Heusen, Jimmy, 214
Vanbrugh Theatre, 45
Venice Preserv'd (Otway), 74, 77–8
Venus Observed (Fry), 80
Vogler, Ian, 54

Wade, Walter, 25
Wagner, Richard, 106–7
Wait Until Dark, 171–5, 233
Walbrook, Anton, 146
Wallace and Gromit, 220–31, 236
Wallace and Gromit: The Curse of the Were-Rabbit, 227–31
Wallach, Eli, 64
Walter, Bruno, 213
Warren, Harry, 214
Way of the World, The (Congreve), 48–53, 73–4, 76, 82, 232
Way to the Stars, The, 196
Weaver, Fritz, 159
Webb, Alan, 136, 138
Webb, Corporal Frank, 4, 29
Weldon, Duncan, 186

Welles, Orson: and Citizen Kane, 28, 106–7, 234; and Moby Dick Rehearsed, 93–108, 110, 150; Around the World with Orson Welles, 108; and Rhinoceros, 135–8; overlapping dialogue technique, 136–7; and The Trial, 147–52; pinscreen technique, 151–2
West Side Story, 157
Wharfe, River, 203
Wharmby, Gordon, 208
When Knights Were Bold, 55
When the Wind Blows (Briggs), 190
Who Cares?, 116–19
Wigmore Hall, 213
Wilde, Brian, 208–9
Wilder, Thornton, 86
Wilding, Michael, 116
Williams, Enid, 190–3
Williams, Harcourt 'Billy', 186
Williams, Kenneth, 97
Williams, Tennessee, 67–8
Williamson, Nicol, 160–5, 158–71, 234–5; ways of working, 168–9
Wilmer, Douglas, 121
Wilson, Angus, 144
Wilson, Don, 121
Wilson, Ronald, 145
Winter Garden Theatre, 125
Withers, Googie, 117–18, 233
Wolfit, Donald, 69
Women Beware Women (Middleton), 73
Wood, Duncan, 200–1
Wordsworth, Richard, 76
Wrede, Casper, 126
Wrong Trousers, The, 223–5
Wymark, Patrick, 157

Yard of Sun, A (Fry), 80

Zetterling, Mai, 109
Zoo Story, The (Albee), 131–5
Zurich, 70–1